Communications in Computer and Information Science 1711

More information about this series at https://link.springer.com/bookseries/7899

Ningyu Zhang · Meng Wang · Tianxing Wu ·
Wei Hu · Shumin Deng (Eds.)

CCKS 2022 - Evaluation Track

7th China Conference
on Knowledge Graph and Semantic Computing Evaluations, CCKS 2022
Qinhuangdao, China, August 24–27, 2022
Revised Selected Papers

Springer

Editors
Ningyu Zhang 🆔
Zhejiang University
Hangzhou, China

Meng Wang
Southeast University
Nanjing, China

Tianxing Wu
Southeast University
Nanjing, China

Wei Hu
Nanjing University
Nanjing, China

Shumin Deng
National University of Singapore
Singapore, Singapore

ISSN 1865-0929   ISSN 1865-0937 (electronic)
Communications in Computer and Information Science
ISBN 978-981-19-8299-6   ISBN 978-981-19-8300-9 (eBook)
https://doi.org/10.1007/978-981-19-8300-9

This Springer imprint is published by the registered company Springer Nature Singapore Pte Ltd.
The registered company address is: 152 Beach Road, #21-01/04 Gateway East, Singapore 189721, Singapore

Preface

This volume contains the papers presented at CCKS 2022: the 16th China Conference on Knowledge Graph and Semantic Computing held during August 24–27, 2022, in Qinhuangdao.

CCKS is organized by the Technical Committee on Language and Knowledge Computing of the Chinese Information Processing Society, and represents the merger of two previously-held relevant forums, i.e., the Chinese Knowledge Graph Symposium (CKGS) and the Chinese Semantic Web and Web Science Conference (CSWS). CKGS was previously held in Beijing (2013), Nanjing (2014), and Yichang (2015). CSWS was first held in Beijing in 2006 and was the main forum for research on the Semantic (Web) technologies in China for a decade. Since 2016, CCKS has brought together researchers from both forums and covered a wider range of fields, including the knowledge graphs, the Semantic Web, linked data, natural language processing, knowledge representation, graph databases, information retrieval, and knowledge aware machine learning. It aims to become the top forum on knowledge graph and semantic technologies for Chinese researchers and practitioners from academia, industry, and government.

The CCKS technology evaluation track aims to provide researchers with platforms and resources for testing knowledge and semantic computing technologies, algorithms and systems, to promote the technical development in the field of domestic knowledge, and to foster the integration of academic achievements and industrial needs. The CCKS 2022 technology evaluation track attracted more than 10,000 teams to participate, forming a highly influential event. This year, following discussion and selection by the evaluation organization committee, CCKS again set up five evaluation topics and 14 evaluation tasks. The task list is given below. The committee also set up bonuses and issued certificates for the top three teams in each task. At the same time, the organization committee specially selected the "innovative technology award" for different tasks, which encourages and rewards the use of innovative technologies.

Topic 1: Information extraction
    Task 1: Evaluation of thousand words general information extraction contest
    Task 2: High-quality article identification based on knowledge graph
Topic 2: Knowledge graph construction and question answering
    Task 3: Hierarchical Multiple-choice QA with Condition
    Task 4: Open knowledge graph QA
    Task 5: Cross-lingual knowledge graph QA evaluation task
    Task 6: Textbook schematic QA
    Task 7: Construction and application of chemical element knowledge graph
Topic 3: Business finance knowledge graph
    Task 8: Few-shot event extraction for financial field
    Task 9: Knowledge graph evaluation for digital commerce
    Task 10: Causal event element extraction and event similarity calculation for financial field

Task 11: Financial NL2SQL evaluation task

Topic 4: Military knowledge graph

Task 12: Event element extraction from open source multimodal military equipment data

Task 13: Foreign army unmanned system knowledge graph construction and evaluation task

Topic 5: Knowledge graph storage

Task 14: Evaluation of custom graph analysis algorithm based on graph database

Having attracted over 10,000 teams for the competition, we encouraged the teams to submit evaluation papers. In total, 42 teams submitted their evaluation papers. All the papers came from the teams ranking in the top three in their competition tasks. After rigorous peer review by experienced researchers, 25 of these papers were accepted (after revision) for inclusion in this volume of proceedings.

September 2022

Ningyu Zhang
Meng Wang
Tianxing Wu
Wei Hu
Shumin Deng

Organization

CCKS 2022 was organized by the Technical Committee on Language and Knowledge Computing of the Chinese Information Processing Society.

Honorary General Chair

Maosong Sun — Tsinghua University, China

General Chairs

Guilin Qi	Southeast University, China
Kang Liu	Institute of Automation, Chinese Academy of Sciences, China
Jiadong Ren	Yanshan University, China

Program Committee Chairs

Bin Xu	Tsinghua University, China
Yansong Feng	Peking University, China

Local Chairs

Yuefeng Qi	Yanshan University, China
Changwu Wang	Yanshan University, China
Peiliang Wu	Yanshan University, China
Jianzhou Feng	Yanshan University, China

Publicity Chairs

Jianfeng Du	Guangdong University of Foreign Studies, China
Hai Wang	Sun Yat-sen University, China

Publication Chairs

Yongbin Liu	University of South China, China
Yubo Chen	Institute of Automation, Chinese Academy of Sciences, China

Evaluation Chairs

Meng Wang   Southeast University, China
Ningyu Zhang   Zhejiang University, China

Sponsorship Chairs

Junyu Lin   Institute of Information Engineering, Chinese
                                   Academy of Sciences, China
Lei Hou   Tsinghua University, China

Website Chair

Yuanzhe Zhang   Institute of Automation, Chinese Academy of
                                   Sciences, China

Evaluation Track Program Committee

Ningyu Zhang   Zhejiang University, China
Meng Wang   Southeast University, China
Tianxing Wu   Southeast University, China
Wei Hu   Nanjing University, China
Shumin Deng   National University of Singapore, Singapore
Weizhuo Li   Nanjing University of Posts and
                                   Telecommunications, China
Xiang Chen   Zhejiang University, China
Yunzhi Yao   Zhejiang University, China
Lei Li   Zhejiang University, China
Zhen Bi   Zhejiang University, China
Yin Fang   Zhejiang University, China
Hongbin Ye   Zhejiang University, China
Wen Zhang   Zhejiang University, China

Contents

A Chemical Domain Knowledge-Aware Framework for Multi-view
Molecular Property Prediction 1
   Rui Hua, Xinyan Wang, Chuang Cheng, Qiang Zhu, and Xuezhong Zhou

A Coarse Pipeline to Solve Hierarchical Multi-answer Questions
with Conditions 12
   Ben Teng, Xuepeng Wang, Xiaodan lv, Xinxin Zhang, and Bo An

A Pipeline-Based Multimodal Military Event Argument Extraction
Framework 21
   Xin Xu, Jian Xu, Guoqing Ruan, Hongyi Bao, and Jiadong Sun

A Search-Enhanced Path Mining and Ranking Method for Cross-lingual
Knowledge Base Question Answering 30
   Zhanglin Wu, Ming Zhu, Min Zhang, Song Peng, Weidong Zhang,
   Ting Zhu, Junhao Zhu, Peng Li, Hao Yang, and Ying Qin

A Translation Model-Based Question Answering Approach
over Cross-Lingual Knowledge Graphs 39
   Jiangzhou Ji, Yaohan He, and Jinlong Li

Cascaded Solution for Multi-domain Conditional Question Answering
with Multiple-Span Answers 47
   Junhao Zhu, Min Zhang, Song Peng, Hao Yang, Ying Qin,
   Weidong Zhang, Han Han, and Miaomiao Ma

Compound Property Prediction Based on Multiple Different Molecular
Features and Ensemble Learning 57
   Wenming Yang, Jiali Zou, and Le Yin

Diagram Question Answering with Joint Training and Bottom-Up
and Top-Down Attention 70
   Ke Zhang, Xiao Li, and Gong Cheng

Element Information Enhancement for Diagram Question Answering
with Synthetic Data 78
   Yadong Zhang, Yang Chen, Yupei Ren, Man Lan, and Yuefeng Chen

Financial Event Extraction of NEC Dataset Based on Pointer Network 87
   Keyu Pu, Hongyi Liu, Yixiao Yang, Yaohan He, and Jinlong Li

High Quality Article Recognition Based on Ernie and Knowledge Mapping 98
  Huihai Liu, Pingfei Cui, and Lin Han

High-Quality Article Classification Based on Named Entities
of Knowledge Graph and Multi-head Attention 107
  Zhancheng Liang, Zhenkun He, and Peipei Jia

Implementation and Optimization of Graph Computing Algorithms Based
on Graph Database 120
  Jiaqi Wei, Shuang Wu, Jinkang Jia, and Ziqian Liu

Knowledge Graph Construction for Foreign Military Unmanned Systems 127
  *Yilin Chen, Jingting Wang, Shutong Zhu, Yuang Gu, Haoyu Dai,
  Jingyi Xu, Yipeng Zhu, and Tianxing Wu*

Knowledge-Enhanced Classification: A Scheme for Identification
of High-Quality Articles 138
  Yanmao Zhou, Yunni Xia, and Yongbo Wang

Learning Seq2Seq Model with Dynamic Schema Linking for NL2SQL 148
  Xingxing Ning, Yupeng Zhao, and Jie liu

Learning to Answer Complex Visual Questions from Multi-View Analysis 154
  Minjun Zhu, Yixuan Weng, Shizhu He, Kang Liu, and Jun Zhao

A Prompt-Based UIE Framework 163
  Fubang Zhao, Yexiang Wang, and YangYang Kang

Multi-modal Representation Learning with Self-adaptive Threshold
for Commodity Verification 172
  Chenchen Han and Heng Jia

Multimodal Representation Learning-Based Product Matching 180
  Changkai Feng, Wei Chen, Chao Chen, Tong Xu, and Enhong Chen

Relation Extraction as Text Matching: A Scheme for Multi-hop Knowledge
Base Question Answering 191
  Ziyan Li, Kan Ni, Haofen Wang, and Wenqiang Zhang

Research on Salient Reasoning for Commonsense Knowledge 202
  Mingxu Ma, Guangshuo Wu, and Jingli Yang

Retrieval-Then-Parsing: A Two-Stage Model for SQL Generation
in Financial Domain 214
  Nengzheng Jin, Dongfang Li, Junying Chen, Yubin Qiu, and Qingcai Chen

Structured Design Solves Multiple Tables of NL2SQL 221
    Xianwei Yi, Ruijie Wang, Hanyi Zhang, and Shiqi Zhen

The Method for Plausibility Evaluation of Knowledge Triple Based on QA 228
    Shutong Jia and Jiuxin Cao

Author Index 237

A Chemical Domain Knowledge-Aware Framework for Multi-view Molecular Property Prediction

Rui Hua, Xinyan Wang, Chuang Cheng, Qiang Zhu, and Xuezhong Zhou[✉]

School of Computer and Information Technology, Beijing Jiaotong University, Beijing 100044, China
{21125171,21120410,21125146,qzhu,xzzhou}@bjtu.edu.cn

Abstract. Molecular property prediction is becoming increasingly important in drug and material discovery, and many research works have demonstrated the great potential of machine learning techniques, especially deep learning. This paper presents our proposed solution for CCKS-2022 task 8, a chemical domain knowledge-aware framework for multi-view molecular property prediction. As a generative self-supervised approach to molecular graph representation learning, the framework is based on Knowledge-guided Pre-training of Graph Transformer (KPGT), which adopts a graph transformer guided by molecular fingerprint and descriptor knowledge. In the fine-tuning stage, combined with practical prediction problems, we fuse functional group information and chemical element knowledge graphs to predict molecular properties. From the perspective of chemical structure, KPGT provides structural information of molecular graphs (especially highlighting chemical bonds), and we further integrate chemical domain knowledge, using functional groups and chemical element knowledge graph, which is the information on physicochemical properties of atoms. From molecular graphs to functional groups, and to atoms, the molecular representation is jointly enhanced by multiple views from coarse to fine. When introducing functional group information and chemical element knowledge graph, we propose a novel BiLSTM-based recurrent module to accumulate domain knowledge. Our framework is able to simultaneously consider molecular graph, functional groups, and atomic physicochemical properties in practical predictions to better predict molecular properties. Finally, without using other external knowledge, the AUC-ROC of the test data reaches 0.88587, ranking second among 140 teams, which validates the performance of our approach.

Keywords: Molecular property prediction · Chemical domain knowledge · Molecular representation

1 Introduction

Accurate prediction of molecular properties enables early discovery of compounds with substandard physicochemical properties, thereby reducing the risk of clinical trial failure

---

R. Hua, X. Wang and C. Cheng—These authors contributed equally to the work.

© The Author(s), under exclusive license to Springer Nature Singapore Pte Ltd. 2022
N. Zhang et al. (Eds.): CCKS 2022, CCIS 1711, pp. 1–11, 2022.
https://doi.org/10.1007/978-981-19-8300-9_1

and improving the success rate of drug development. Traditional molecular property prediction analysis generally needs experiments, which is expensive and time-consuming. Many research works have demonstrated the great potential of machine learning techniques, especially deep learning, in predicting the molecular properties. These works use sequences (SMILES expressions or molecular fingerprints) or graphs (where nodes correspond to atoms and edges correspond to chemical bonds) to represent molecules, and apply sequence modeling or graph neural networks (GNNs) to predict the molecular properties which can assist drug research and development to improve efficiency and reduce costs [1–3].

However, the chemical space is vast, preventing these methods from being generalized in potential compounds. On the other hand, labeled data for molecular representation learning tasks are expensive and far from sufficient, especially compared to the size of the latent chemical space. Obtaining labels of molecular property often requires complex and time-consuming laboratory experiments [4]. As a result, the number of labels in most molecular learning benchmarks is insufficient, and machine learning models trained on such limited data tend to perform poorly. Due to the limited labeled data and huge chemical space, supervised learning strategies are prone to overfitting, poor generalization, and weak robustness in predicting molecular sets different from the training set.

Following the great success of Self-Supervised Learning (SSL) methods in Computer Vision (CV) [5] and Natural Language Processing (NLP) [6], many recent works in molecular representation learning adopt self-supervised learning strategies [7]. The main goal of self-supervised learning is to learn transferable knowledge from a large amount of unlabeled data through elaborately designed pretext tasks, and then transform the learned knowledge to downstream tasks [8]. Graph SSL can help GNN-based models learn more generalized representations for better performance on downstream tasks. Unlike CV, however, molecular graphs are constructed based on the rules in the field of chemistry, that the bonds (edges) between atoms (nodes) in molecular graphs are defined by chemical bond theory. During self-supervised learning, operations on molecular graphs may lose the initial semantics of their structures resulting in abrupt changes in their identities and properties [9]. Current self-supervised learning strategies for molecular graphs can only capture the structural similarity of superficial graphs, instead of intrinsic semantics closely related to molecular properties from chemical structures. Besides, graphs are usually formed by domain-specific rules, which means that domain knowledge can be incorporated into the design of the learning process. However, most current methods only consider the structural information of molecules, ignoring the chemical domain knowledge [10].

In response to these problems, combined with the task requirements of CCKS-2022 task8, we propose a coarse-to-fine multi-view molecular property prediction framework, which is based on the pre-training model KPGT [9], a self-supervised learning framework. In the fine-tuning stage, combined with the actual prediction problem, the chemical domain knowledge is integrated to predict the molecular properties. From the perspective of chemical structure, KPGT provides information of molecular graph (especially highlighting chemical bonds), and we further integrate functional group information, and finally incorporates the chemical element knowledge graph. From molecular graphs to functional groups, and then to atoms, the molecular representation is jointly enhanced by multiple views from coarse to fine. We also propose a novel BiLSTM-based recurrent module to accumulate domain knowledge when introducing functional group and chemical element knowledge graph. All these allow our framework to simultaneously consider molecular graph, functional group and atomic physicochemical properties in practical predictions to better predict molecular properties.

Finally, without using other external knowledge, the AUC-ROC of the test data reaches 0.88587, ranking second among 140 teams, which validates the performance of our approach.

2 Related Work

CCKS-2022 Task 8 is the task of molecular property prediction, which means that the core lies in Molecular Representation Learning (MRL). Therefore, the related work revolves around MRL. According to the learning methods, supervised MRL and self-supervised MRL are mainly introduced. Furthermore, since our approach emphasizes functional groups and chemical element knowledge, related methods based on domain knowledge will also be briefly discussed.

2.1 Supervised MRL

Traditional supervised learning employs feature-based methods to learn fixed representations from chemical descriptors and molecular fingerprints. In order to utilize the structural information of molecular graphs, relying on the rapid development of graph neural networks, molecular representation learning models applying GNN models have received considerable attention. Duvenaud et al. [11] were the first to apply graph convolutional networks to map molecules into neural fingerprints. Gilmer et al. [3] developed a message-passing framework MPNN for molecular property prediction. Its variant DMPNN [12] subsequently learned to encode molecular by using bond-centric convolutions instead of atoms, performing an edge-based message passing process on edge-directed graphs; CMPNN [13] further extended this work by improving the node and edge interaction kernel. The message passing operators used in GNNs only aggregated local information and fail to capture long-range dependencies in molecules. Recently, CoMPT [14] applied the transformer framework to capture long-term dependencies.

However, all the above works are supervised models that require molecular labels, which are rare and expensive, and the actual property prediction process is often prone to overfitting, poor generalization, and weak robustness.

2.2 Self-supervised MRL

Compared with supervised learning, self-supervised learning learns transferable knowledge from large amounts of unlabeled data by designing pretext tasks, and then generalizes learned knowledge to downstream tasks. Self-supervised methods can learn more general molecular representations, which has gained widely attention of researchers. Chithrananda et al. [15] proposed ChemBERTa, which used RoBERTa to pre-train on

PubChem to learn the sequence features of SMILES, but ignored the molecular graph structure information. Wang et al. [16] proposed a self-supervised graph neural network framework MolCLR, which enhanced molecular graphs with atomic masking, bond deletion and subgraph deletion strategies, and adopted the idea of contrastive learning to perform self-supervised learning on a large number of unlabeled data. Li et al. [9] used a knowledge-guided graph transformer for pre-training that converted molecular graphs into line graphs, employing a generative self-supervised learning strategy to learn more generalized representations of molecular graphs by predicting masked information.

2.3 Domain Knowledge Based MRL

Utilizing chemical knowledge (such as chemical elements, functional groups, etc.) in MRL is crucial for property prediction and drug discovery [20]. DMAX [17] proposed a new method to represent molecular graphs by inserting additional nodes with corresponding edges for each functional group and ring structure identified in the molecule. The proposed augmentation method improved the prediction performance, but the problem is that the open-source tool maintained by this method is not easily applicable to a large number of molecules. KCL [10] integrated basic chemical domain knowledge into molecular graph representation learning, and guided the enhancement process of the original molecular graph through the constructed chemical element knowledge graph, which made the molecular graph contain two types of information: the structural information of the molecular graph and the atomic property information extracted from the chemical element knowledge graph. However, the properties of general atoms usually do not have a decisive influence on the properties of molecules, and the introduction of physicochemical properties for all atoms of a molecule may bring some noise to the graph structure information.

3   Our Approach

We propose a coarse-to-fine multi-view molecular property prediction framework. The framework is chemical domain knowledge-aware and it's based on the pre-trained model KPGT. It integrates the functional group information of molecules and the chemical elements knowledge graph to predict molecular properties. KPGT provides information on the structure of molecular graphs (especially highlighting chemical bonds), and we further integrate functional group information, and then incorporates the chemical element knowledge graph, allowing our framework to learn molecular representations from multiple views. Specifically, our framework is divided into three parts: KPGT, functional group embedding, and knowledge graph embedding.

3.1   KPGT

Our framework is based on the proposed Knowledge-Guided Pre-training of Graph Transformer (KPGT), which is briefly introduced in this section. For more details, please refer to [9].

KPGT, which pre-training strategy is based on a generative self-supervised learning scheme, randomly selects a subset of nodes in the molecular graph for prediction, and adopts cross-entropy loss after masking to predict the type of the original node.

The difference is that KPGT does not use a simple molecular graph for pre-training, but converts it into a molecular line graph according to the rules. Specifically, it constructs a new node for each edge (chemical bond) in the original molecular graph, so as to highlight the chemical bond, and converts the common node of the molecular graph into a new edge. The molecular line graph is then fed into the Line Graph Transformer (LiGhT), which encodes the molecular line graph and learns a global feature representation for molecular property prediction. It is worth mentioning that KPGT introduces path encoding and distance encoding in LiGhT to ensure that the model can encode the structural information of molecular line graphs.

KPGT also introduces the knowledge of molecular fingerprints and descriptors in the pre-training process to guide the prediction of masked nodes. To incorporate the knowledge to guide predictions, a special node, called a knowledge node (K-node), is defined for each molecular line graph. The initial features of the K-node are initialized by quantitative molecular descriptors and molecular fingerprints. In pre-training, we follow KPGT to randomly mask a portion of initial features of the K-node, and learn to predict the masked molecular descriptors and fingerprints. Prediction of masked molecular descriptors is represented as a regression task with RMSE loss, while prediction of fingerprints is described as a binary classification task with cross-entropy loss.

KPGT provides our framework with structural information of molecular graphs (especially chemical bonds), and it incorporates knowledge of the molecules themselves in the learning process.

3.2 Functional Group Embedding

From the intuition of the chemistry discipline, it is often not just the graph structure that really determines the properties of a molecule, but the functional groups (FGs).

Since we did not find an official functional group identification method and property summary, we selected RDKit which is a publicly available cheminformatics tool to identify functional groups and utilize the FG class information. There are some important chemical functional groups built in RDKit, a total of 39, the specific structures are shown in Fig. 1. In particular, we use RDKit to get a list of FGs in SMILES (see Fig. 2), and then feed the functional group sequence into the Bidirectional LSTM (BiLSTM) encoder (see Fig. 3) to learn the embedding representation of functional groups.

3.3 Knowledge Graph Embedding

The chemical elements knowledge graph also contains chemical domain knowledge, and the introduction of atomic physicochemical properties can enhance molecular representation to some extent. We propose two strategies for embedding representations of knowledge graphs: BiLSTM-based recurrent module and knowledge graph embedding method.

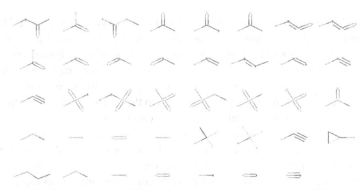

Fig. 1. Summary of 39 chemical functional groups built in RDKit.

SMILES		Sequences
COC(=O)C1CC2C=CC=CC(=O)C2(C)C1		[35, 2]
CSC(SC)=C1CC(=O)Nc2ccccc2C1=O	RDKit	[24, 24, 35]
CCCCN1C(=O)C(O)(NC(C)=O)C1COC(C)(C)C		[35, 0, 34, 28]

Fig. 2. The sequence acquisition process of functional groups. RDKit can directly recognize SMILES and output the functional group serial number contained in it.

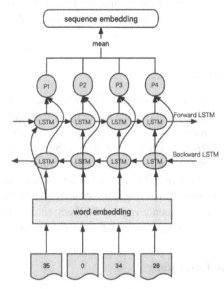

Fig. 3. The BiLSTM-based recurrent module. Input the sequence into BiLSTM to obtain the functional group information representation corresponding to SMILES.

BiLSTM-based Recurrent Module. In this part, we convert SMILES and knowledge graphs into sequences through key-value methods, and encode them with BiLSTM to obtain the final embedding representation. SMILES sequences usually contain multiple chemical atoms, and some atoms combine into functional groups and lose their properties. Therefore, we only consider independent atoms in SMILES. Then we use the atoms as the key to query the knowledge graph to get additional information about the atom. We combine them into sequences according to the format of atomic number of atoms and atomic properties, and finally send them into BiLSTM to encode the sequence information. Figure 4 shows the generation process of BiLSTM input sequence.

Knowledge Graph Embedding. We adopt knowledge graph embedding methods (e.g., Rotate and Complex) to learn entity and relation embeddings for chemical element knowledge graphs. We use the individual atoms in SMILES as indices to query the embedding matrix to obtain entity and relation embeddings. For the entity and relation vectors of different atoms, we obtain the entity and relation embeddings of the entire SMILES through linear mapping, and finally concatenate the two vectors to obtain the final embedding representation.

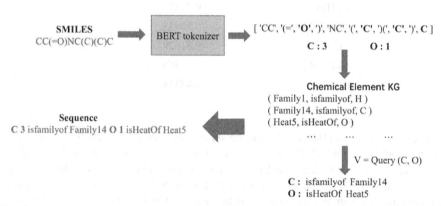

Fig. 4. The generation process of BiLSTM input sequence. We first identify the number of atoms in SMILES, splicing the atomic properties in the chemical element knowledge graph into a sequence and send it to BiLSTM.

4 Experiments

4.1 Dataset

The datasets provided in this competition include SMILES Expression Dataset and a Chemical Element Knowledge Graph. The SMILES Expression Dataset includes training set, validation set and test set. The training set has a total of 32901 SMILES expressions which has 1179 positive samples and 31722 negative samples. The validation set and test set respectively contain 4113 samples. The Chemical Element Knowledge Graph is constructed based on the Periodic Table of Elements which includes 117 attribute entities and 17 relation entities and helps build microscopic correlations between atoms.

4.2 Parameter Settings

In the fine-tuning phase, the seed is set to 22, the learning rate is 5e−5, the batch size is 32, the epoch is 100, and the early-stopping mechanism is used. The size of the epoch affects the learning rate. The graph embedding dimension of Rotate is 128 × 64, and the Complex is 128×128. For other parameter settings, please refer to KPGT.

4.3 Results

During the validation phase, we tried some baseline models and the results on the validation set are shown in Table 1.

Table 1. The results of baseline models on the Valid dataset.

Baseline Models	ROC-AUC
FastText	0.76406
GCN(DGL-LifeSci)	0.78953
KCL	0.81929
MolCLR	0.85940
KPGT	**0.88349**

It can be seen from the results that the supervised model FastText (binary classification model based on "SMILES" string) and the simple GNN (GCN model based on molecular graph structure) are far less effective than the self-supervised model. While in the self-supervised model, KCL, a contrastive learning framework that uses chemical element knowledge graphs to guide molecular augmentation, performs mediocrely, not as good as MoCLR, which augments molecular graphs through atom masking, bond deletion, and subgraph deletion strategies. We think it may be related to the molecules data in the valid dataset. The generative self-supervised model KPGT achieved the best result.

Therefore, during the testing phase, we used KPGT as the foundation and adjusted it in combination with our proposed multi-view molecular property prediction architecture based on actual test data. The results of test dataset are shown in Table 2.

Table 2. The results of our models on final test datasets.

Our Models	ROC-AUC
KPGT + FGs	0.88256
KPGT + KG(BiLSTM)	**0.88586**
KPGT + KG(ComplEx)	0.88507
KPGT + FGs + KG(ComplEx)	0.87302

We try to introduce functional group information and chemical element knowledge graph information respectively based on KPGT, and finally incorporated these two kinds of information together.

Introduce FGs. When introducing functional group information, since we did not find an official functional group identification method and property summary, we adopt RDKit, which is an open-source chemical information toolkit with 39 chemical functional groups built-in. We initialize the molecular representation by using an BiLSTM-based recurrent module to accumulate functional groups information.

Introduce KG. When introducing the chemical element knowledge graph, we employ two strategies: sequence and knowledge graph embedding. The sequential approach still uses our proposed BiLSTM-based recurrent module to accumulate atomic property information. When using the knowledge graph embedding, we divided the test data on the training set by ourselves, and tried two classic methods: ComplEx, and RotatE. ComplEx has the better result, so it is used on the final test data.

4.4 Discussion

From the intuition of chemistry, what really determines the properties of molecules is often the properties of functional groups [18], but our experiment shows that the results of using functional groups alone do not meet expectations. This may be due to the fact that we only used we only use functional group classes and do not have corresponding properties information. At the same time, the number of functional groups in RDKit is limited, and only a few functional groups frequently appear in the train/valid/test data, which leads to the fact that the specific functional group information aiming at properties is not introduced in the process, resulting in suboptimal ROC-AUC.

For methods using chemical element knowledge graph individually, the result of using our proposed BiLSTM-based recurrent module is slightly better than using ComplEx. BiLSTM has more parameters and is richer than ComplEx which may explain this phenomenon [19, 21].

Finally, the result of incorporating functional group information and ComplEx-based chemical element properties knowledge into molecular representations is not as good as introducing them individually. This may be because we add the three representations together in the final fusion. The fusion method is too simple, and the functional group and atomic property information may affect the graph structure information, resulting in poor performance. If there is no limit on the number of submissions, we plan to try other fusion methods such as concatenation, attention mechanism, etc.

5 Conclusion

This paper presents our proposed solution for task 8 of CCKS-2022, a chemical domain knowledge-aware, multi-view molecular property prediction framework. As a generative self-supervised approach to molecular graph representation learning, the framework is based on the pretrained model KPGT. In the fine-tuning stage, combined with practical prediction problems, our model perceives chemical domain knowledge. From molecular graphs to functional groups, and to atoms, the molecular representation is jointly enhanced by multiple views from coarse to fine. When introducing functional group information and chemical element knowledge graph, we propose a BiLSTM-based recurrent module to accumulate domain knowledge. Our framework can simultaneously consider molecular graph, functional group information, and atomic physicochemical properties in practical predictions to better predict molecular properties. Finally, without using other external knowledge, the AUC-ROC of the test data reaches 0.88587, ranking second among 140 teams, validating the performance of our method.

References

1. Kontogeorgis, G.M., Gani, R.: Computer Aided Property Estimation for Process and Product Design: Computers Aided Chemical Engineering. Elsevier (2004)
2. Xu, Z., Wang, S., Zhu, F., et al.: Seq2seq fingerprint: an unsupervised deep molecular embedding for drug discovery. In: Proceedings of the 8th ACM International Conference on Bioinformatics, Computational Biology, and Health Informatics, pp. 285–294. Association for Computing Machinery, New York (2017)
3. Gilmer, J., Schoenholz, S.S., Riley, P.F., et al.: Neural message passing for quantum chemistry. In: Proceedings of the 34th International Conference on Machine Learning, pp. 1263–1272. PMLR, Sydney (2017)
4. Brown, N., Fiscato, M., Segler, M.H.S., et al.: GuacaMol: benchmarking models for de novo molecular design. J. Chem. Inf. Model. **59**(3), 1096–1108 (2019)
5. Jing, L., Tian, Y.: Self-supervised visual feature learning with deep neural networks: a survey. IEEE Trans. Pattern Anal. Mach. Intell. **43**(11), 4037–4058 (2020)
6. Devlin, J., Chang, M.W., Lee, K., et al.: Bert: Pre-training of deep bidirectional transformers for language understanding. arXiv preprint arXiv:1810.04805 (2018)
7. Guo, Z., Nan, B., Tian, Y., et al.: Graph-based Molecular Representation Learning. arXiv preprint arXiv:2207.04869 (2022)
8. Chang, D.T.: Embodied-Symbolic Contrastive Graph Self-Supervised Learning for Molecular Graphs. arXiv preprint arXiv:2205.06783 (2022)
9. Li, H., Zhao, D., Zeng, J.: KPGT: Knowledge-Guided Pre-training of Graph Transformer for Molecular Property Prediction. arXiv preprint arXiv:2206.03364 (2022)
10. Fang, Y., Zhang, Q., Yang, H., et al.: Molecular contrastive learning with chemical element knowledge graph. In: Proceedings of the AAAI Conference on Artificial Intelligence, vol. 36, pp. 3968–3976 (2022)
11. Duvenaud, D.K., Maclaurin, D., Iparraguirre, J., et al.: Convolutional networks on graphs for learning molecular fingerprints. Adv. Neural Inf. Process. Syst. **28** (2015)
12. Yang, K., Swanson, K., Jin, W., et al.: Analyzing learned molecular representations for property prediction. J. Chem. Inf. Model. **59**(8), 3370–3388 (2019)
13. Song, Y., Zheng, S., Niu, Z., et al.: Communicative representation learning on attributed molecular graphs. In: Proceedings of the Twenty-Ninth International Joint Conference on Artificial Intelligence, pp. 2831–2838 (2020)
14. Chen, J., Zheng, S., Song, Y., et al.: Learning attributed graph representations with communicative message passing transformer. arXiv preprint arXiv:2107.08773 (2021)
15. Chithrananda, S., Grand, G., Ramsundar, B.: ChemBERTa: large-scale self-supervised pretraining for molecular property prediction. arXiv preprint arXiv:2010.09885 (2020)
16. Wang, Y., Wang, J., Cao, Z., et al.: Molecular contrastive learning of representations via graph neural networks. Nat. Mach. Intell. **4**(3), 279–287 (2022)

17. Grave, K.D., Costa, F.: Molecular graph augmentation with rings and functional groups. J. Chem. Inf. Model. **50**(9), 1660–1668 (2010)
18. Al-shammari, A.K., Al-Bermany, E.: Polymer functional group impact on the thermo-mechanical properties of polyacrylic acid, polyacrylic amide-poly (vinyl alcohol) nanocomposites reinforced by graphene oxide nanosheets. J Polym Res **29**, 351 (2022)
19. Belkin, M., Hsu, D., Ma, S., et al.: Reconciling modern machine-learning practice and the classical bias–variance trade-off. In: Proceedings of the National Academy of Sciences, pp. 15849–15854 (2019)
20. Zhang, N., et al.: OntoProtein: protein pretraining with gene ontology embedding. In International Conference on Learning Representations (2022)
21. Nakkiran, P., Kaplun, G., Bansal, Y., et al.: Deep double descent: where bigger models and more data hurt. J. Stat. Mecha. Theory Exper. 12, 124003 (2021)

A Coarse Pipeline to Solve Hierarchical Multi-answer Questions with Conditions

Ben Teng[1], Xuepeng Wang[1], Xiaodan lv[1], Xinxin Zhang[1], and Bo An[1,2(✉)]

[1] BAAI, Beijing, China
anbo724@163.com
[2] The Institute of Ethnology and Anthropology, Chinese Academy of Social Sciences, Beijing, China

Abstract. Span extraction is an important task of machine reading comprehension (MRC). Traditionally, for a question, the answer is expected to be a single text span from the given context. However, in practice, the answer to a question may exist in multiple spans. Besides, multiple answers to a question may be of different granularity and hierarchically related to each other. In this paper, we propose a simple but effective pipeline to solve the hierarchical multi-answer questions with conditions, an evaluation task introduced in CCSK 2022. The pipeline mainly contains two components: the answer span detection and relation classification. Answer span detection focuses on finding multiple answer spans while relation classification aims to determine whether there is a relationship between two answers. In addition, some helpful strategies are also introduced. Finally, our pipeline achieved an F1 score of 0.759 on online testing data and ranking second among 181 teams.

Keywords: Span extraction · MRC · Relation classification

1 Introduction

Span extraction is one of machine reading comprehension (MRC) tasks. Most traditional models extract a span of text (continuous subsequence) from the given context as the answer to the question. However, forcing an answer to be a single span may be too strict. In practice, the answer to a question may exist in multiple spans in the context. Recent work has taken some steps to handle multi-span questions [1] casts question answering as a sequence tagging task, predicting for each token whether it is a part of the answer. At inference time, they decode the answer with standard decoding methods, such as Viterbi.

CCKS2022 presents a more complex span extraction task. First of all, due to the lack of relevant domain knowledge, the question raised by the user is not clear enough, resulting in the need to answer according to different conditions. Secondly, multiple answers to a question may be of different granularity and hierarchically related to each other. All of this makes serious challenges for multi-answer questions.

The task of CCKS2022 can be described as the followings:

N. Zhang et al. (Eds.): CCKS 2022, CCIS 1711, pp. 12–20, 2022.
https://doi.org/10.1007/978-981-19-8300-9_2

*Given the context **C** and question **Q**, the model should give the correct answers **A**, including **condition answers**, **coarse answers**, **fine answers** and the **relations** among them* (Fig. 1).

In this work, we propose a simple but effective pipeline, as shown in Fig. 2, to solve the hierarchical multi-answer questions with conditions. There are two components in this pipeline: (1) the answer span detection; (2) the relation classification. In the answer span detection stage, the answers with red colors in Fig. 1 will be extracted, while in the relation classification stage, the blue ones will be predicted.

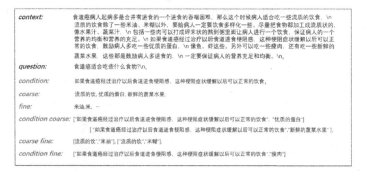

Fig. 1. The illustration of the CCKS2022 question answering task

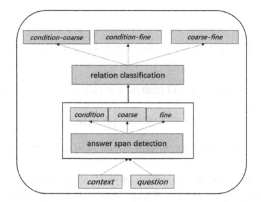

Fig. 2. The pipeline to solve the hierarchical multi-answer questions with conditions

Several experiments have been conducted to validate our pipeline. Results of online testing data indicate that our pipeline can obtain competitive performance (F1 = 0.7591) on this task, which ranks second in the competition of CCKS 2022 question answering task.

2 Method

As stated in the introduction, we decompose the question answering task into two sub-problems: an answer span detection problem and a relation classification problem. The answer span detection aims to find the condition spans, coarse spans and fine spans while the relation classification is to decide whether there is a relation between a pair of detected <condition, coarse>, <condition, fine > and <coarse, fine>.

In the following section, we will describe the solution to the above two sub-problems in detail.

2.1 Answer Span Detection

Span extraction a common task in natural language processing, such as named entity recognition and is commonly cast as a sequence tagging problem [2]. In this work, we model multi-answer questions as a *multi-span exaction task*.

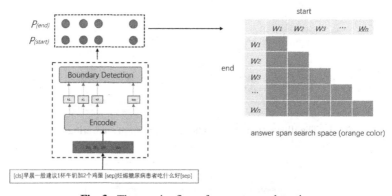

Fig. 3. The concise flow of answer span detection

First, we encode the question and context with a pre-trained language model:

$$h = \text{Encoder}([q, c]),\tag{1}$$

where $h = (h1, h2, ..., hm)$ is a sequence of contextualized representations for all input tokens.

Then we carry out the boundary detection to identify whether a word is the first or last word of an answer span. We predict the start and end positions with two token-wise classifiers. In this task, we feed the contextual representation hi into a multi-layer perceptron (MLP) classifier, and apply a soft-max layer to obtain the probability $P_{(i, s)}$ of the word w_i being the first word of an answer span.

$$P_{(i, s)} = \text{softmax}(\text{MLP}_{\text{start}}(h_i))\tag{2}$$

Similarly, we apply an MLP classifier to obtain the probability $P_{(i, e)}$ of the word w_i being the last word of an answer span.

$$P_{(i, e)} = \text{softmax}(\text{MLP}_{\text{end}}(h_i))\tag{3}$$

During training, we label the span boundaries of all answers as the ground-truth. Then, we define the training objective function as the average of two cross-entropy losses in detecting the start and end boundaries.

$$L = (L_{\text{start}} + L_{\text{end}})/2 \tag{4}$$

For the predicted start/end label of each word, value 1 means this word is a start/end position of an answer span and 0 means not. After the start/end label of one word is obtained, we use a basic strategy to extract spans from the context sentence. The searching space of the answer span is shown in Fig. 3 (right part). We start with the first word, and if that word is a span starting position, we look backward from that word to find the first word with an ending label is 1. The span between them is one of our detected answers.

In this task, since each answer span has a span type, such as condition, fine or coarse, we should assign a tag for each detected span. To solve it, many ways can be taken. For example, a span classification model can be used to classify detected spans to the corresponding tags. In the proposed method, we take a different approach: three distinct boundary detection models are trained for different answer span types. Two reasons are considered: (1) each model only learns one piece of information, which is easier; (2) we can make different attempts for different span types.

In the experiments, we adopt 5-fold cross-validation to train answer span detection models. In the prediction stage, the average pooling is used to ensemble the outputs of five models. The flow is illustrated in Fig. 4.

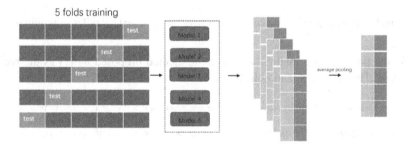

Fig. 4. The training and the predicting flow of answer span detection

2.2 Relation Classification

After detecting the types of answer spans, we build models to classify the relationships between two answer spans. Assuming that there are m condition spans, n coarse spans and l fine spans are detected, we need to classify $m*n$ condition-coarse pairs, $m*l$ condition-fine pairs and $n*l$ coarse-fine pairs.

In our pipeline, we build three binary classification models for the above three relation types, respectively. These three models are similar except that they have different inputs. The base model is Bert For Sequence Classification from package Transformers[8]. Two categories of inputs are experimented with to get better performance for each relation type. We will take the condition-coarse relation classification model as an example to illustrate the details of the method in the following part.

The first type of input is simply encoding the candidate pairs <condition, coarse> and <question, context> with a pre-trained language model:

$$h = \text{Encoder} ([condition, \, coarse, \, context, \, question]), \tag{5}$$

Then an MLP classifier is applied to obtain the probability of relation between the candidate pair.

However, this input ignores the position information. As shown in Fig. 5, two coarse spans "青菜" are detected in the context. They have different positions.

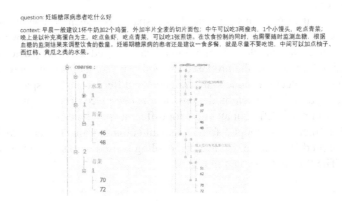

Fig. 5. An example that two coarse spans have the same text but different positions.

To add position information, we adopt the method proposed by [7] as the second input type. The input text is modified as follows:

$$[cls] + \, context + [sep] + \, question + < condition > < /condition > < coarse > < /coarse > + [sep]$$

where $< condition >$ $< /condition >$ $< coarse >$ $< /coarse >$ are four type markers to indicate the condition start position, condition end position, coarse start position, coarse end position, respectively.

The position ids of four type markers are assigned with the corresponding condition/coarse start position id and end position id.

2.3 Additional Strategies

2.3.1 Strategy 1

Due to the nature of this task, as stated in the task description, it is difficult to unify the boundaries of the condition fragments, so the start and end positions of the annotated condition fragments are extended to the nearest stop character in the published training dataset. Based on this rule, we extend the detected condition span answers to the nearest stop character, such as ",", "。" and ".".

2.3.2 Strategy 2

As stated in the relation classification stage, detected coarse/fine spans may have the same text but different positions. Although some modifications are made to add position information, we find that some rules can directly improve the classification performance. In experiments, we adopt the rule that if two candidate pairs contain the same text but different positions, the one which has a shorter distance between elements in the pair is selected.

3 Experiments

3.1 Data Processing

The dataset provided in this task contains 5000 training samples and 1000 online testing samples. In the answer span detection stage, we use the ground-truth answer spans to tag the tokens of the context for each training sample. For the relation classification, the training samples are generated by the steps in Fig. 6.

training data generation for relation classification

```
for sample in samples :
  for condition in sample :
    for coarse  in sample :
      if <condition, coarse> in sample :
        add [<condition, coarse>, 1] into training data
      else :
        add [<condition, coarse>, 0] into training data
```

Fig. 6. The algorithm to generate training samples

3.2 Experiments of Answer Span Detection

With the same network structure, we test the effect of three different pre-trained models on training samples: ERNIE-gram [5], pert-large [4] and macbert-large [6]. The results are shown in Table 1, 2 and 3, respectively. We can find that models with pert-large are fit for condition span detection while models with the ERNIE-gram are fit for coarse span detection.

No model is perfect. Thus, for the online testing, we ensemble the spans obtained from the three pre-trained models by voting as the final result.

Table 1. The valid result of condition span detection

Condition	Fold 1	Fold 2	Fold 3	Fold 4	Fold 5
ERNIE-gram	7329/7611/7468	7523/7506/7514	7527/7481/7504	7334/7916/7614	7470/7602/7535
pert-large	7524/7581/7553	7365/7959/7650	7545/7580/7562	7565/7733/7648	7283/8104/7688
macbert-large	7612/7709/7660	7341/7797/7562	7736/7390/7559	7565/7565/7565	7625/7625/7626

Table 2. The valid result of fine span detection

Fine	Fold 1	Fold 2	Fold 3	Fold 4	Fold 5
ERNIE-gram	8636/8669/8653	8683/8882/8781	8661/8866/8763	8711/8690/8700	8617/8530/8573
pert-large	8623/8510/8567	8546/8910/8724	8660/8782/8720	8643/8623/8633	8354/8791/8567
macbert-large	8504/8832/8665	8669/8845/8756	8827/8702/8764	8599/8793/8695	8407/8772/8583

Table 3. The valid result of coarse span detection

Coarse	Fold 1	Fold 2	Fold 3	Fold 4	Fold 5
ERNIE-gram	6673/6956/6812	6683/7281/6969	6299/7363/6790	6292/7665/6911	6246/7722/6906
pert-large	6502/7126/6800	6481/7407/6913	6279/7518/6843	6295/7198/6716	6673/6926/6797
macbert-large	6690/6891/6789	6845/7083/6962	6457/7028/6730	6396/7108/6733	6505/7095/6787

Table 4. The experiment result of relation classification

Input type	Pair type	dev acc
1	<condition, coarse>	0.978
2	<condition, coarse>	0.964
1	<condition, fine>	0.991
2	<condition, fine>	0.956
1	<coarse, fine>	0.994
2	<coarse, fine>	0.970

3.3 Experiments of Relation Classification

In the relation classification stage, pert-large is used as pretrained model. We divide the generated training samples into training set and development set by a 9:1 ratio. The results of the two category inputs are shown in Table 5.

Should note that due to the random seed is not fixed when we train the models, the development dataset changes for different input types and pair types.

3.4   Online Result

WE test different combinations on testing data. The final scores are listed in Table 5. "Ensemble*" in Table 5 means that we find "Voting Ensemble" may lead to empty answers for some questions. Thus, for these questions, we assign answer spans from pert (ERNIE-gram/macbert) to the final ensembled results.

Table 5. Scores for different combinations on testing data

Combination	Score
pert + Input type 1	0.7470
Voting Ensemble + Input type 1	0.7528
Voting Ensemble + Strategies + Input type 1	0.7582
Voting Ensemble + Strategies + Input type 2	0.7581
Ensemble* + Strategies + Input type 1	0.7591

4   Discussion

IN this article, we propose a simple but valid pipeline to solve the hierarchical multi-answer questions with conditions. During the training process, we conduct a lot of experiments to test our ideas. Here we present some interesting attempts that are not described in the Methods section.

4.1   First Attempt

In the answer span detection stage, for different span types, we add some heuristic texts to the questions. For example, "寻找句子中的条件" (find conditions in the sentence) is concatenated with the question text when the condition span detection model is trained.

4.2   Second Attempt

In the relation classification stage, we present two types of input. We can find that although position information has been considered, text information is passed to the model in an indirect way. Combing first and second category inputs, we propose the third category input.

$$[cls] + condition + [sep] + coarse + [sep] + context + [sep] + question + [sep]$$

The position ids for *condition* and *coarse* should be aligned with themselves in the context.

4.3 Third Attempt

In the answer span detection, we use the average pooling method to ensemble the results of five-fold models. We also test a stacking method to do that. The outputs of five-fold models are treated as features, and then traditional machine learning methods, such as decision tree, LightGBM, are employed to make a fusion.

4.4 Fourth Attempt

IN the answer span detection, we also test UIE [9], the first Chinese general information extraction model of Baidu PaddleNLP, to jointly extract coarse and fine answer spans. In the training stage, the prompt is set to "Abstract" (抽象) and "Detail" (具体体), corresponding to coarse-answer and fine-answer, respectively.

In the reasoning phase, considering the predicted spans contains all granularities and there will be more than one label for a span, we added two limitations to ensure the uniqueness of the span tag: only the coarsest granularity (delete the nested entities) and the highest probability (the highest confidence) will be selected.

4.5 Future Work

Since we do the above attempts in a coarse way, the final performance of these attempts is not very well. In future work, we will refine the methods and take some novel methods, such as models based on joint extraction of answer spans and relations.

References

1. Elad, S., Avia, E., Mor, S., Amir, G., Jonathan, B.: A simple and effective model for answering multi-span questions. In: Proceedings of the 2020 Conference on Empirical Methods in Natural Language Processing (EMNLP), pp. 3074–3080 (2020)
2. Tan, C., Qiu, W., Chen, M., Wang, R., Huang, F.: Boundary enhanced neural span classification for nested named entity recognition. In: Proceedings of the AAAI Conference on Artificial Intelligence, vol. 34, no. 05, pp. 9016–9023 (2020)
3. Li, X., Feng, J., Meng, Y., Han, Q., Wu, F., Li, J.: A Unified MRC Framework for Named Entity Recognition, pp. 5849–5859 (2020)
4. Cui, Y., Yang, Z., Liu, T.: PERT: Pre-training BERT with Permuted Language Model (2022)
5. Xiao, D., et al.: ERNIE-Gram: pre-training with explicitly N-gram masked language modeling for natural language understanding, 1702–1715 (2021)
6. Cui, Y., Che, W., Liu, T., Qin, B., Wang, S., Hu, G.: Revisiting pre-trained models for chinese natural language processing. In: Findings of the Association for Computational Linguistics: EMNLP 2020, pp. 657–668 (2020).
7. Zhong, Z., Chen, D.: A frustratingly easy approach for entity and relation extraction. In: Proceedings of the 2021 Conference of the North American Chapter of the Association for Computational Linguistics: Human Language Technologies, pp. 50–61 (2021)
8. Wolf, T., Debut, L., Sanh, V., Chaumond, J., Delangue, C., et al.: Transformers: state-of-the-art natural language processing. In: Proceedings of the 2020 Conference on Empirical Methods in Natural Language Processing: System Demonstrations, pp. 38–45 (2020)
9. Lu, Y., et al.: Unified Structure Generation for Universal Information Extraction. ACL (2022)

A Pipeline-Based Multimodal Military Event Argument Extraction Framework

Xin Xu, Jian Xu[✉], Guoqing Ruan, Hongyi Bao, and Jiadong Sun

Science and Technology on Information System Engineering Laboratory, Nanjing Research Institute of Electronic Engineering, Nanjing 210023, China
461629348@qq.com

Abstract. This paper presents a winning solution for the CCKS2022 Competition of Event Argument Extraction from Open Source Multimodal Military Equipment Data. The task is to match the textual information extracted from the text corpus with the visual information from images for event argument extraction. For this aim, we introduce a pipeline-based multimodal information extraction framework consisted of three models. The first one is a global pointer model which extracts entity information from the given text corpus, the second one is a yolo model which detects the bounding boxes of entities in the images and the last one is a multimodal matcher which matches the textual information with the visual information of entities for event argument extraction. With our pipeline-based multimodal information extraction framework, we have achieved the first place in the CCKS-2022 competition with a F1-score of 54.15%.

Keywords: Pipeline · Framework · Event argument extraction · Image and Text association

1 Introduction

The CCKS-2022 task of multimodal military information extraction aims at matching entity information from both the text corpus and images for event argument extraction. Fig. 1 gives an example of entity information matching between text and images. Suppose the textual information of an entity in a structural event argument of type investigation is "MQ-9 无人机" with a role of initiator and the visual information of the same entity is contained in a bounding box of the image below, then we would annotate the matching result as one. In the other case, suppose the entity information in the structural event argument is "地面或海面目标", with a role of receiver and there is no corresponding visual information, then we would annotate the matching result as zero. Please note that, a text may contain more than one event argument and have more than one event type.

As for the competition data, we have discovered that nearly 50% of texts do not contain event arguments. Meanwhile, a text may contain multiple event types, thus resulting in multiple role types for the same entity. Specifically, in the labeled training

---

X. Xu and J. Xu —Contributed equally to the work.

N. Zhang et al. (Eds.): CCKS 2022, CCIS 1711, pp. 21–29, 2022.
https://doi.org/10.1007/978-981-19-8300-9_3

Text:这就意味着MQ-9无人机可以在挂载武器装备的情况下，长时间滞留于9千米的高空，对地面或海面目标进行监视，甚至视情况展开打击，性能相当先进。

Image:

Event elments:
(5,12,'MQ-9无人机',侦查事件,发起者,[88.58548895899054,255.5714285714285,1123.3766561514194,616.0])
(40,47,'地面或海面目标',侦查事件,承受者,-1)
(5,12,'MQ-9无人机',攻击事件,发起者,[88.58548895899054,255.5714285714285,1123.3766561514194,616.0])
(40,47,'地面或海面目标',攻击事件,承受者,-1)

Fig. 1. An example of entity matching between text and images.

and validation data, about 4% of entities have more than one role type. For images, we discover that it is better to use the visual information of the detected bounding boxes for entity matching instead of using the entity categories since they are hard to infer due to small samples and sparse data.

To address these challenges, we propose a pipeline-based multimodal information extraction framework consisted of the three models as below:

i.   Global Pointer Model for Named Entity Recognition
     The global pointer is a pointer-based information extraction model which judges both the head and tail of entity together on a global view. The model enumerates all the text fragments in a sentence, and utilizes a loss function to ensure that the score of labeled entities is higher than that of non-entities. This provides a good solution to identifying entities with multiple role types. Furthermore, we perform an auxiliary task to determine the event type of the texts and incorporate the information of event type into the global pointer model.

ii. Yolo Model for Object Detection
     We only make use of the information about the presence and coordinates of objects, without inferring object categories. By doing so, we avoid the problem of target category detection with sparse samples.

iii. Multimodal Matcher for Matching Textual with Visual Information

If the textual information of entities matches the visual information of entities in the bounding boxes of the images for event argument extraction, our multimodal matcher model would output one otherwise zero.

With the pipeline-based multimodal information extraction framework, we have achieved the first place in the CCKS2022 Competition of Event Argument Extraction from Open Source Multimodal Military Equipment Data with a F1-score of 54.15%.

2 Method

Suppose a pair of textual and visual information for an entity is provided, denoted as $<X, I>$. We first tokenize the text as $x = [[CLS], x_1, x_2, ..., x_{l-2}, [SEP]]$, , where [CLS] and [SEP] are special tokens in the BERT [1] vocabulary. Then we obtain the token embedding vector $e = [e_0, e_1 ..., e_l]$, each element with a hidden dimension d_0. Finally, we derive the contextualized token embedding $\mathbf{h}(\textbf{text}) = [h_0, h_1, ..., h_{l-1}]$ by applying BERT transformer, where h_0 represents the context of overall sentence. Similarly, for the visual information of entity, we can obtain the image hidden vector with a hidden dimension d_1 after applying the swin transformer [2] $\mathbf{h}(\textbf{image}) = [h_1, h_2 ... h_n]$.

We propose a pipeline-based multimodal information extraction framework to extract the textual and visual information of entities in pair for event argument extraction. The entity information include the textual entity name, its starting and ending positions in the text and also the visual information of its bounding box in the image (Table 1).

Table 1. A pipeline-based multimodal information extraction framework.

A pipeline-based multimodal information extraction framework
Input: a set of samples of text and image pairs
Output: a list of the multimodal entity information
resultList=[]
for sample in range(samples):
image, text=sample
entlist= TextInfoExtract(text)
boxlist= VisualInfoExtract(image)
for box in boxlist:
for ent in entlist:
match=MultiModalMatch(ent, box)
if match==1:
resultList.append(ent+box)
return resultList

2.1 Global Pointer Model for Named Entity Recognition

Since a text may contain multiple events, the same entity mention may have different role types, thus resulting in the problem of nested named entities that existing crf-based models [3] cannot handle. One solution [4–8] is to construct a 3-dimensional matrix for each text $\mathbf{S} \in \mathbf{R}^{r*l*l}$ to evaluate the consistency of boundary information about starting and ending positions and role types in term of entity scores, where r represents the number of role types and l denotes the text length. For example, element $s_{\alpha,s,e}$ represents one entity's score, whose entity type is α that starts at position s and ends at position e.

We add a classifier token c (as highlighted in red in Fig. 2) to represent the context of overall sentence to the BERT encoder h, (whereas ∘ denotes concatenation)

$$\mathbf{h}' = e(s) \circ h \tag{1}$$

After passing through two project matrix $\mathbf{w_q}, \mathbf{w_k}$,

$$q_{i,\alpha} = W_{q,\alpha} h_i' + b_{q,\alpha} \tag{2}$$

$$k_{i,\alpha} = W_{k,\alpha} h_i' + b_{k,\alpha} \tag{3}$$

We transformer h' into a pair of query and key vectors:

$$q_\alpha = [q_{0,\alpha},\ q_{1,\alpha} \cdots q_{l,\alpha}] \tag{4}$$

$$k_\alpha = [k_{0,\alpha}, k_{1,\alpha} \cdots k_{l,\alpha}] \tag{5}$$

Then we define the entity score for the entity with starting position i, end position j and entity type α as follows:

$$s_\alpha(i,j) = q_{i,\alpha}^T k_{j,\alpha} \tag{6}$$

Then we apply the following loss function to keep entity scores of entities significantly greater than those of non-entities:

$$loss(ner) = \log(1 + \sum_{(i,j)\in P_\partial} e^{-s_\partial(i,j)}) + \log(1 + \sum_{(i,j)\in N_\partial} e^{s_\partial(i,j)}) \tag{7}$$

where i and j represent the starting and ending positions in the text, and $0 <= i <= j <= l; p_\alpha$ is the set of all entities with type α for the sample and N_α is the set of all non-entity spans or entities not with type α for the sample (Fig. 2).

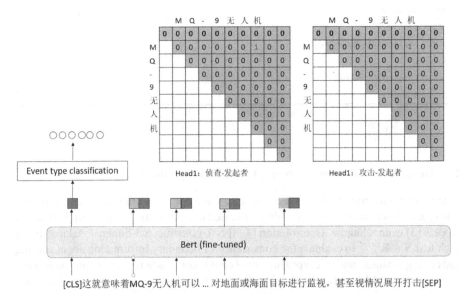

Fig. 2. Global pointer model for named entity recognition.

2.2 Yolo Model for Object Detection

We use yolo v5 [9] for object detection. Please note that we only detect whether the object exists or not, ignoring the object categories. If the object does exist, we would obtain the visual information in its bounding box. In the later training of Multimodal Matcher, we only use the visual information of these bounding boxes.

During the process of object detection, a loss function is applied to evaluate the degree of consistency between the predicted value and the real value of the model. The loss function of our yolo model includes two parts: positioning loss (box_loss), and confidence loss (obj_loss).

$$loss = l_{giou} + l_{conf} \tag{8}$$

Box_loss calculates the error between the prediction box and the real labeling box using the GIoU_loss function. Its principle is shown in Eq. (9): for two arbitrary convex shapes A and B, it finds the smallest convex shape C enclosing both A and B, then:

$$L_{giou} = \sum_{i=0}^{S^2} \sum_{j=0}^{B} I_{i,j}^{obj} [1 - IoU + \frac{A^c - U}{A^c}] \tag{9}$$

here S^2 denotes the number of grids and B denoted the number of bounding boxes in each grid. When an object exists in the bouding box, the value of $I_{i,j}^{obj}$ equals to 1 else 0.

Obj_loss estimates the confidence error of the prediction box, and use the cross-entropy loss function, as shown in Eq. (10):

$$l(y, \hat{y}) = -\frac{1}{n} \sum_{x} [y \ln \hat{y} + (1 - y) \ln(1 - \hat{y})] \tag{10}$$

where x is the sample, y is the label value, $\hat{y}$ is the predicting value of the model and n is the total number of samples.

2.3 Multimodal Matcher

BERT uses stacks of Transformer blocks where Each block $F^{(l)}$ receives as input a matrix of token embeddings $H^{(l-1)} \in R^{|t|*d}$ and outputs a new matrix of embeddings $H^{(l)} \in R^{|t|*d}$. Each block consists of a multi-head self-attention layer and a feed-forward layer, surrounded by layer normalization and residual connections.

The input to the first Transformer block, $H^{(0)}$, is a matrix of non-contextualized embeddings from an embedding lookup layer with parameter $W \in R^{|L|*d}$. For most pretrained Transformers, L is a moderately-sized vocabulary for either word pieces or sentence pieces.

The span's BERT embeddings (highlighted in red in Fig. 3) are combined using a fusion $f(e_i, e_{i+1,...,}e_{i+k})$. We use the mean-pooling as the fusion function and obtain both the token embeddings and position embeddings after combining the textual and visual information. We concatenate the two embeddings and utilize a binary classifier with an output of dimension one, indicating whether the textual and visual information of entities are matched for event argument extraction.

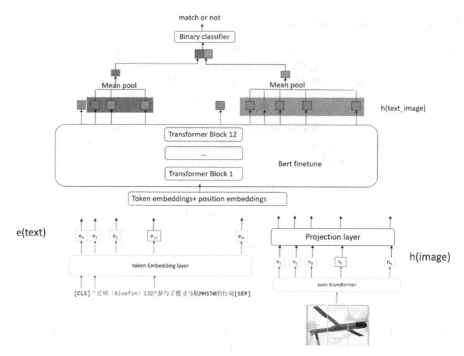

Fig. 3. Multimodal matcher (Color figure online)

3 Experiment

This section introduces the dataset provided in the CCKS2022 Competition and the experimental results to evaluate our pipeline-based multimodal information extraction framework.

3.1 Dataset

The data sets provided in the competition includes a training set which is finely labeled and also a test data set with no labels. The following experimental results are provided for the offline validation.

3.2 Implementation

The pipeline-based multimodal information extraction framework is consisted of three models. The first one is the global pointer model for named entity recognition, with the nezha-base-wwm as the pretrained model. During experiments, the number of training epochs is set as 100, the learning rate is set as $3e-5$ and the batch size is set as six. The early stop strategy is applied such that if the F1 value during validation does not improve for 3 consecutive times, the training procedure would be stopped. The second model is the Yolo model for object detection. We use yolov5 as the pretrained backbone model and set the input image size as 1280 * 1280, the number of training epochs as 20. The last one is the multimodal matcher model which matches the textual and visual information of entities for event argument extraction. We use the swin-tiny-patch4-window7–224 for feature extraction and set the learning rate as 3e−5.

3.3 Main Result

We use F1 as the evaluation metric and the evaluation process is shown in Algorithm 1. There are two different cases of evaluation, depending on whether the condition highlighted in red is met or not. If the condition is not met, we only evaluate the performance of event argument extraction from text, otherwise we evaluate the performance of textual and visual event argument extraction instead (Table 2).

Table 2. Performance evaluation.

Performance Evaluation

Input: prediction list-[prelist] , ground truth list- [gtlist]

\# The two lists have the same length and each element of the lists indicates the information of role types,

starting and ending positions and the bounding boxes of entities.

Output: F1 value

\# number of information pieces correctly predicted

matchNo=0

\# number of information pieces predicted

preNo=0

\# number of ground-truth information pieces

gtNo=0

\# For each piece of predicted information

for i in range(len([prelist]):

  samplePres= [prelist]$_i$

  sampleGts=[gtlist]$_i$

  preNo+= len(samplePres)

  gtNo+=len(sampleGts)

  for preEnt in samplePres:

    \# For each piece of ground-truth information

    for gtEnt in sampleGts:

      if preEnt and gtEnt share the same role type 事件类型一致 **&&** share the same starting position **&&**

share the same ending position **&&** the intersection over union is larger than 0.5:

        matchNo+=1

        break

precison= matchNo/preNo

recall=matchNo/gtNo

f1=(2*precison*recall)/(precison+recall)

return f1

We use 3/4 of the training data set for model training and the remaining 1/4 for validation. When we ignore the condition of intersection over union and evaluate the performance of event argument extraction only, the F1 value of validation is 0.61. When we consider the condition of intersection over union and evaluate the performance of textual and visual information matching for entities, the F1 value of validation is 0.52. The F1 value of our trained model on the independent test data set is 0.47 (Table 3).

Table 3. Results on validation data.

Global pointer	Yolo	Multimodal matcher	Event type classification	F1 (validation)	F1 (test)
√	×	×	×	61	–
√	√	√	×	52	47
√	√	√	√	–	51
√ + ensemble	√	√	√	–	54

In the final round of competition, due to the constraint of model size, we ensemble four Global Pointer Models with a voting strategy. The F1 value on the validation data set was 0.55 while that on the independent test data set is 0.54. We have achieved the first place in both the preliminary and final rounds of the competition.

4   Conclusion

To cope with the problems of limited event arguments of text corpus, multiple role types and sparse samples, we have proposed a pipeline-based multimodal information extraction framework. It is consisted of a global pointer model, a yolo model and a multimodal matcher. The global pointer model is able to extract entity augments from the text corpus with event type classification, the yolo model is able to detect the bounding boxes of entities without identifying their categories, and the multimodal matcher model is able to match the textual and visual information of entities for event argument extraction. The experimental results show that our framework has performed significantly well that we have achieved the first place in the CCKS2022 Competition of Event Argument Extraction from Open Source Multimodal Military Equipment Data in both the preliminary and final rounds.

References

1. Devlin, J., Chang, M.W., Lee, K., et al.: BERT: Pre-training of deep bidirectional transformers for language understanding. arXiv preprint arXiv:1810.04805 (2018)
2. Liu, Z., Lin, Y., Cao, Y., et al.: Swin transformer: hierarchical vision transformer using shifted windows. In: Proceedings of the IEEE/CVF International Conference on Computer Vision, pp. 10012–10022 (2021)

3. Wu, G., Tang, G., Wang, Z., et al.: An attention-based BiLSTM-CRF model for Chinese clinic named entity recognition. IEEE Access **7**, 113942–113949 (2019)
4. 苏剑林. GlobalPointer: 用统一的方式处理嵌套和非嵌套 NER [Blog post]. https://kexue.fm/archives/8373. Accessed 01 May 2021
5. Wang, Y., Yu, B., Zhang, Y., et al.: TPLinker: Single-stage joint extraction of entities and relations through token pair linking. arXiv preprint arXiv:2010.13415 (2020)
6. Bekoulis, G., Deleu, J., Demeester, T., et al.: Joint entity recognition and relation extraction as a multi-head selection problem. Expert Syst. Appl. **114**, 34–45 (2018)
7. Li, Y., Liu, L., Shi, S.: Empirical analysis of unlabeled entity problem in named entity recognition. arXiv preprint arXiv:2012.05426 (2020)
8. Yu, J., Bohnet, B., Poesio, M.: Named entity recognition as dependency parsing. arXiv preprint arXiv:2005.07150 (2020)
9. Ultralytics. YOLOv5. https://github.com/ultralytics/yolov5. Accessed 1 Nov 2020
10. Deng, S, et al.: OntoED: low-resource event detection with ontology embedding. In: Proceedings of the 59th Annual Meeting of the Association for Computational Linguistics and the 11th International Joint Conference on Natural Language Processing (Volume 1: Long Papers), pp. 2828–2839 (2021)
11. Lou, D., Liao, Z., Deng, S., Zhang, N., Chen, H.: MLBiNet: a cross-sentence collective event detection network. In: Proceedings of the 59th Annual Meeting of the Association for Computational Linguistics and the 11th International Joint Conference on Natural Language Processing (Volume 1: Long Papers), pp. 4829–4839 (2021)
12. Deng, S., Zhang, N., Kang, J., Zhang, Y., Zhang, W., Chen, H.: Meta-learning with dynamic-memory-based prototypical network for few-shot event detection. In: Proceedings of the 13th International Conference on Web Search and Data Mining, pp. 151–159 (2020)

A Search-Enhanced Path Mining and Ranking Method for Cross-lingual Knowledge Base Question Answering

Zhanglin Wu, Ming Zhu, Min Zhang, Song Peng, Weidong Zhang, Ting Zhu, Junhao Zhu, Peng Li, Hao Yang[✉], and Ying Qin

Huawei Technologies Co., Ltd., Beijing 100080, China
{wuzhanglin2,zhuming47,zhangmin186,pengsong2,zhangweidong17, zhuting20,zhujunhao,lipeng372,yanghao30,qinying}@huawei.com

Abstract. Knowledge Base Question Answering (KBQA) is a popular research direction in knowledge graphs, and most of KBQA work focuses on natural language parsing. In order to enhance the application of cross-lingual knowledge, the 16th China Conference on Knowledge Graph and Semantic Computing (CCKS2022) has released a cross-lingual knowledge base question answering (CKBQA) task. This paper presents the submission of our team (HW-TSC) to the CKBQA task, in which we propose a search-enhanced path mining and ranking method. The method divides the process of CKBQA into four parts: question classification, principal entity extraction, search-enhanced candidate path mining and candidate path ranking. Finally, both the preliminary and final evaluation results prove the effectiveness of our method.

Keywords: KBQA · CCKS2022 · CKBQA · Search-enhanced

1 Introduction

Knowledge graph is a knowledge base that uses a graph structure to describe entities and their relationships. As early as 2006, Berners Lee [1] put forward the idea of data link and called for the promotion and improvement of relevant technical standards. Subsequently, the research on semantic networks also arose. Until 2012, Google [2] formally proposed "knowledge graph" intended to improve the performance of search engines and the quality of search results. Subsequently, knowledge graph developed rapidly and was widely used in KBQA, personalized recommendation [3] and other fields.

KBQA is an important application of knowledge graphs. The mainstream methods of KBQA can be divided into semantic parsing [4, 5] and information retrieval [6, 7]. Semantic parsing-based methods typically convert natural languages to intermediate semantic representations, and then transform these representations into descriptive languages that can be executed in knowledge graph. Information retrieval-based methods first identify the entities in user questions to match against the subject entities in the knowledge graph, take relevant subgraphs as candidate answer sets, then extract features from queries and candidate answers and rank these answers.

© The Author(s), under exclusive license to Springer Nature Singapore Pte Ltd. 2022
N. Zhang et al. (Eds.): CCKS 2022, CCIS 1711, pp. 30–38, 2022.
https://doi.org/10.1007/978-981-19-8300-9_4

Compared with the traditional knowledge graph question and answer task, the CCKS 2022 CKBQA task is more challenging, their main gap lies in the integration of cross-lingual knowledge. We have made several attempts to align cross-lingual entities. In the following sections, the methods and experimental results are presented.

2   Task Description

The evaluation task aims to answer questions in different languages using a cross-lingual knowledge graph. The question-and-answer dataset for this task consists of parallel path questions in Chinese, English and French, including 2-hop and 3-hop types. We need to predict and generate the multi-hop reasoning path of the input question. The sponsor provides 14,262 question-and-answer data for model training, as well as some entity triples in the knowledge graph.

3   Method

Our method is divided into four parts: question classification, principal entity extraction, search-enhanced candidate path mining, and candidate path ranking. The pipeline is shown in Fig. 1. Question classification determines whether the answer to a question is two-hop or three-hop. Principal entity extraction extracts principal entities in user questions. Search-enhanced candidate path mining obtains possible answer paths. Candidate path ranking selects the top path as the correct answer.

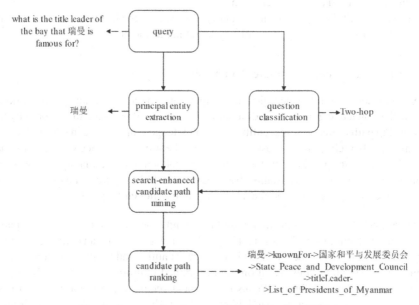

Fig. 1. An example of our method pipeline for CKBQA.

3.1 Question Classification

According to the CKBQA task description, we find that the number of answer hops is either two or three. Therefore, we use the bert-based text classification model [8] to identify the number of answer hops. To achieve better performance, we apply the xlm-roberta-base pre-training model [9] as the encoder, and use the adversarial learning strategy of FGM [10] to improve the robustness of classification model.

3.2 Principal Entity Extraction

According to the analysis of CKBQA task, the principal entity mentioned in the question is the first entity of the answer, and no additional entity link is required. Therefore, we use the answers from training data to mark the entities of the question in the second step. The corresponding entity extraction model is trained based on W2NER [11]. In addition, entity recognition model based on neural network may have some errors. We use all the first entities of the entity triples to build an entity library that sorts entities based on their character lengths and discovers the principal entity in question by whole-word matching. Based on the rules, the whole-word matching principal entity can be fused with the NER result to achieve a more accurate extraction. The specific rules are as follows:

(1) If NER result is part of the whole-word matching result or the whole-word matching result is part of NER result, then the whole-word matching result is used as the principal entity.
(2) If the result of whole-word matching is completely different from that of NER, then the latter is used as the principal entity.
(3) If NER result does not exist in the entity library, then the most similar entity in the entity library is obtained by similarity matching as the principal entity.

3.3 Search-Enhanced Candidate Path Mining

After the principal entity is identified, it is important to obtain candidate paths for questions with knowledge graphs. In traditional KBQA tasks, all paths are mined only by the relationship path of the principal entity in the knowledge graph, while in CKBQA tasks, path mining also relies on the cross-lingual parallel entity pairs. Since the cross-lingual parallel entity pairs provided by the sponsor are incomplete, we mainly extend them through vector search and translation-based ES search [12]. Figure 2 shows the process of two search methods to extend the cross-lingual parallel entity pairs.

Vector Search. Vector search can be used to extend cross-lingual parallel entity pairs. We construct all entities in Chinese and English-French graphs into an entity set, and use langid [13] tool to divide the entity set into Chinese entities and English-French entities. Then, we embed all entities based on the pre-trained multilingual model LaBSE [14] to build a vector search library. We also implement vector search of entities with faiss [15], an open-source similarity search library. Ultimately, we can find each entity's most similar cross-lingual entity by vector search.

Translation-Based ES Search. Translation-based ES search is another method we use to extend cross-lingual parallel entity pairs. Likewise, we add all header entities in the knowledge graph to the ES search base. To highlight the finer-grained differences, we adopt the open-source Sentencepiece [16] model to divide entities into sub-words as indexes for ES search when we construct the ES search library. After the library is built, we first employ the multilingual NMT model mbart [17] to translate the tail entities in the knowledge graph into other languages, and then use ES search to find their most similar entities to establish cross-lingual parallel entity pairs. To improve the accuracy, we also adopt the following strategies:

(1) Convert traditional Chinese to simplified Chinese.
(2) Re-rank search results using LaBSE similarity.
(3) Strictly distinguish ES search libraries by language.

After extending cross-lingual parallel entity pairs, we mine all paths that satisfy the conditions in the knowledge graph as candidate paths.

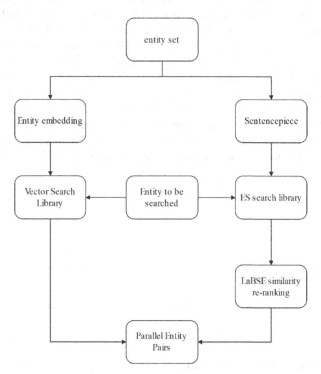

Fig. 2. The process of search methods to extend cross-lingual parallel entity pairs.

3.4 Path Ranking

Path ranking is the last step of our method, which selects the most suitable candidate path for answering questions from all candidate paths. In our method, we treat it as a binary classification task, and use the probability of being correctly classified to represent the matching between questions and answers. We train the classification model based on four different pre-trained models: xlm-roberta-base [9], xlm-roberta-large [9], infoxlm [18] and mbert [8]. Finally, we ensemble the classification probabilities by different models to select the best candidate path for each question. The main techniques we use to train the binary classification model are as follows:

Data Augmentation. In order to expand the training data scale of binary classification model, we translate questions in the original training data into two other languages, and construct new question and answer sentence pairs, in which principal entities are not translated.

Negative Sampling Training. Each question has more candidate paths in the knowledge graph and fewer correct candidate paths. If all incorrect candidate paths are used as negative samples for the training of binary classification model, it will cause serious data balance, which will lead to low classification accuracy. Therefore, we design a simple negative sampling method to randomly obtain negative samples from incorrect candidate paths. It is not necessary to pursue a complete balance of positive and negative samples during the construction of negative sample data. Because the number of negative samples is much larger than that of positive samples in the real prediction process. If the number of negative samples is too small, the binary classification model will not be able to adequately learn the patterns of the negative sample data. In addition, we also incorporate curriculum learning into negative sampling training. The process of negative sampling training based on curriculum learning is shown in Fig. 3:

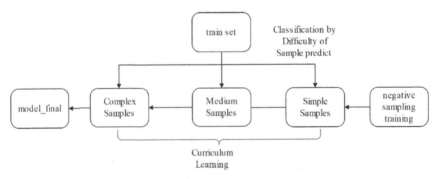

Fig. 3. Negative sampling training based on curriculum learning.

Path Feature Extraction. We also tried to use only relations to build candidate paths. For example, for the candidate path < 茶裏王, related, 伊藤園>, <Ito_En, logo, File:ITO_EN-logo.jpg>, we remove the entities and construct a new relationship path

<related, [sep], logo>. However, our experimental results show that the representation method of this relationship path is not as good as that of entity relationship path.

Curriculum Learning. Curriculum learning [19] was first proposed by a research team led by Bengio, a leader in machine learning. Its main idea is to simulate the learning order of human beings which starting from easy to difficult, allowing models to learn from easy to complex samples. Therefore, we use the initially constructed negative sample data to forecast the full data. Data whose similarity ranked from 1 to 5 are difficult samples, and those ranked from 6 to 10, 11 to 20, and above 20 are easy samples.

Model Ensemble. Model ensemble is an effective method to improve the accuracy. To further improve the performance of path ranking, we selected four pre-trained multi-lingual models mentioned above to train the binary classification model, and used the ensemble probability of multiple models as the final prediction result.

4 Experiment Result

On CCKS 2022 CKBQA task, we divide the training data into training set and development set, and use the development set to verify our method.

4.1 Question Classification

We construct a question classification model based on xlm-roberta-base to predict the number of answer hops, and we also validate the FGM training strategy based on this model. As shown in the comparative experimental results in Table 1, the model with the FGM training strategy is more accurate.

Table 1. Question classification accuracy

Model	Accuracy
xlm-roberta-base	0.9964
xlm-roberta-base + FGM	**0.9993**

4.2 Principal Entity Extraction

We validate and compare whole-word matching or NER alone and these two methods together for primary entity extraction. The specific experimental results are shown in Table 2. Although the whole-word matching and NER may make mistakes in entity extraction alone, they can complement each other and achieve the best results when working together.

Table 2. Experimental results of principal entity extraction

Method	P	R	F1
NER	0.9948	0.9940	0.9944
Whole-word matching	0.9982	0.9982	0.9982
NER + Whole-word matching	**1.0**	**1.0**	**1.0**

4.3 Search-Enhanced Candidate Path Mining

The difficulty of candidate path mining lies in insufficient cross-lingual parallel entity pairs provided officially in IIL File. Therefore, we design two search-enhanced methods for more cross-lingual parallel entity pairs, and conduct related experiments.

Table 3. Coverage of different search methods

Method	Coverage of cross-lingual parallel entity pairs in IIL File (%)
Vector search (top1)	**54.0**
ES search (top1)	**47.7**
ES search (re-rank top1)	**53.7**
Vector search (top1) + ES search (re-rank top1)	**66.6**
Vector search (top3) + ES search (re-rank top3)	**77.3**

For vector search, we use LaBSE for embedding, faiss for indexing, and remove bucketing and quantization to improve accuracy. While for ES search, we first apply mbart to translate the search entity for cross-lingual ES search. After the search is completed, we employ LaBSE model to calculate the similarity to rerank all search results. We also widen the candidate range of search results to improve its coverage on correct cross-lingual parallel entity pairs.

4.4 Path Ranking

Path ranking can be regarded as a binary classification task, that is, to determine whether a candidate path is the correct answer. We train four binary classification models based on different pre-trained models, and use the results of the model ensemble for the submission. Table 4 presents the experimental results of the model using HIT@1 and HIT@5 algorithms.

Table 4. Path ranking hit@1 and hit@5

Model	HIT@1	HIT@5
xlm-roberta-base	0.914	0.964
xlm-roberta-large	0.932	0.967
mbert	0.936	0.968
Infoxlm	0.938	0.967
Ensemble	**0.951**	**0.976**

4.5 End-To-End Evaluation Result

The end-to-end evaluation result of CKBQA is shown in Table 5. To test the performance of our path ranking model on the official test set, we manually supplement a batch of cross-lingual parallel entity pairs.

Table 5. End-to-end CKBQA accuracy

	F1
Preliminary	0.6780
Preliminary + Artificial cross-lingual parallel entity pairs	**0.9107**
Final	0.6453
Final + Artificial cross-lingual parallel entity pairs	**0.9173**

5 Conclusion

We propose a search-enhanced path mining and ranking method for CKBQA task. It consists of four modules: question classification, principal entity extraction, search-enhanced candidate path mining and candidate path ranking. Since the cross-lingual parallel entity pairs provided by the sponsor is incomplete, we extend the cross-lingual parallel entity pairs through vector search and translation-based ES search in the process of path mining to improve the coverage of correct answers. And in the process of path ranking, we use multiple strategies and models to enhance the hit rate of correct answers. Ultimately, the system based on our method has ranked first in the preliminary and second in the final, with the F1 values of 0.9107 and 0.9173 respectively.

References

1. Shadbolt, N., Berners-Lee, T., Hall, W.: The semantic web revisited. IEEE Intell. Syst. **21**(3), 96–101 (2006)

2. Singhal,A.: Introducing the knowledge graph: things, not strings. Offic. Blog Google **5**, 16 (2012)
3. Wang, H., Zhang, F., Zhao, M., et al.: Multi-task feature learning for knowledge graph enhanced recommendation. In: The World Wide Web Conference, pp. 2000–2010 (2019)
4. Berant, J., Chou, A., Frostig, R., et al.: Semantic parsing on freebase from question-answer pairs. In: Proceedings of the 2013 Conference on Empirical Methods in Natural Language Processing, pp. 1533–1544 (2013)
5. Abujabal, A., Yahya, M., Riedewald, M., et al.: Automated template generation for question answering over knowledge graphs. In: Proceedings of the 26th International Conference on World Wide Web, pp. 1191–1200 (2017)
6. Bordes, A, Chopra, S, Weston, J.: Question answering with subgraph embeddings. In: Proceedings of the 2014 Conference on Empirical Methods in Natural Language Processing (EMNLP), pp. 615-620 (2014)
7. Yao, X., Van Durme, B.: Information extraction over structured data: question answering with freebase. In: Proceedings of the 52nd Annual Meeting of the Association for Computational Linguistics (Volume 1: Long Papers), pp. 956–966 (2014)
8. Kenton, J.D.M.W.C., Toutanova, L.K.: BERT: Pre-training of deep bidirectional transformers for language understanding. In: Proceedings of NAACL-HLT, pp. 4171–4186 (2019)
9. Conneau, A., Khandelwal, K., Goyal, N., et al.: Unsupervised cross-lingual representation learning at scale. In: Proceedings of the 58th Annual Meeting of the Association for Computational Linguistics, pp. 8440–8451 (2020)
10. Miyato, T., Dai, A.M., Goodfellow, I.: Adversarial training methods for semi-supervised text classification. arXiv preprint (2016)
11. Li, J., Fei, H., Liu, J., et al.: Unified named entity recognition as word-word relation classification. In: Proceedings of the AAAI Conference on Artificial Intelligence, vol. 36, no. 10, pp. 10965–10973 (2022)
12. Gormley, C., Tong, Z.: Elasticsearch: the Definitive Guide: a Distributed Real-Time Search and Analytics Engine. O'Reilly Media, Inc. (2015)
13. Lui, M., Baldwin, T.: langid. py: An off-the-shelf language identification tool. In: Proceedings of the ACL 2012 System Demonstrations, pp. 25–30 (2012)
14. Feng, F., Yang, Y., Cer, D., et al.: Language-agnostic BERT sentence embedding. In: Proceedings of the 60th Annual Meeting of the Association for Computational Linguistics, pp. 878–891 (2022)
15. Johnson, J., Douze, M., Jégou, H.: Billion-scale similarity search with gpus. IEEE Trans. Big Data **7**(3), 535–547 (2019)
16. Kudo, T., Richardson, J.: Sentencepiece: A simple and language independent subword tokenizer and detokenizer for neural text processing. In: Proceedings of the 2018 Conference on Empirical Methods in Natural Language Processing: System Demonstrations, pp. 66–71 (2018)
17. Tang, Y., Tran, C., Li, X., et al.: Multilingual translation with extensible multilingual pretraining and finetuning. arXiv preprint (2020)
18. Chi, Z., Dong, L., Wei, F., et al.: InfoXLM: An information-theoretic framework for cross-lingual language model pre-training. In: NAACL-HLT (2021)
19. Bengio, Y., Louradour, J., Collobert, R., et al.: Curriculum learning. In: Proceedings of the 26th Annual International Conference on Machine Learning, pp. 41–48 (2009)

A Translation Model-Based Question Answering Approach over Cross-Lingual Knowledge Graphs

Jiangzhou Ji[(✉)], Yaohan He, and Jinlong Li

China Merchants Bank Artificial Intelligence Laboratory, Shenzhen 518000, China
{jesse,heyh18,lucida}@cmbchina.com

Abstract. Question answering is a typical application of knowledge graphs and it develops fast recent years. However, there are still some difficulties in this topic like QA over cross-lingual knowledge graphs. CCKS2022 holds a benchmark competition on QA over cross-lingual knowledge graphs. In this paper, we present a three-stage approach leveraging translation model to this benchmark. Our approach outperforms in the benchmark, which reaches 0.9320 as the precision score ranking the first place on the leaderboard.

Keywords: Question answering · Knowledge graph · Cross-lingual

1 Introduction

Question answering is a fundamental application of knowledge graphs, and the Knowledge-based Question Answering(KBQA) develops fast recent years. The key task to KBQA is to find a path in knowledge graphs, which connects entities and relations, to answer the given query.

As more and more non-English users have participated in the establishment and maintenance of knowledge graphs in recent years, the distribution of online knowledge has changed from a single language rich in resources (English) to complementary multilingual resources. However, current KBQA method on cross-lingual knowledge graphs mainly focus on natural language question parsing, while ignoring the joint application of cross-lingual knowledge.

CCKS2022 holds a benchmark on QA over cross-lingual knowledge graphs, which requires that the solution should leverage knowledge graphs in different languages. The definition of the task is: for given natural language query Q, model outputs a answer path p, which lies in the given knowledge graphs $\mathbf{K_{cn}}$ and $\mathbf{K_{en}}$ (in Chinese and in English). For the query Q, it may contains multi languages among Chinese(simplified and traditional), English and French. The given label is in DBpedia format. A sample is shown in Fig. 1. In this sample, we could find that there is a transition between the entity from one language to another.

The dataset consists of parallel path questions in Chinese, English and French, including 2-hop and 3-hop question types (the corresponding answer path contains 2 or 3 triples).

N. Zhang et al. (Eds.): CCKS 2022, CCIS 1711, pp. 39–46, 2022.
https://doi.org/10.1007/978-981-19-8300-9_5

Fig. 1. A sample in the train set

In this paper, we propose an approach to this benchmark which outperforms in the competition. The rest of the paper is organized as following: Sect. 2 describes the design of our approach; Sect. 3 presents our experiment implementations; Sect. 4 concludes our approach and sketches some directions for future works.

2   Approach

In this section, we'll describe the overview of the pipeline and the design of each stage.

2.1   Overview

Regrading to the inputs and outputs of this benchmark, we design 3 stages to finish the cross-lingual QA task. Stage-1 Named Entity Recognition(NER): to recognize the key entity in the query text, Stage-2 Path Proposal: to propose the candidate answer path leveraging the translation model, Stage-3 Path Ranking: to rank the paths by scoring model. By the three stages procedure, a query input with question text could be answered by a path among the given Chinese and English Knowledge Graph. This pipeline is illustrated as Fig. 2.

2.2   Design of Stages

Stage-1: NER. To answer the input question text, we need to recognize the key entity where the answer path starts. Hence, we see this as a NER task in mix-language(Chinese, English and French) text with only one category. According to the characteristics of the given train set, we construct a global pointer network model based on a pre-trained BERT model.

In detail, we choose BERT-base [1], which pre-trained on the top 104 languages with the largest Wikipedia using a masked language modeling (MLM) objective, as the encoder part. After that, the encoder part connects to a pointer network which uses the global pointer mechanism [4]. The train set of Stage-1

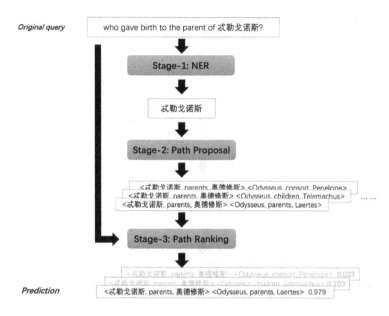

Fig. 2. The pipeline of the three stages

is the query part and the start entity of the labelled path. The loss function is as Eq.(1) [3].

$$L = \log\left(1 + \sum_{(i,j)\in P_\alpha} e^{-r_\alpha(i,j)}\right) + \log\left(1 + \sum_{(i,j)\in Q_\alpha} e^{r_\alpha(i,j)}\right) \quad (1)$$

where $r_\alpha(i,j)$ is the biaffined score of span from i to j. P_α is the set of heads and tails of category α, and Q_α is the set of heads and tails of category non-α or non-entity. Note that only $i \leq j$ should be considered.

The structure of Stage-1 is illustrated as Fig. 3.

Stage-2: Path Proposal. In overview, Stage-2 receives a key entity as input, and outputs all possible answer paths, that satisfy the requirements of the benchmark rules and including the transition between knowledge graphs, regarding to the key entity.

By the Stage-1, the key entity is recognized from the input query. Hence, we see the recognized entity as the start of the answer path. By analysis of the given train set, the answer path has and must have only one transition from the knowledge graph in one language to another. To solve this transition cross the knowledge graphs in different languages, we build a translation model based on transformer encoder-decoder model.

We use the English-Chinese subset of WMT17(Workshop on Machine Translation 2017) mixed with the given cross-lingual mappings as training set for

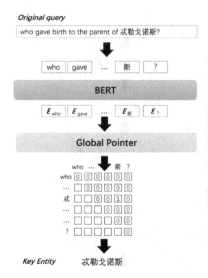

Fig. 3. The structure of Stage-1

the translation model, and the train process are followed by [2]. After we got an English-Chinese bi-direction translation model, we use ElasticSearch for the entity linking.

Based on the given knowledge graphs in two languages, the Stage-2 propose all answer paths with two or three triplets and only one transition between knowledge graphs. The structure of Stage-2 is illustrated as Fig. 4.

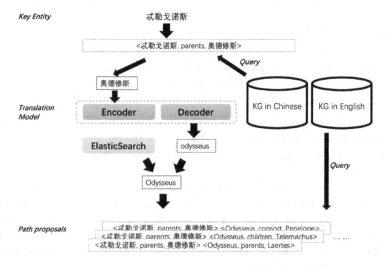

Fig. 4. The structure of Stage-2

Stage-3: Path Ranking. In overview, Stage-3 receives the original input query and corresponding paths proposed by Stage-2 and outputs the most matched answer path, which will be final prediction of our pipeline.

In detail, the input of Stage-3 model is the text concatenated the original input query and one candidate path(the start entity and the predicates afterwards), and the output is the match score. The model is a BERT-like classification model and its output sigmoid of [**CLS**] token logit is the match score. The path with the highest match score among the proposed paths will be the final prediction.

The positive samples of train set is sampled from the given original train set. Meanwhile for every sample of original train set, we construct the negative samples by some false answer paths proposed by Stage-2. The ratio of positive samples and negative samples is 1:3.

The structure of Stage-3 is illustrated as Fig. 5.

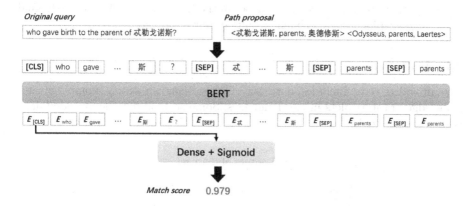

Fig. 5. The structure of Stage-3

2.3 Our Strategies

To improve the performance of our pipeline, we also apply some strategies on modeling and data processing.

Multi Base Model Choice. For Stage-1 and Stage-3, we choose BERT-base and RoBERTa-large as the encoder part, and both are pre-trained on large-scale multi-language corpus. And we ensemble the outputs of these models to the final submission.

Entity Linking. Though the Stage-2's translation model could translate entity name into another language, the translated name usually doesn't match the entity in knowledge graphs. All entity names are recorded in ElasticSearch, and the the target entity is linked by ElasticSearch. During this procedure, the transition of simplified Chinese and traditional Chinese is applied.

Negative Sampling. In detail, we iterate the negative samples in Stage-3 train set by adding the false positive predictions by the previous trained models. So that, the model could be trained by the original positive samples and indistinguishable negative samples. The final train set of Stage-3 is iterated twice by such procedure.

3   Experiments

In this section, we'll describe the data set in the CCKS 2022 QA on cross-lingual knowledge graphs and experiment results of our approach.

3.1   Data Set

The provided data includes data set, Chinese-English entity mappings and knowledge graph triplets in two languages. Some stats about the provided data is shown in Table 1.

Table 1. Stats of data sets

Item	Quantity
Train set	14,262
Test set A	1,500
Test set B	1,500
Chinese-English entity mappings	13,636
Triplets in K_{cn}	104,941
Entities in K_{cn}	77,541
Relation types in K_{cn}	1,156
Triplets in K_{en}	162,554
Entities in K_{en}	122,525
Relation types in K_{en}	1,639

The length of the query is short than 150, hence the regular position embeddings is available. Moreover, there are simplified Chinese and traditional Chinese text mixed in the data sets.

3.2   Implementation

All programs are implemented by TensorFlow framework, and trained on nvidia Tesla V100 GPU.

Stage-1. For Stage-1, we set the learning rate to 1×10^{-5} using AdamW optimizer, the batch size is set to 16 and the model is trained for 15 epochs. We train 2 models on BERT-base and RoBERTa-base, ensemble the results of these models. For data set, we spilt the provided labelled data (the query and the start entity) into train set and validation set randomly as the ratio of 95:5. All models are trained on the split train set and evaluated on the split evaluation set.

In evaluation phase, we predict all entities in test set and randomly choose only one entity for each sample.

Stage-2. For Stage-2, we set the learning rate to 3×10^{-5} using AdamW optimizer, the batch size is set to 16 and the model is trained for 20 epochs. For data set, we combined with WMT17 dataset and given Chinese-English entity mappings as the whole dataset.

We import all entity names into ElasticSearch, and link the document with *match* function by default parameters. The top-1 document is chosen to be the next subject in triplet.

In the evaluation phase, we translate every object of triplet and link to a subject in the knowledge graph in another language.

Stage-3. For Stage-3, we set the learning rate to 1×10^{-5} using AdamW optimizer, the batch size is set to 16 and the model is trained for 20 epochs. We train 2 models on BERT-base and XLM-RoBERTa, ensemble the results of these models by average the logits of outputs. For data set, we construct the dataset by the strategy described in Sect. 2.3.

In the evaluation phase, we predict all possible answer paths for a sample, choose the highest score one to be the output path and reformat the path into the required form.

3.3   Experiment Results

For Stage-1, the precision on our split valid set is up to 0.987 by the NER model. For Stage-2, the BLEU-1 of our translation model on split valid set is 27.2. For Stage-3, the classification precision on our constructed valid set is 0.941.

3.4   Competition Results

The competition score is evaluated by accuracy. On Test Set A, we got an accuracy of 0.8887. On Test Set B, we got an accuracy of 0.9320, ranking 1st place.

4   Conclusion

In this paper we propose a 3-stage pipeline to the CCKS-2022 question answering on cross-lingual knowledge graphs benchmark. And our approach leverage the translation model, NER model and classification model so that this approach reach the precision of 0.9320, ranking the first place of the benchmark.

In future, we're looking forward to optimizing the pipeline by the graph models, simplifying the procedure to form an effective end-to-end solution.

References

1. Devlin, J., et al.: BERT: pre-training of deep bidirectional transformers for language understanding. arXiv preprint arXiv:1810.04805 (2018)
2. Vaswani, A., et al.: Attention is all you need. In: Advances in Neural Information Processing Systems 30 (2017)
3. Jianlin, S.: Apply softmax cross-entropy loss function to multi-label classification. https://kexue.fm/archives/7359. Accessed 10 Aug 2022
4. Jianlin, S.: GlobalPointer: unified way to process with non-nested and nested NER. https://kexue.fm/archives/8373. Accessed 10 Aug 2022

Cascaded Solution for Multi-domain Conditional Question Answering with Multiple-Span Answers

Junhao Zhu[✉], Min Zhang, Song Peng, Hao Yang, Ying Qin, Weidong Zhang, Han Han, and Miaomiao Ma

Huawei Technologies Co., Ltd. 2012 Laboratories, Beijing, China
{zhujunhao,zhangmin186,pengsong2}@huawei.com

Abstract. This paper introduces our technical solution for CCKS-2022's task of "A Dataset of Conditional Question Answering with Multiple-Span Answers". The solution consists of Data Analysis and Processing, Condition-Answer Extraction, Post-extraction Processing, Condition-Answer Relation Classification, and Post-classification Processing. The rule-based post-extraction and Post-classification Processing modules consist of seven cascaded modules. Because the training data of the task contains multi-domain questions and answers and is constrained, we have designed a prediction method based on the conditions, coarse-grained answers, and fine-grained answers of the fine-tuned pre-trained language model for multi-domain scenarios. Binary classification is used for relation extraction of conditions, coarse-grained answers, and fine-grained answers, and the constraint extraction method is based on rules. The proposed solution obtains an F1 value of 0.74487 on the test set (ranking 3rd), and its effectiveness in multi-domain scenarios is verified.

Keywords: Condition-answer extraction · Condition-answer relation classification · Multi-domain scenario · Pre-trained language model

1 Background and Task Introduction

Text question answering (QA) is an important research task in linguistic text analysis. With the development of machine reading comprehension datasets and significant progress of language models, QA systems have attracted extensive attention from academic and industrial circles. Extractive QA is an important form of QA tasks, which requires the model to extract a span from the corresponding context as the answer. Different from the current common single-span extraction task, in practical application, the answer to a question may exist in multiple positions of the context, which is called extractive multi-span QA. By analyzing samples of the Internet QA community, we find that the samples of multiple answers generally have two characteristics: (1) The questions asked by users who lack relevant domain knowledge are not clear. As a result, these questions need to be answered separately according to different conditions. (2) A

N. Zhang et al. (Eds.): CCKS 2022, CCIS 1711, pp. 47–56, 2022.
https://doi.org/10.1007/978-981-19-8300-9_6

question may have multiple answers that have different granularities but a hierarchical relation between them. They together pose a serious challenge to multi-span QA.

Given 5000 samples from Tencent's external QA community, the original data contains a question and context that can answer that question. All samples contain multiple answer spans, including not only labeled answer spans (where the answer span is labeled with two granularities: coarse and fine) but also labeled condition spans needed to answer the question. That is, three context spans are labeled: conditional, coarse-grained, and fine-grained answers. In addition to the context spans, the relation between the condition and the answer as well as the hierarchical relation between the coarse-grained and fine-grained answers are also labeled in all samples. Under the condition that only the provided sample data can be used, the conditional answers and their relations of the users' questions in the test set are calculated and inferred.

2   Technical Solution

The technical solution of this paper consists of five modules: Data Analysis and Processing, Condition-Answer Extraction, Post-extraction Processing, Condition-Answer Relation Classification, and Post-classification Processing, as shown in Fig. 1. Among them, Data Analysis and Processing includes data cleaning, entity dictionary generation, and splitting by period. The Condition-Answer Extraction module extracts the condition, coarse-grained answer, and fine-grained answer spans from user questions based on RoBERTa [3], fine-tunes the data three times, and ensembles the two models (for details, see Fig. 3). The Post-extraction Processing is to correct and supplement the model extraction results. The Condition-Answer Relation Classification module is based on BERT [4] to determine whether there is a relation between the condition, coarse-grained answer, and fine-grained answer. The rule-based Post-extraction and Post-classification Processing modules correct and supplement the relation according to the characteristics of sample data, and finally output the result according to the above modules (i.e.,

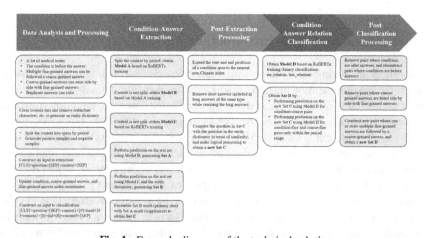

Fig. 1. Example diagram of the technical solution

condition, coarse-grained answer and fine-grained answer set, condition-coarse pairs, condition-fine pairs, and coarse-fine pairs).

2.1 Data Analysis and Processing

Analysis of Data Characteristics

- A large number of medical terms, with 77% of medical-related QA samples labeled:

  An entity dictionary is created to improve the recall of fine-grained answers.

- Condition span before answer span:

  In relation classification, only coarse-grained answers and fine-grained answers after the condition span need to be processed.

- One or more fine-grained answers followed by the coarse-grained answer:
  The coarse-fine pair is created by relating the fine-grained answer and the coarse-grained answer following it (the threshold of distance between the two answers is set to at most 5 characters, and these characters must contain Chinese characters like " 等" and " 这").
- The coarse-grained answer can be listed side by side with the fine-grained answer:
  The coarse-grained answer can appear together with the fine-grained answer. In this case, it is necessary to remove the coarse-fine pair (if any).

Data Processing

- Generating an entity dictionary:

  The conditions, coarse-grained answers, and fine-grained answers of the labeled data set are extracted to generate an entity dictionary. The key is the Question, and the value is the set of corresponding conditions, coarse-grained answers, and fine-grained answers.

- Context processing:

  Operations, such as uppercase to lowercase, traditional Chinese to simplified Chinese, full-width to half-width, Chinese digit to Arabic digit, and error correction, are performed.

2.2 Condition-Answer Extraction

Answers are classified into the following three types (labeled sample data) (Table 1):

Table 1. Answer type and quantity

Answer Type	Quantity
Condition	6559
Coarse-grained Answer	7843
Fine-grained Answer	29,668

The quantity of fine-grained answers is much greater than that of conditions and coarse-grained answers. Therefore, extracting fine-grained answers will be the main point to improve the Score.

Table 2. Context length and quantity

Length	Quantity
≤100	496
>100 && ≤200	2281
>200 && ≤300	1999
>300 && ≤400	213
>400 && ≤500	11
>500	0

In this solution, RoBERTa is used to perform encoding, and the concatenated token input is "[CLS] + Question + [SEP] + Context + [SEP]". The string length distribution is as follows Table 2 (Fig. 2):

You can see that the length does not exceed 512 characters and most of the samples are between 100 and 300 characters. Therefore, you do not need to process token input through the sliding window.

After the token is generated, the position coordinates are refreshed (the length of Question + [SEP] is added to all coordinates) and fine-tuning is started.

This solution proposes two stages of extracting condition, coarse-grained answer, and fine-grained answer spans:

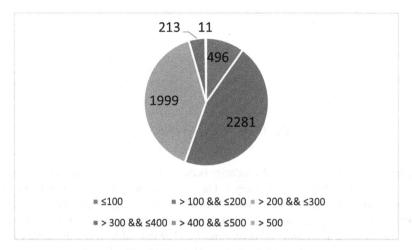

Fig. 2. Context length distribution

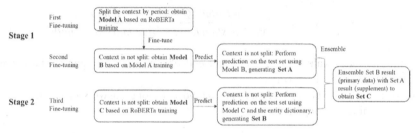

Fig. 3. Two-stage method for condition and answer extraction

Each stage is described as follows:

- Stage 1: The first fine-tuning is performed based on the RoBERTa + LSTM network [1], and the labeled data is split by period (multiple context spans are obtained) to obtain model A. In the second fine-tuning, the original context is not split. Based on the Model A training, Model B is obtained, and prediction is performed on the test set to obtain Set A.
- Stage 2: The third fine-tuning is performed based on the RoBERTa + LSTM network [1] to obtain Model C, and prediction is performed on the test set to obtain Set B.

The prediction results of Stage 1 and Stage 2 are ensembled to obtain Set C, with the prediction result of Stage 2 as the primary data and that of Stage 1 as the supplement.

2.3 Post-extraction Processing

After the model extraction results are ensembled, some answers need to be recalled to compensate for the insufficiency of model prediction, as shown in the following Fig. 4:

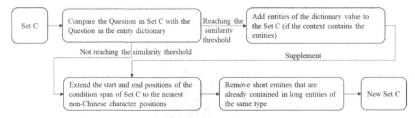

Fig. 4. Post-extraction processing

- Calculate the edit distance and similarity between the question of the test set and the key of the entity dictionary (the key is Question). If the edit distance and similarity meet the specified threshold (2 and 0.4 respectively in the experiment), obtain the value of the entity dictionary (the value is a set of conditions, coarse-grained answers, and fine-grained answers), and determine whether the value of the dictionary exists in the context field of Set C. If it exists, add the answers to Set C; otherwise, ignore the answers. The formula for calculating the similarity is as follows:

$$\text{Similarity} = 1 - \frac{Editdistance\ Question, Dictionary key}{\max\ Question\ length, Dictionary\ key\ length} \tag{1}$$

- Extend the index values of the start and end of the condition span to the nearest non-Chinese character positions.
- Remove short answers that are already included in long answers of the same type while retaining the long answers.

2.4 Condition-Answer Relation Classification

There are four types of pairs: condition-coarse pair, condition-fine pair, coarse-fine pair, and unrelated pair. The existing correct pairs (positive samples) are directly generated from the labeled data in the samples, while the incorrect unrelated pairs (negative samples):

- Consist of the unpaired conditions and answers in the positive samples.
- Consist of conditions and answers across the pairs in positive samples if positive samples do not contain these pairs.

Data Distribution (Fig. 5):

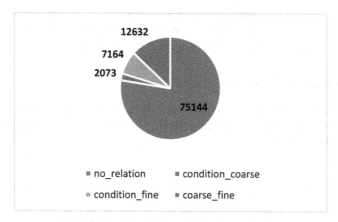

Fig. 5. Data distribution of four types of pairs

As shown in the preceding figure, the data distribution is extremely unbalanced. For multi-class classification, even if the weight parameter is set, or downsampling is used for large categories, the prediction accuracy is not high. The analysis shows that only the relations between three types of answers (condition span, coarse-grained answer span, and fine-grained answer span) need to be identified. Therefore, the binary classification processing is adopted (for details, see Fig. 6).

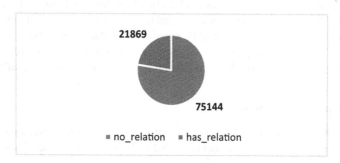

Fig. 6. Data distribution of the two relations

Relation Classification model:

- The same as the other relation classification models, in our Relation Classification mode, the input is a sentence containing two labeled answers. Not only the semantic information of the input sentence, but also information of the two answers in the sentence need to be considered. To enable the BERT to identify the two answers, a symbol (e.g. # or $) is added before and after each answer (e.g. [CLS] + question + [SEP] + context1 + [#] + head + [#] + context2 + [$] + tail + [$] + context3 + [SEP]), so that the BERT can extract local information of the two answers.

- This solution uses labeled data to fine-tune the BERT-based multi-class classification model [2] to obtain Model D.
- Model D is used to perform prediction on the new Set C for condition-coarse pairs, and to perform prediction on the new Set C for condition-fine and coarse-fine pairs only within the period range. In this way, the Set D is obtained.

2.5 Post-classification Processing

In some scenarios where the prediction result of the Relation Classification model is inaccurate, some rules need to be adopted to correct the model prediction error, as shown in the following Fig. 7:

Fig. 7. Post-classification processing

3 Experiment

The organizer of CCKS-2022's task "A Dataset of Conditional Question Answering with Multiple-Span Answers " provided 5000 labeled samples and 1000 pieces of unlabeled test data for the preliminary and final competitions. During model training, the Condition-Answer Extraction model and Condition-Answer Relation Classification model divide 5000 samples into training set and test set on a 9:1 basis. All model parameters use the default settings. It should be noted that the data distribution of condition-coarse, condition-fine, and coarse-fine relation pairs is imbalanced. Therefore, binary classification, instead of multi-class classification, is used for relation classification.

3.1 Model Effect Evaluation

The experimental results of the Condition-Answer Extraction model and the Condition-Answer Relation Classification model are listed in Table 3, Table 4, and Table 5.

Table 3. Condition-answer extraction model result

Answer	Precision	Recall	F1	EM
Condition	0.87642	0.88968	0.883	0.758
Coarse answer	0.74940	0.77243	0.76074	0.57
Fine answer	0.83366	0.88504	0.85858	0.494
All	0.82342	0.86005	0.84134	0.282

Table 4. Condition-answer relation classification model result

Relation	Precision	Recall	F1	EM
Condition-coarse answer	0.80645	0.80894	0.80769	0.802
Condition-fine answer	0.70984	0.70771	0.70877	0.678
Coarse answer-fine answer	0.67726	0.66844	0.67282	0.578
All	0.71243	0.70752	0.70997	0.362

Table 5. Pipeline model result

	Precision	Recall	F1	EM
Result	0.78144	0.80054	0.79087	0.234

3.2 End-To-End Effect Evaluation

The evaluation results on the preliminary test set and the final test set are shown in Table 6.

Table 6. End-to-end effect evaluation

Test Set	Score
Preliminary	0.73171
Final	0.74487

4 Conclusion

This paper proposes a cascaded question answering solution for the conditional question answering with multiple-span answers in multi-domain scenarios. The solution consists of five modules: Data Analysis and Processing, Condition-Answer Extraction, Post-extraction Processing, Condition-Answer Relation Classification, and Post-classification Processing. In the case of a small data set, the model + rule approach achieves good generalization ability, and the system reaches an F1 score of 0.74487 on the test set.

References

1. Li, J., et al.: Unified Named Entity Recognition as Word-Word Relation Classification (2022)
2. Wu, S., He, Y.: Enriching Pre-trained language model with entity information for relation classification. In: Proceedings of the 28th ACM International Conference on Information and Knowledge Management (CIKM '19), pp. 2361–2364. Association for Computing Machinery, New York, NY, USA, (2019). https://doi.org/10.1145/3357384.3358119

3. Zhuang, L., Wayne, L., Ya, S., Jun, Z.: A robustly optimized BERT pre-training approach with post-training. In: Proceedings of the 20th Chinese National Conference on Computational Linguistics, pp. 1218–1227, Huhhot, China. Chinese Information Processing Society of China (2021)
4. Devlin, J., et al.: BERT: pre-training of deep bidirectional transformers for language understanding. In: NAACL. 2019, Association for Computational Linguistics, pp. 4171–4186 (2019)
5. Ashish, A., et al.: Attention is all you need. In: Proceedings of the 31st International Conference on Neural Information Processing Systems (NIPS' 17). Curran Associates Inc., Red Hook, NY, pp. 6000–6010 (2017)
6. Zhu, Y., Wang, G., Karlsson, B.F.: CAN-NER: Convolutional attention network for Chinese named entity recognition. arXiv preprint arXiv:1904.02141 (2019)
7. Kishimoto, Y., Murawaki, Y., Kurohashi, S.: Adapting bert to implicit discourse relation classification with a focus on discourse connectives. In: Proceedings of the 12th Language Resources and Evaluation Conference, pp. 1152–1158 (2020)
8. Cao, X., Liu, Y.: Coarse-grained decomposition and fine-grained interaction for multi-hop question answering. J. Intell. Inf. Syst. 1–21 (2021). https://doi.org/10.1007/s10844-021-006 45-w
9. Huang, P., Huang, J., Guo, Y., Qiao, M., Zhu, Y.: Multi-grained attention with object-level grounding for visual question answering. In: Proceedings of the 57th Annual Meeting of the Association for Computational Linguistics, pp. 3595–3600 (2019)
10. Krishna, K., Iyyer, M.: Generating question-answer hierarchies. arXiv preprint arXiv:1906.02622 (2019)
11. Liu, B., Wei, H., Niu, D., Chen, H., He, Y.: Asking questions the human way: scalable question-answer generation from text corpus. In: Proceedings of The Web Conference 2020, pp. 2032–2043 (2020)

Compound Property Prediction Based on Multiple Different Molecular Features and Ensemble Learning

Wenming Yang[(✉)], Jiali Zou, and Le Yin

METiS, Hangzhou, China

ywm108@163.com, {jlzou,lyin}@metispharmaceuticals.com

Abstract. China Conference on Knowledge Graph and Semantic Computing (ccks2022) proposed the task of chemical element knowledge graph construction and compound properties prediction.

For this task, we proposed to generate vector representations of chemical molecules by using molecular descriptors and pharmacophore fingerprints, and using large-scale chemical molecular data for unsupervised training to generate vector representations of chemical molecules. Then we discussed the performance of molecular representations generated by different methods in molecular properties prediction. The vector representations generated based on different ways were concatenated, and they were input into the ensemble model for prediction. Finally, the score of 0.8985 was obtained in the test dataset, and won the first place.

Keywords: Feature fusion · Pharmacophore fingerprint · Functional group · Voting

1 Introduction

It is not easy to find drug candidates. The traditional method is to screen potential compounds from tens of millions by the participation of pharmaceutical chemists, and then their effect in inhibiting viral activity is verified through experiments. The success rate depends on the experience of chemical experts, which is not only costly but also time-consuming. Before deep learning is proposed, density functional theory (DFT), as a widely used computational method, has long become a powerful tool in the field of chemistry. DFT can predict a variety of molecular properties with high accuracy but without a large amount of experimental data. However, DFT is very time-consuming and generally takes several hours to complete the calculation of a single molecule. The traditional quantum chemical calculation method requires huge time cost. If the number of screened compounds is large, it is difficult to complete the molecular property prediction in a short time and screen the appropriate compounds. If there is a large amount of experimental data accumulated in the past and with an accurately trained machine learning model, the computational cost of DFT will not become a major obstacle to the prediction of molecular properties. Virtual screening of huge molecular spaces is

N. Zhang et al. (Eds.): CCKS 2022, CCIS 1711, pp. 57–69, 2022.
https://doi.org/10.1007/978-981-19-8300-9_7

possible using data-driven AI technology, which can not only accelerate the screening process, but also expand the search space. Usually more than 100 molecules with the best comprehensive performance will be firstly screened out, and then their key properties are further predicted through high-precision quantum physical calculation. After all, in combination with the additional selection by pharmaceutical chemists, dozens of drug candidate molecules that are most likely to be successfully developed are identified and processed into targeted experimental validation.

A large number of studies show that machine learning or deep learning have made great progress in compound properties prediction. In these works, the factors affecting the accuracy of properties prediction are not only related to the model itself and experimental data, but also to the representation of chemical molecules. Good molecular representation plays a key role not only in property prediction, as well as in downstream tasks such as similar molecular generation.

This competition is launched on the base of the construction of the knowledge graph of chemical elements, and enhancement of the original molecular graph by using the knowledge in the chemical field. Starting with the expression of compound SMILES (simplified molecular input line entry system) and the simple knowledge Graph, players can expand the knowledge graph of chemical elements as needed, and then use machine learning or deep learning technology to predict the molecular properties.

Next, this paper introduces the scheme by exhibiting related work, methods, experiments and summaries.

2   Related Work

Different molecular representation methods have different effects on downstream tasks. This section introduces the molecular representation methods involved in this scheme.

2.1   Molecular Descriptor

Molecular descriptors refer to the measurement of the properties of a molecule in a certain aspect, which can be either the physical and chemical properties of the molecule or the numerical indexes derived by various algorithms according to the molecular structure. Molecular descriptors can be divided into quantitative descriptors and qualitative descriptors. Qualitative descriptors are generally called molecular fingerprints, that is, the structure, properties, fragments or substructures of molecules are expressed by some kind of coding. The commonly used molecular fingerprints include Daylight fingerprints, MACCS keys, PubChem molecular fingerprints, etc., they are different in the definition of substructures and the coding methods. At present, there are more than 5000 kinds of molecular descriptors provided by various software. For example, 208 kinds can be provided in rdkit. Mordred is an extended descriptor library established based on rdkit, which can calculate 1826 molecular descriptors. The above software is written in C++ and there is an API in python. By combining different molecular descriptors into vectors, every molecule can be represented by a vector, which is adopted in property prediction or drug design. Molecular fingerprints transform a molecule into a row of bit vector of 0 or 1 for computer processing and calculation. The bits in the fingerprints indicate whether there are some substructures in the molecules.

Fingerprint Based on Substructure. MACCS [1] fingerprint: MACCS fingerprint is a fingerprint based on substructure. The substructure encoded by smarts has two variants according to the type and number of substructures: one is 166 bits long and the other is 960 bits long. The shorter fingerprint is commonly used. Although it is only 166 bits short, it covers most of the chemical characteristics of interest in drug discovery and virtual screening. PubChem fingerprint [2] is also a substructure-based fingerprint, which has 881 bits, covering a wide range of different substructures and functional groups, and is mainly used for molecular similarity search.

Circular Fingerprints. Morgan molecular fingerprint is an extended connectivity fingerprints (ECFP) derived from Morgan algorithm [3], thus it is a circular fingerprint. Morgan fingerprints have become the industry standard method for circular molecular fingerprints, they are specially designed for structure-activity relationship studies. FCFP (functional class fingerprints), as a variant of ECFP, is further abstracted from the latter. The main software packages supporting ECFP fingerprints basically also support FCFP.

Pharmacophore Fingerprint. Pharmacophore fingerprint is also a common molecular fingerprint.

Pharmacophore is a summary of the structural characteristics that play the most important role in a series of bioactive molecules reactivities. Pharmacophore fingerprint adopts the fingerprint coding method based on substructure, it also considers the distance between atom. It is usually classified according to the distance range to form a bit string of 0 or 1. Pharmacophore fingerprints include 2D pharmacophore fingerprints and 3D pharmacophore fingerprints. Gobbi 2D pharmacophore fingerprint is used in this evaluation task. This fingerprint is designed and implemented by Gobbi et al.

2.2 SMILES

SMILES (simplified molecular input line entry system), as a simplified molecular linear input specification, is a specification that explicitly describes the molecular structure with ASCII strings. The smiles symbol is consist of a series of uninterrupted letters, and the chemical structure is transformed by the vertical first traversal tree algorithm. The five coding elements of smiles are atom, chemical bond, branch chain, closed loop and unconnected structure. The isomers of chemicals follow the coding rules of isomeric smiles. As an example, given "smiles: CC (= O) n1c2cccc2sc2c1ccc1ccccc21", it can be converted into 2D or 3D structure diagram of molecules by tools. Shown in Fig. 1.

Chemical molecules can be directly converted into smiles sequences as input into the deep learning model for molecular properties prediction. GB Goh [4] et al. proposed the SMILES2Vec model by using deep recurrent neural network (RNN),which automatically extracted features from SMILES to predict the properties of compounds. Due to the scarcity of data in the field of drug research and development, we can imitate the technology in the field of natural language processing, use a large number of unlabeled data for model pre-training, and generate molecular representations from the pre-trained model, and then input them into deep learning or machine learning models for properties prediction. S Jaeger [5] and other authors proposed the mol2vec model by imitating

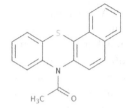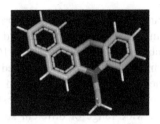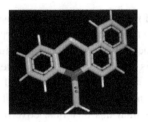

Fig. 1. Molecular formula (2D and 3D structures) and SMILES

word2vec in natural language processing. Like in the word2vec model, the vectors of similar words are relatively close in space. Mol2vec learns the vector representation of molecular substructure, and the relevant chemical substructures with similar directions. The vector obtained by mol2vec overcomes the shortcomings of common feature representation, such as sparsity and bit collision.

Bert model has been widely used in the text field and image processing, and has achieved good results. By processing smiles in the same way, we can obtain the pretraining model of chemical molecules on Bert. Chithranda S [6] and other researchers released Bert model called ChemBERTa, which trained with PubChem's 77m smiles data. Wang s [7] and others proposed the smiles-bert model by using similar methods, they used a large number of unlabeled data for unsupervised training, and showed the effectiveness and generalization ability of the pre training model in the downstream tasks. The latest paper published by Wu Z [8] is also based on the Bert model, but the author proposed a new pre training strategy. By learning the molecular and atomic features predefined by computational chemists, the model extracts features from smiles like computational chemists. The general fingerprint K-BERT-FP generated by K-BERT shows the same prediction ability as MACCS on 15 drug datasets.

2.3 Molecular Graph Representation

In recent years, with the rise of graph networks, many researchers regard molecules as a type of graph data, and use graph neural networks to predict molecular properties. For a molecule, atoms are regarded as nodes, and chemical bonds are regarded as edges. Through continuous iteration, the properties of adjacent atoms and bonds are merged into every single this atom. The neural network takes the original molecular graph as input, adopts convolutional layers to extract features, and then combines the features of all atoms through global pooling. This approach allows us to perform molecular prediction end-to-end. The method of pretrainning and finetunning has been widely used in natural language processing and image fields, and applying this method on molecular graphs has also become a research hotspot.Hu W [9] et al. proposed a pre-training method that simultaneously learns at the node level and the entire graph level, which can learn both local and global representations of the graph well. For node-level pre-training of GNNs, the authors use readily available unlabeled data and natural graph distributions to capture domain-specific knowledge or rules in graphs, and propose two self-supervised methods: Context Prediction and Attribute Masking.

The research work published jointly by researchers such as Sun M et al. [10] from Michigan State University and Agios Pharmaceutical Company believes that in general graph data enhancement, nodes will be masked or edges will be discarded, but in molecular graphs, such enhancement will change the molecular structure and semantic information. In view of this, the authors investigate graph contrastive learning in the biomedical domain and propose a new framework named MoCL, which utilizes domain knowledge at both local and global levels to assist representation learning. The author implements a molecular graph enhancement scheme based on local-level domain knowledge through substructure replacement, so that the semantics of the graph does not change during the enhancement process. Using similarity information between molecular graphs, the global structure of the data is encoded into the graph representation by adding a global contrastive loss. The author also provide a theoretical basis for the learning objectives related to triple loss in metric learning, illustrating the effectiveness of the whole framework. MoCL is evaluated on various molecular datasets and demonstrated to outperform other state-of-the-art methods.

Most current methods of graph contrastive learning mainly focus on the topological structure of the graph, and rarely consider the domain knowledge contained in the graph. The authors Fang Y [11] pointed out that for molecular graphs, the addition or deletion of chemical bonds or functional groups will largely change the identity and properties of molecules. This paper proposes a new method: a knowledge-enhanced molecular graph contrastive learning framework (KCL). KCL uses the information of chemical elements to build a chemical element knowledge graph to guide the enhancement process of the original molecular graph, and at the same time designs a Knowledge-aware Message Passing Neural Network (KMPNN) encoder to maximize the difference between positive and negative sample pairs to construct a contrastive loss function and optimize Model. For each atom in the original molecular graph, find the triplet that has the atom as a tail entity in the chemical element knowledge graph. Taking the head entities in these triples as new nodes and the relations as edges between the head and tail entities, the molecular augmentation graph is obtained. Molecular-enhanced graphs, as positive samples of original molecular graph, contain richer and more complex information and are able to capture microscopic connections between atoms.

Zhang Z [12] et al. proposed a graph self-supervised learning framework based on functional groups, which can effectively learn the functional group information in molecules, called MGSSL. The innovativeness of this method lies in the consideration of molecular functional groups in the process of pre-training, and proposes a set of methods for molecular rupture and the construction of functional group tree. At the same time, pre-training is carried out at the node level and the functional group level, and different weights are automatically assigned.

Xiaomin Fang [13] et al. proposed the geometry enhanced molecular Representation Learning by introducing the 3D structure of molecules into molecular characterization. In this paper, the defects of the sequence model with smiles sequence as input are analyzed. For example, the string syntax is difficult to understand, and two adjacent atoms may be far apart in the text sequence; a small change in the string may lead to a large change in the molecular structure. For example, the string syntax is difficult to understand, and two adjacent atoms may be far apart in the text sequence; A small change in the string may lead to a large change in the molecular structure. In order to better learn the knowledge of molecular space, in addition to taking geometric information as input, the research team designed a number of self supervised learning tasks.

Rong Y [14] and others hope to capture semantic information and structural information from a large amount of unlabeled data. The main structure of the model is borrowed from Transformer, which is called GTransformer. In the OGB competition, Ying C [15] proposed the Graformer model in order to introduce the powerful expressive power of the Transformer model into the graph-structured data. Zhang x C et al. [16] inspired by the pre training model, the authors proposed the MG-Bert model based on the molecular graph, by randomly covering some atoms in the molecular graph and then using the MG-Bert model to recover the covered atoms. There are also some researchers who integrate other information for pre training, For example, the work from Zeng Z [17] proposed a KV-PLM for cross-modal learning, which fuses molecular structure information with knowledge texts for Masked Language Model pre-training. Inspired by the latest research results in the field of computer vision, Qian Y et al. [18] proposed a new perspective, that is, using molecular images to characterize molecular structural information and predict compound and protein interactions.

3   Method

This section focuses on the models and methods in this evaluation task. The representation of chemical molecules is very important to the prediction of molecular properties. Good molecular representation will obtain high prediction accuracy. Although there are many pre-training models based on large-scale unlabeled data, traditional molecular descriptors and molecular fingerprints are still very effective in compound properties prediction.

3.1   Molecular Vector Representation

The following methods and pre-training models are selected for this evaluation task to generate molecular representation vectors.

Molecular Descriptor. A large number of calculation methods for molecular descriptors are built in RDKit, these methods are mainly located in rdkit.Chem.Descriptors. For missing or other non-standard data, it is uniformly treated as 0.

The name of the feature vector is: rdkit_descriptor_vec,dim=208.
code repository: https://github.com/rdkit/rdkit.

Pharmacophore Fingerprint (Gobbi 2D). The pharmacophore fingerprint is generated by Rdkit, the feature vector is composed of 0 or 1, and the vector length is 39972. Since the dimensionlity is too high, Sparse AutoEncoder is used for dimensionality reduction. The model structure is shown in Fig. 2, and the dimensionality after dimension reduction is 256.

The name of the feature vector is: rdki_gobbi_ae_vec,dim=256.
code repository: https://github.com/rdkit/rdkit.

Pre-trained Model KCLGNN [11]. There are two different encoding methods in the model. After verification, KMPNN encoder is selected.

The name of the feature vector is: kclgnn_vec,dim=128.

code repository: https://github.com/ZJU-Fangyin/KCL.

3D Structural Characterization of Chemical Mmolecules: GeoGNN [13]. The name of the feature vector is:geognn_vec,dim=32.

code repository: https://github.com/PaddlePaddle/PaddleHelix/tree/dev/apps/pretrained_compound/ChemRL/GEM.

Pretrain-Gnns. The Pretrain-gnns model [9] has various pretraining parameters. After verification, the parameter "supervised_contextpred.pth" provided by the author of the paper is selected to generate a molecular representation. The name of the feature vector is: pregnn_vec,dim=300.

code repository: https://github.com/snap-stanford/pretrain-gnns.

MGSSL Model [12]. The name of the feature vector is: mgssl_vec,dim=300.

code repository: https://github.com/zaixizhang/MGSSL.

The different eigenvectors are shown in Table 1.

Table 1. Vectors obtained according to different models

Feature serial number	Feature name	Model	Dim
feature_1	rdkit_descriptor_vec	rdkit	208
feature_2	rdki_gobbi_ae_vec	rdkit	256
feature_3	kclgnn_vec	KCLGNN	128
feature_4	geognn_vec	GeoGNN	32
feature_5	pregnn_vec	Pretrain_gnn	300
feature_6	mgssl_vec	MGSSL	300

3.2 AutoEncoder Model

The model structure of the AutoEncoder model is shown in Fig. 2. The model consists of two parts, one is the Sparse Auto Enocder (SAE). The network of SAE consists of three layers of network: the input layer (Encoder), the middle layer (Hidden), and the output layer (Decoder).

loss function (see Formula 1):

$$loss\_1 = Huber\,loss + KL(p||q) \tag{1}$$

The second part is the binary classification model. Due to the imbalance of the samples, the loss function adopts GHM [19].

loss function (see Formula 2):

$$loss\_2 = GHM\ Loss \tag{2}$$

The two-part loss function is added (see Formula 3), and both models are trained at the same time.

$$loss = loss\_1 + loss\_2 \tag{3}$$

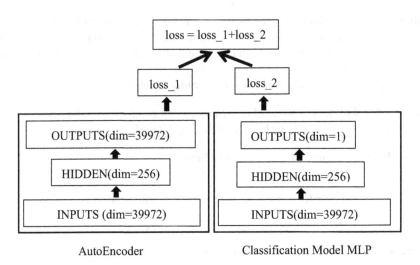

Fig. 2. Pharmacophore fingerprint dimensionality reduction AutoEncoder model

In the reasoning stage, only the SAE model is used, the pharmacophore fingerprint vector which the dimension is 39972 is input and the output of the hidden layer is taken to obtain the final vector.

3.3 Ensemble Model

Concatenate Feature
concatenate feature 1:kclgnn_geognn_rdkit-descriptor_mgssl_pregnn_rdkit-gobbi_vec

kclgnn_vec	geognn_vec	rdkit_descriptor_vec	mgssl_vec	pregnn_vecn	rdki_gobbi_ae_vec

concatenate feature 2:kclgnn_geognn_rdkit-descriptor_mgssl_rdkit-gobbi_vec

kclgnn_vec	geognn_vec	rdkit_descriptor_vec	mgssl_vec	rdki_gobbi_ae_vec

Ensemble Model Process. Different machine learning models are used for integration, as shown in Fig. 3. We construct four lightgbm models with different parameters. The prediction result_1 is obtained by voting with 'votingclassify' in sklearn, which includes four machine learning models: RandomForest,XGBoost,LightGBM,Catboost. As described in Fig. 3, results the predicted by lightgbm-1 are added to the results generated by voting classifier, and then averaged to obtain the result_1. A similar calculation method is applied to obtain result_4.

4   Experiment

4.1   Data Introduction

Introduction To Knowledge Ggraph of Chemical Eelements. The construction of chemical element knowledge graph needs to obtain all chemical elements and their basic chemical properties from the periodic table of chemical elements. The knowledge graph data contains 1643 triples, 17 relationships, 225 entities, 107 attributes, and 118 elements.

Training Data. The dataset used in this competition mainly includes the smiles formula and labels. The competition task is mainly a binary classification task. For the binary classification task, ROC-AUC is used to evaluate the prediction performance.

The training dataset contains 32902 smiles data and labels. There are 4113 data items in the validation set, including two columns of smiles and id. The test dataset also contains 4113 items.Example of the training set:

smiles,label

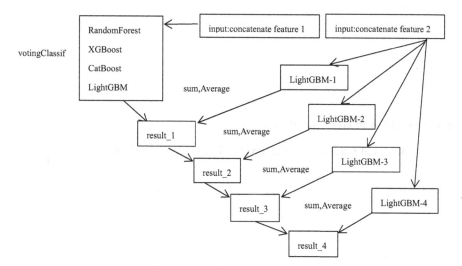

Fig. 3. Ensemble model method

O=C1c2c(O)cc(O)c(OC3OC(CO)C(O)C(O)C3O)c2OC(c2ccc(O)c(O)c2)C1O,0
Cc1ccccc1-n1c(SCC(=O)NC(=O)Nc2cccc(Cl)c2)nc2c(Br)cc(Br)cc2c1=O,0
CCOC(=O)CNC(=O)CNC(=O)CNC(=O)CNNc1c(OCc2ccccc2)c(=O)c1=O,0
Cc1cc(CC(=O)NCCO)n(CCO)c(=O)c1,0

4.2 Experimental Setup

Software and Hardware. Operating system:linux; GPU:NVIDIA V100 32 GB; Deep Learning Framework:pytorch; Machine Learning Framework:sklearn; Rdkit-pypi == 2022.3.4.

SAE Model. Optimization:ADAM,   Learning   Rate=0.001,   Hidden   dim   = 256.BATCH_SIZE = 128.

```
ClassificationModelMLP(
    (linear1): Linear(in_features=39972, out_features=256, bias=True)
    (activation): GELU()
    (batch_normal): BatchNorm1d(256, eps=1e-05, momentum=0.1, affine=True, track_running_stats=
True)
    (linear2): Linear(in_features=256, out_features=1, bias=True)
);
AutoEncoder(
    (encoder): Sequential(
        (0): Linear(in_features=39972, out_features=256, bias=True)
        (1): ReLU()
    )
    (decoder): Sequential(
        (0): Linear(in_features=256, out_features=39972, bias=True)
        (1): ReLU()
    )
)
```

4.3 Model Parameters and Result

The parameters of models included in votingClassify are as follows.

RandomForest:{min_samples_leaf=2, n_estimators=1250,n_jobs=-1, criterion='entropy',class_weight=
{0:1, 1:10},random_state=3,   bootstrap = True,oob_score = True,max_depth= None};
XGBoost:{learning_rate=0.05,max_depth=4,colsample_bytree=0.8,n_estimators=1342,n_jobs=-1,rand
om_state=70,reg_alpha=1,reg_lambda=1,scale_pos_weight=10,subsample=0.9,objective='binary:logist
ic'};
CatBoost:{iterations=1350,depth = 6,learning_rate = 0.05,custom_loss='AUC',eval_metric='AUC',
bagging_temperature=1,rsm = 0.78,od_type='Iter',od_wait=400,metric_period = 400,l2_leaf_reg =
5,thread_count = 10,random_seed = 68,loss_function = 'Logloss',scale_pos_weight = 20};
LightGBM:{boosting_type='gbdt',objective='binary',n_estimators=1200,learning_rate=0.05,max_depth
=-1,num_leaves=31,bagging_fraction= 0.85,feature_fraction=0.9,reg_alpha=0.5,reg_lambda=0,metric=
'auc',bagging_freq=5,min_split_gain=0.0,min_child_weight=0.001,random_state=32,scale_pos_weight
=9}.

The voting results of 4 different models on test dataset is shown in Table 2.

Table 2. Results from concatenate feature 1 and model voting

Feature	Model	Ensemble method	Test result
Concatenate feature 1	RandomForest	VotingClassifier	0.89637
	XGBoost		
	CatBoost		
	LightGBM		

The parameters of LightGBM are as follows.

LightGBM:{learning_rate=0.05,max_depth=-1,num_leaves=31,bagging_fraction=0.85,feature_fraction
=0.9,reg_alpha=0.5,reg_lambda=0,metric='auc',bagging_freq=5,min_split_gain=0.0,min_child_weight
=0.001,random_state=76,scale_pos_weight=9 }.
By adjusting the parameters n_estimators , 4 different lightgbm models can be obtained.
LightGBM-1(n_estimators=1200),LightGBM-2(n_estimators=1240),LightGBM-3(n_estimators=1230)

LightGBM-4(n_estimators=1250).

The results of LightGBM-1 on test dataset is shown in Table 3.

Table 3. Concatenating features 2 results from LightGBM-1

Feature	Model	Parameter	Test result
Concatenate feature 2	LightGBM-1	n_estimators = 1200	0.89341

According to the calculation process described in Fig. 3, the final result on test dataset is 0.8985.

5 Summary

In this evaluation task, in order to find the best molecular representation, we verified the current mainstream models and methods, which include traditional molecular descriptors and molecular fingerprints. After experimental verification, we found that the performance of traditional molecular representations on this task is even better than most current pre-trained models based on graph neural networks. This indicates that molecular representation methods such as molecular descriptors can be considered when actually solving similar tasks. We also verified that the large-scale pre-trained graph neural network model greatly improve the performance of downstream tasks, especially the pre-trained model that incorporates 3D features with GeoGNN. When choosing the features that be concatenated, we consider it from different perspectives and cover as comprehensively as possible. For example, MGSSL focuses on functional groups, and KCLGNN integrates the knowledge graph of chemical elements. The pharmacophore is the spatial orientation of various structural features of molecules that interact with biological targets and trigger biological effects. Incorporating of pharmacophore fingerprints in this task enhances the ability of the power of molecular representation. In the future, fusing the results or parameters generated by molecular simulations into graph neural networks could be explored to further improve the capabilities of molecular representation.

References

1. Durant, J.L., Leland, B.A., Henry, D.R., Nourse, J.G.: Reoptimization of MDL keys for use in drug discovery. J. Chem. Inf. Comput. Sci. **42**(6), 1273–1280 (2002). https://doi.org/10.1021/ci010132r
2. Cereto-Massagué, A., Ojeda, M.J., Valls, C., Mulero, M., Garcia-Vallvé, S., Pujadas, G.: Molecular fingerprint similarity search in virtual screening. Methods **71**, 58–63 (2015). https://doi.org/10.1016/j.ymeth.2014.08.005
3. Morgan, H.L.: The generation of a unique machine description for chemical structures-a technique developed at chemical abstracts service. J. Chem. Doc. **5**(2), 107–113 (1965). https://doi.org/10.1021/c160017a018
4. Goh, G.B., Hodas, N.O., Siegel, C., Vishnu, A.: Smiles2vec: an interpretable general-purpose deep neural network for predicting chemical properties. arXiv preprint arXiv:1712.02034 (2017)
5. Jaeger, S., Fulle, S., Turk, S.: Mol2vec: unsupervised machine learning approach with chemical intuition. J. Chem. Inf. Model. **58**(1), 27–35 (2018)
6. Chithrananda, S., Grand, G., Ramsundar, B.: ChemBERTa: large-scale self-supervised pretraining for molecular property prediction. arXiv preprint arXiv:2010.09885 (2020)
7. Wang, S., Guo, Y., Wang, Y., et al.: SMILES-BERT: large scale unsupervised pre-training for molecular property prediction. In: Proceedings of the 10th ACM International Conference on Bioinformatics, Computational Biology and Health Informatics, pp. 429–436 (2019)
8. Wu, Z., Jiang, D., Wang, J., et al.: Knowledge-based BERT: a method to extract molecular features like computational chemists. Briefings Bioinform. **23**(3), bbac131 (2022)

9. Hu, W., Liu, B., Gomes, J., et al.: Strategies for pre-training graph neural networks. arXiv preprint arXiv:1905.12265 (2019)
10. Sun, M., Xing, J., Wang, H., et al.: MoCL: data-driven molecular fingerprint via knowledge-aware contrastive learning from molecular graph. In: Proceedings of the 27th ACM SIGKDD Conference on Knowledge Discovery & Data Mining, pp. 3585–3594 (2021)
11. Fang, Y., Zhang, Q., Yang, H., et al.: Molecular contrastive learning with chemical element knowledge graph. In: Proceedings of the AAAI Conference on Artificial Intelligence, vol. 36, no. 4, pp. 3968–3976 (2022)
12. Zhang, Z., Liu, Q., Wang, H., et al.: Motif-based graph self-supervised learning for molecular property prediction. Adv. Neural Inf. Process. Syst. **34**, 15870–15882 (2021)
13. Fang, X., Liu, L., Lei, J., et al.: Geometry-enhanced molecular representation learning for property prediction. Nat. Mach. Intell. **4**(2), 127–134 (2022)
14. Rong, Y., Bian, Y., Xu, T., et al.: Self-supervised graph transformer on large-scale molecular data. Adv. Neural Inf. Process. Syst. **33**, 12559–12571 (2020)
15. Ying, C., Cai, T., Luo, S., et al.: Do transformers really perform badly for graph representation? Adv. Neural Inf. Process. Syst. **34**, 28877–28888 (2021)
16. Zhang, X.C., Wu, C.K., Yang, Z.J., et al.: MG-BERT: leveraging unsupervised atomic representation learning for molecular property prediction. Briefings Bioinform. **22**(6), bbab152 (2021)
17. Zeng, Z., Yao, Y., Liu, Z., et al.: A deep-learning system bridging molecule structure and biomedical text with comprehension comparable to human professionals. Nat. Commun. **13**(1), 1–11 (2022)
18. Qian, Y., Li, X., Wu, J., et al.: Picture-word order compound protein interaction: predicting compound-protein interaction using structural images of compounds. J. Comput. Chem. **43**(4), 255–264 (2022)
19. Li, B., Liu, Y., Wang, X.: Gradient harmonized single-stage detector. In: Proceedings of the AAAI Conference on Artificial Intelligence, vol. 33, no. 01, 8577–8584 (2019)
20. Zhang, N., et al.: OntoProtein: protein pretraining with gene ontology embedding. In: International Conference on Learning Representations, 29 September 2021
21. Wu, F., et al.: Molformer: motif-based transformer on 3D heterogeneous molecular graphs. arXiv preprint arXiv:2110.01191, 4 October 2021

Diagram Question Answering with Joint Training and Bottom-Up and Top-Down Attention

Ke Zhang[✉], Xiao Li, and Gong Cheng

State Key Laboratory for Novel Software Technology, Nanjing University, Nanjing, China
{kzhang,xiaoli.nju}@smail.nju.edu.cn, gcheng@nju.edu.cn

Abstract. Diagram question answering is a challenging multi-modal machine learning task that focuses on answering questions according to given diagrams on specific fields. Compared to natural imaged, these diagrams have more abstract expressions and complex logical relations, which makes diagram question answering more difficult. In this paper, we propose a new approach for diagram question answering task. We add bottom-up and top-down attention to identify regions of interest to questions and use a same model to jointly train multiple choice questions and true false questions. Our approach on test dataset of official CCKS2022 textbook diagram question answering session achieves the accuracy of 58.09%.

Keywords: Diagram understanding · Visual question answering · Joint learning

1 Introduction

IN recent years some research on both computer vision and natural language processing including image-text retrieval, image captioning, and visual question answering have been hot spots. Visual question answering task is to answer the natural language questions according to visual image context. Compared with image-text retrieval and image captioning, visual question answering is a more challenging task that requires advances in vision, language, problem-solving, and learning theory.

Existing visual question answering datasets are limited to natural images such as COCO [1], Flickr [2], and VQA [3] constructed from real-world scenes. However, for visual question answering in educational scenes, visual contest becomes diagrams instead of natural images. Diagram is an abstract expression in educational scenes, which is often constructed from geometric shapes and logic symbols and used for expressing information such as logic and concepts. Visual question answering tasks on this more abstract visual context is helpful for machines to understand human cognitive behaviors and learning habits.

Recently Wang et al. [4] proposed CSDia, a novel geometric type of diagrams datasets in Computer Science field. Compared to other visual question answering datasets, CSDia has more abstract expressions and complex logical relations. It has about 1,300 diagrams and 3,500 question-answer pairs that covers 12 different knowledge categories of

N. Zhang et al. (Eds.): CCKS 2022, CCIS 1711, pp. 70–77, 2022.
https://doi.org/10.1007/978-981-19-8300-9_8

Computer Science and are divided two different types: multiple choice question-answer pairs and true false question-answer pairs. Wang et al. also proposed diagram question answering task, a question answering task similar to visual question answering on the CSDia dataset. Figure 1 shows an example diagram with corresponding multiple choice question and true false question from the CSDia dataset.

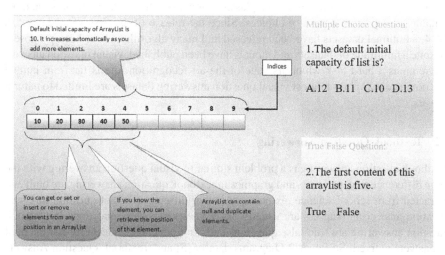

Fig. 1. Example diagram with corresponding multiple choices question and true false question from the CSDia dataset.

In comparison to visual question answering, the diagram question answering task has several characteristics that makes it more challenging. Firstly, the graphics in CSDia dataset does not have specific semantics, only when attached to a particular knowledge concept. This makes extracting and understanding visual features more difficult, since in graphics one object can be given different semantics under different knowledge concepts and one knowledge concept in diagrams have various expressions. Another challenge is that diagram resources are scarce and expensive to label, thus CSDia has a small number of diagrams, which makes diagram question answering a few-shot learning task.

To overcome these challenges, in this paper we propose a new approach to solve diagram question answering task. In this approach, we use bottom-up and top-down attention to extract and learn regions of interest in the diagram that are relevant for the question in hand. We also use the joint learning of multiple choice questions and true false questions to overcome the few-shot challenge. Experiment shows that our approach can efficiently solve diagram question answering task on the CSDia dataset. The remainder of the paper is structured as follows. Section 2 describes related work. Section 3 introduces our approach, including bottom-up and top-down attention and how to jointly learn multiple choice questions and true false questions. Section 4 we present our experimental results. Finally, Sect. 5 concludes.

2 Related Work

2.1 Visual Question Answering

Visual question answering is a problem in computer vision and natural language processing where system is given a text-based question about an image, and it must infer the answer. It is usually regarded as a classification task where model predicts the most suitable answer from a pool of choices. Since the release of the first VQA dataset in 2014, additional datasets have been released and many algorithms have been proposed. Despite a multitude of datasets and models have been published, visual question answering remains a hard task which its state-of-the-art recognition rate is far from human performance. Graphics in most visual question answering datasets are limited to natural images.

2.2 Textbook Question Answering

Textbook question answering is a problem similar to visual question answering with the main difference that questions and graphics in textbook question answering are built and extracted from school science textbooks. Another difference is that question in visual question answering datasets are usually essay questions, while questions in textbook question answering are true false questions and multiple choice questions that the pool of answers is fixed. So far, AI2 Diagrams dataset [5] and Textbook Question Answering dataset [6] are the most widely used for textbook question answering. Specifically, Kembhavi et al. studied the problem of diagram interpretation land reasoning, introduced Diagram Parse Graphs as the representation to model the structure of diagrams and conducted experiments on AI2 Diagrams dataset, which contains diagrams from elementary school science textbooks. They also tested three different types of deep learning models on Textbook Question Answering dataset, which contains diagrams from life, earth and physics textbooks. However, datasets used for textbook question answering task such as AI2 Diagrams dataset and Textbook Question Answering dataset still focus on natural disciplines and real-world objects, instead of pure geometric shapes and logical relations.

2.3 Diagram Question Answering

Diagram question answering is similar to textbook question answering. The main difference is that diagrams in diagram question answering are constructed from pure geometric shapes and logic symbols, which makes diagrams more abstract and difficult to understand for machines. Wang et al. proposed diagram question answering tasks and corresponding dataset CSDia, which has exhaustive annotations of objects and relations for about 1,300 diagrams and 3,500 question-answer pairs. They also proposed the Diagram Paring Net that focuses on analyzing the topological structure and text information of diagrams. Experiments showed CSDia is more complex compared to previous natural image understanding datasets.

3 Approach

3.1 Model Framework

In order to achieve diagram question answering task on CSDia dataset, we propose a new model. Its framework is shown in Fig. 2.

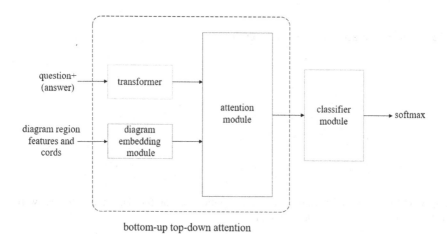

bottom-up top-down attention

Fig. 2. Framework of model for diagram question answering.

As diagram question answering task depends on both visual features and text features and thus is more complicated, we divide the model into three modules: embedding module, attention module and classifier module.

Embedding Module. Embedding module extracts the text features (for multiple choice questions, it includes the question text and the answer text; for true false questions, only question text is included) and visual features from the CSDia dataset. For text features, we use a transformer (specifically, roberta-large) to extract features that contain the overall information of input text. For image features, we divide the diagram into multiple sub-images through the CORD of each question and feed them with original diagram into diagram embedding module (specifically, resnet101) to obtain the image features of the objects corresponding to each CORD ang the overall image.

Attention Module. Attention module fuses the text features and visual features via bottom-up and top-down attention. It examines the importance of sub-image visual features obtained in embedding module to the text feature, so as to extract the features of salient regions that contribute greatly to the question (and answer) text. Considering that CORD is null for some questions in CSDia dataset and some questions have answers that are related to the overall image, we also involve the overall image visual features in the process, which differs from original bottom-up and top-down attention methods. The embedding module and attention module constitute bottom-up and top-down method part of the model, which will be detailed in Sect. 3.2.

Classifier Module. Classifier module classifies the fusion features into different answers via a dense layer and a classifier layer. It has two outputs that respectively correspond to true and false in true false questions. For multiple choice questions, the first output that corresponds to true in true false questions is used as the value of softmax function of input answer in embedding module. Classifier module will be detailed in Sect. 3.3.

3.2 Bottom-Up and Top-Down Attention

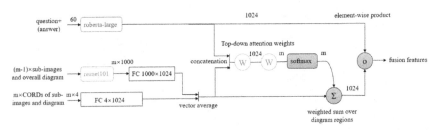

Fig. 3. Overview of embedding module and attention module for diagram question answering, including bottom-up and top-down attention.

Since diagram question answering task involves both text and diagrams, we need to address both branches in embedding module and merge them in attention module in order to answer the questions based on both text and visual information (see Fig. 3). To encode the text part, we use roberta-large to extract text features. For the visual part, we apply bottom-up and top-down attention to take the features of the regions of interest detected bottom-up in the diagram and then apply top-down attention on the question. Since CORD is null for some questions in CSDia dataset and some questions have answers that are related to the overall image, we also feed overall diagram into the bottom-up process.

Specifically, we use roberta-large to extract the text feature from input text. Suppose a question has $(m-1)$ CORDs, we feed sub-images corresponding to these CORDs and the overall diagram into restnet101 to extract the visual features and use a fully connected layer to align the size of vectors. Since the position of sub-images also influence the answers of diagram questions, we use another fully connected layer to extract positional feature vectors and average them with visual feature vectors. Then, we concatenate text feature vectors and positional visual feature vectors, generate an unnormalized top-down attention weight for each position visual feature vector and assign them to corresponding vectors. Finally, we calculate the element-wise product of visual feature vectors and weighted positional visual feature vectors and obtain fusion feature vectors.

3.3 Joint Training

Since the CSDia dataset for diagram question answering has a small number of diagrams and questions, it is important to take full advantage of given questions of CSDia dataset.

We address that the multiple choice questions and the true part of true false questions have similar learning functions, thus we use joint learning to enhance the performance of our approach. Specifically, we use the same model to train true false questions and multiple choice questions. The main difference between the structure of multiple choice questions and true false questions is that multiple choice questions have 4 choices containing corresponding answer texts, while true false question have only 2 fixed answers "True" and "False". To overcome this problem, we use different methods to deal with the inputs of multiple choice questions and true false questions. For true false questions, we use each question as a sample and use the whole question text as the input text. For multiple choice questions, we divide each question into 4 samples according to different choices, which use question text followed with corresponding answer text as the input text.

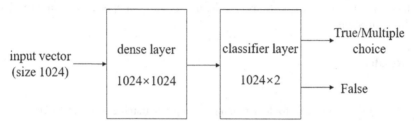

Fig. 4. Overview of classifier module for diagram question answering.

Different methods of input samples need different methods to deal with outputs. The overview of classifier for diagram question answering is shown in Fig. 4. It contains a 1024×1024 dense layer and a 1024×2 classifier layer with a dropout layer between these two layers. The classifier layer has two outputs. For true false questions, the two outputs are respectively used as the parameters of softmax function corresponding to "True" and "False". For multiple choice questions, since a question is divided into 4 samples, we use the "True" output of these 4 samples and use softmax function to calculate the training probability of the 4 choices. In our experiment, joint training can significantly enhance the accuracy of both true false questions and multiple choice questions, which will be detailed in Sect. 4.

4 Experiment

4.1 Datasets

WE use the CSDia dataset as the experiment dataset for diagram question answering. CSDia is the first diagram question answering dataset in computer science, containing 1,294 diagrams and over 3,400 question answering pairs. Among them, all the diagrams are from the real data in the education scene, including two English textbooks, five Chinese textbooks, several blogs, knowledge encyclopedia and other sources. Questions in CSDia dataset includes true false questions and multiple choice questions in which the proportion of number of questions is roughly 1:1. All the questions can also be divided into short-answer (one-step reasoning) questions and complex (two-step reasoning) questions according to their difficulty, and the proportion of number of questions is roughly 4:1.

4.2 Settings

In the embedding module and attention module, we use the model parameters obtained after pretraining on AI2 Diagram dataset in ISAAQ model [7] as initial input. The maximum length of sequence in Roberta-large is set as 60. The optimization algorithm is Adam algorithm, the learning rate is set as 1e-6 and the batch size is 8. Considering that we jointly trained the multiple choice questions and true false questions and they have different bias requirements for the model, we used the model after 24 epochs to obtain results of multiple choice questions and the model after 58 epochs to obtain results of true false questions.

4.3 Results

Table 1. Accuracy for joint training and separate training of our approach

Training	True false questions	Multiple choice questions
Joint training	66.67%	49.51%
Separate training	65.70%	48.22%

Table 1 shows the experiment results of our approach. With joint training, our approach achieves an accuracy of 66.67% on true false questions and 49.51% on multiple choice questions. In comparison, with separate training the model achieves an accuracy of 65.70% on true false questions and 48.22% on multiple choice questions, which means joint learning can significantly improve the performance for diagram question answering and confirms that our approach is effective for diagram question answering.

5 Conclusion

IN this paper, we propose a new approach for diagram question answering task. We use bottom-up and top-down attention to identify question-related regions and use joint learning of multiple choice questions and true false questions to improve the performance. Our approach on test dataset of official CCKS2022 textbook diagram question answering session achieves the accuracy of 58.09%, with 66.67% on true false questions and 49.51% on multiple choice questions, which confirms that our approach is effective for diagram question answering. Experiment shows that joint learning can significantly improve the performance.

Acknowledgements. This work was supported in part by the NSFC (62072224) and in part by the Beijing Academy of Artificial Intelligence (BAAI).

References

1. Lin, TY., et al.: Microsoft COCO: common objects in context. In: Fleet, D., Pajdla, T., Schiele, B., Tuytelaars, T. (eds.) ECCV 2014. LNCS, vol. 8693, pp. 740–755. Springer, Cham (2014). https://doi.org/10.1007/978-3-319-10602-1_48
2. Young, P., Lai, A., Hodosh, M., Hockenmaier, J.: From image descriptions to visual denotations: new similarity metrics for semantic inference over event descriptions. Trans. Assoc. Comput. Linguist. **2**, 67–78 (2014)
3. Antol, S., Agrawal, A., Lu, J., et al.: VQA: visual question answering. In: Proceedings of the IEEE International Conference on Computer Vision, pp. 2425–2433 (2015)
4. Wang, S., Zhang, L., Luo, X., et al.: Computer science diagram understanding with topology parsing. ACM Trans. Knowl. Discov. Data (TKDD) **16**(6), 1–20 (2022)
5. Kembhavi, A., Salvato, M., Kolve, E., Seo, M., Hajishirzi, H., Farhadi, A.: A diagram is worth a dozen images. In: Leibe, B., Matas, J., Sebe, N., Welling, M. (eds) ECCV 2016. LNCS, vol. 9908, pp. 235–251. Springer, Cham (2016). https://doi.org/10.1007/978-3-319-46493-0_15
6. Kembhavi, A., Seo, M., Schwenk, D., et al.: Are you smarter than a sixth grader? Textbook question answering for multimodal machine comprehension. In: Proceedings of the IEEE Conference on Computer Vision and Pattern recognition, pp. 4999–5007 (2017)
7. Gómez-Pérez, J.M., Ortega, R.: ISAAQ-mastering textbook questions with pre-trained transformers and bottom-up and top-down attention. EMNLP (1) 2020

Element Information Enhancement for Diagram Question Answering with Synthetic Data

Yadong Zhang[1], Yang Chen[1], Yupei Ren[1,2], Man Lan[1,2(✉)], and Yuefeng Chen[3]

[1] School of Computer Science and Technology, East China Normal University,
Shanghai, China
{yadongzhang,51255901090,52265901023}@stu.ecnu.edu.cn,
mlan@cs.ecnu.edu.cn
[2] Shanghai Institute of AI for Education, East China Normal University,
Shanghai, China
[3] Shanghai Transsion Co., Ltd., Shenzhen, China
yuefeng.chen@transsion.com

Abstract. Unlike natural pictures, diagrams are a highly abstract vehicle for knowledge representation, and Diagram Question Answering involves complex reasoning processes such as diagram element detection. However, due to low resource constraints, achieving efficient extraction of diagram elements is challenging. In addition, vision tasks rely on image feature extraction, and most feature extraction today is based on real scenario images on ImageNet. To solve the above problems, we programmatically synthesized a diagram dataset to implement diagram element prediction and put its feature extraction module to use on downstream task. In the actual task, we explicitly input the predicted image elements from the diagram into the model. The experimental comparison shows a significant improvement in our model compared to the baseline.

Keywords: Diagram question answering · Low resource · Data synthesis

1 Introduction

In recent years, there have been exciting developments in the research of Visual Question Answering (VQA). A VQA system takes as input an image and a free-form, open-ended, natural-language question about the image and produces a natural-language answer as the output [1]. Current VQA datasets focus on answering questions related to natural images, such as Vqa [1], Clevr [2], and Visual genome [3]. However, abstract diagrams with rich semantics occupy much of the visual world in realistic scenarios. Schematic diagrams are a highly abstract vehicle for knowledge expression, usually consisting of geometric shapes such as rectangles and circles and logical symbols such as arrows and dashes. Compared to VQA, Diagram Question Answering (DQA) has more distinct visual and linguistic inference characteristics.

N. Zhang et al. (Eds.): CCKS 2022, CCIS 1711, pp. 78–86, 2022.
https://doi.org/10.1007/978-981-19-8300-9_9

Diagrams are a prevalent visual form in education, and they express various knowledge concepts in a more abstract semantic sense [4]. Giving a diagram to answer natural language questions related to that knowledge point based on visual information is the work of this paper, the CCKS 2022 Textbook Diagram Question Answering task. The difficulty of this task is mainly twofold. First, schematic diagrams are scarce resources, expensive to annotate, and have a natural small sample scenario. Second, schematic diagrams are abstract in expression and sparse in features yet rich in technical and semantic information, leading to challenges in understanding conceptual diagrams and making accurate and comprehensive cognitive reasoning. This work focuses on effectively capturing and understanding the knowledge embedded in abstract diagrams.

Through investigation of the data, we found that many DQA questions related to elements in the diagram. For example, "The first value of the current list is?" or "How many nodes are there?". For questions such as these, an intuitive idea is to predict the elements of the diagram and input them into the DQA model, thus improving the DQA model's ability to answer these questions. As mentioned before, one of the difficulties of this competition was the small amount of data with hundreds of diagrams and without the labeling of diagram elements. Therefore, it is impractical to use this data for diagram element detection.

To meet the challenge above, we programmatically synthesized a task-related diagram dataset. We train diagram element detection on the synthesized data, make predictions on the real competition data, and feed the detection results explicitly into the DQA model. With the help of the input of element content (position, value), we significantly improved the baseline model. In addition, the feature extraction module we train on diagram element detection can improve the DQA model simultaneously.

2 Related Work

DQA Datasets. As an emerging multimodal task, DQA has released several abstract diagram datasets in recent years. For example, diagram datasets generated based on fixed templates: NLVR [5], FigureQA [6], and DVQA [7]. This class of DQA datasets is generated from a limited number of figure or question templates that may result in unintended visual or linguistic shortcuts in question answering. The subject DQA datasets involve different subjects in real educational scenarios, such as mathematics [8] or physics [9]. It is worth noting that the dataset in this paper is from the computer science discipline [4]. Subject abstract datasets need to combine domain-specific knowledge for question reasoning, and thus there is a large variability between datasets. Recently, Lu et al. developed a new dataset: IconQA [10]. This dataset contains only abstract diagrams and basic common sense. It rarely covers complex domain knowledge, which provides a new benchmark for understanding different visual reasoning skills in abstract diagrams and real learning scenarios.

DQA Methods. In recent years, deep learning-based methods have been widely used for DQA tasks. Common ones are attention and transformers [12]. With the attention mechanism, the model can jointly process multimodal data from diagram regions and question text. Using pre-trained models based on transformers to learn visual and linguistic features in the dataset can significantly improve the performance of downstream DQA tasks. This paper uses the patch cross-modal Transformer model (Patch-TRM) [10] in IconQA as a baseline, which applies a pyramid cross-modal Transformer with an input diagram embeddings pre-trained on the icon dataset.

3   Method

Figure 1 shows the complete process of our approach. We synthesize a diagram dataset to train a diagram element extraction model. Based on the Patch-TRM baseline [10], we feed the model explicitly with the predicted diagram elements to improve the model's ability to answer questions related to the diagram elements.

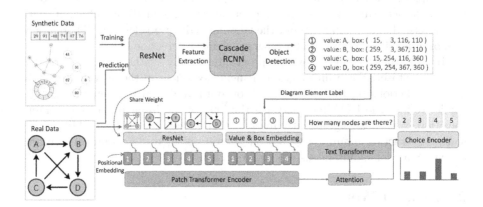

Fig. 1. The overview of our approach.

3.1   Diagram Data Synthesis

Many questions in the competition data relate to elements in the diagram, such as "The first value of the current list is?". Faced with the challenge of low resources in the competition, we argue that the available data resources cannot support the training process for the detection of diagram elements.

By investigating the data, we found that most diagram data is the data structure in computer science. These data structures have in common that the diagram node elements are geometry shapes with node values and that these nodes are placed according to the type of data structure to which they belong. Based on these characteristics, We performed a synthesis of the diagram data. The details of our implementation are described below.

Data Structure. In computer science, a wide variety of data structures exist, such as trees and graphs. From these data structures, we selected the following six data types for data synthesis.

1. Linear data structures: Array, Linked List, Stack, Queue.
2. Edge-based data structures: Tree, Graph.

In the actual competition data, there are also flowcharts, deadlock, etc. These data are more focused on the textual content (descriptions rather than weights of nodes) of the diagram elements and are more challenging to synthesize programmatically.

Synthesis Variation. In order to make the synthesized data more closely resemble the real data, we use several methods to enhance the diversity of the synthesized results, resulting in a more generalizable element detection model. These methods include fonts, colors, etc., and detailed descriptions can be found in Table 1. In Appendix Fig. 2 we show some synthetic data samples.

Table 1. Variations in synthetic data.

Item	Application	Variations
Position	Border, Text, Edges	Random fluctuations at the centre point
Font	Node weight, Edge Weight	Arial, Calibri, Cambria, etc.
Color	Border, Text, Edges	Gray, Random HSV color
Blur	Full diagram	Gaussian Blur, Box Blur, No blur

3.2 Diagram Element Detection

Based on the synthetic diagram dataset, we trained a Cascade RCNN object detection model [11]. Cascade RCNN consists of a sequence of detectors trained with increasing IoU thresholds, to be sequentially more selective against close false positives. The detectors are trained stage by stage, leveraging the observation that the output of a detector is a good distribution for training the next higher quality detector. The resampling of progressively improved hypotheses guarantees that all detectors have a positive set of examples of equivalent size, reducing the overfitting problem.

We use the model to predict the value and coordinate information of the elements in the competition diagram. Our accuracy on the validation set of the synthetic data is 96%.

3.3 Baseline and Diagram Element Embedding

We use Patch-TRM [10] in IconQA as our baseline model. The diagrams are first scaled to different sizes and splitted into ordered patches according to a hierarchical pyramid layout, encoded by a pre-trained ResNet [14]. In the actual implementation, we designed 5 layers with 79 patches, which allows the model to focus on both local and global information in the diagram. After ResNet extracts the features from these diagrams, the representations of all the patches are passed into the Transformer as input. To solve the position insensitivity of the Transformer, we also add the position embedding for each patch. Regarding the question and the choice text information, we use Bert [13] and GRU [15] to encode them respectively. Finally, we use the attention mechanism to let the diagram information and the text information interact, and use the softmax function to obtain the final prediction results.

We concatenate the predicted numerical and coordinate information of diagram element together with the patch information of the diagram and feed it into the Patch Transformer Encoder. We use relative values for the coordinates to reduce the effect of the element size.

4   Experiments

To verify the accuracy of our idea, we set up two sets of ablation experiments. And the details of our experiments are provided.

4.1   Datasets and Settings

Datasets. The dataset we use is a subset of CSDQA [4]. Computer Science Diagrams Question Answering (CSDQA) is a computer science domain dataset with rich annotations. It contains 1,294 diagrams in 12 categories with over 3,400 question-answer pairs from five undergraduate courses: Data structure, Principles of Computer Networks, Computer Architecture, Digital Logic Circuit, and Computer Operating System. Detailed statistics about the dataset we use in the competition are shown in Table 2.

Table 2. Results of dataset segmentation

	Image	Question
Train	713	1996
Val	238	664
Test	238	618

Implementation Details. We first use the Cascade RCNN model [11] to perform element recognition on the diagrams, predicting the numerical and coordinate information of the elements, which are subsequently fed into the Patch Transformer Encoder along with the diagram vectors. Following the setup in the IconQA [10], in Patch Transformer Encoder, we use 79/30 patch blocks and try to use Cascade RCNN Backbone for feature extraction on the diagrams. For the

Text Transformer, we encode it using the Bert-small model [13] with a maximum length limit of 25/34. For the Choice Encoder, we use the GRU model [15] with a word embedding size of 300.

4.2 Ablation Studies

Backbone. We use ResNet models pre-trained by ImageNet or Icon645 datasets, respectively, and Backbone from the Cascade RCNN object detection network for feature extraction. Results are presented in Table 3. We find that ResNet pre-trained with ImageNet is better than pre-trained on the Icon645 dataset, which indicates that Icon645 and the competition data are not strongly correlated. In addition, we found that the overall results of ResNet, which comes from the diagram element detection model, are better than those of the pre-training under ImageNet. It indicates that the extracted diagram features are more suitable for the later task by using more similar data for model pre-training.

Table 3. Effect of different backbones. Each row corresponds to a model with varied pre-trained ResNet and fixed other settings. All experiments are based on the training set given by the competition, and the training set is divided into training and validation datasets in the ratio of 8:2.

Model	Val accuracy
Patch-TRM with ImageNet Pretrain	48.94
Patch-TRM with Icon645 Pretrain	44.57
Patch-TRM with Cascade RCNN Backbone	**49.54**

Image Element Detection and Embedding. We try to interact the results of the diagram element detection with the diagram information and feed it into our model together. The results are shown in Table 4. Adding the detection results of the diagram elements, we found a significant improvement in the model. It shows that our diagram element detection model trained on synthetic data works on real competition data and also shows the importance of diagram element detection for DQA.

Table 4. The accuracy of model with/without element embedding

Model	Accuracy
Patch-TRM	48.94
Patch-TRM with element embedding	**50.90**

4.3   Ensemble

We adjust the model's hyperparameters, such as the number of patches after diagram splitting, the max length of the question text encoding, etc., and try to set the weight decay to constrain the model and mitigate overfitting. The model configuration used for the ensemble is shown in Table 5.

During the model ensemble stage, the predictions of the four models on the test set were voted, and the option with the highest number of votes was used as the final answer. The final voting accuracy on the test set is 55.01%.

Table 5. Different configurations of the models. At the time of Ensemble, we have already acquired the answers for the validation set, so these models have more training data compared to some of the experiments above.

Id	Patch	Max length of question	Weight decay	Accuracy
1	79	25	no	53.61
2	79	34	no	54.06
3	79	34	yes	52.71
4	30	25	no	54.97

5   Conclusion

We synthesized diagram data for the low-resource DQA task to achieve an effective diagram element detection. We explicitly fed the detection result into the DQA model to improve the model's response to questions related to diagram elements. The feature extraction module used in the element detection also benefits the subsequent DQA model as the input data is more similar to the actual task. In DQA, diagrams and questions are equally important. In future work, consideration could be given to simultaneous generation and pre-training of diagrams and questions to alleviate the low resource problem in DQA.

Acknowledgements. We appreciate the support from Pudong New Area Science & Technology Development Fund (Project Number: PKX2021-R05).

Appendix

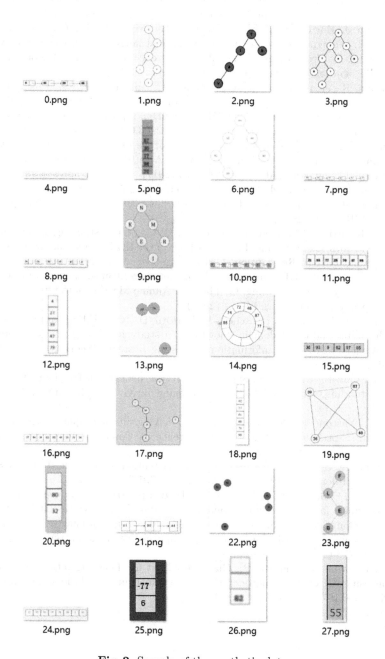

Fig. 2. Sample of the synthetic data.

References

1. Antol, S., et al.: VQA: visual question answering. In: Proceedings of the IEEE International Conference on Computer Vision, pp. 2425–2433 (2015)
2. Johnson, J., Hariharan, B., Maaten, L.V.D., Fei-Fei, L., Zitnick, C.L., Girshick, R.: CLEVR: a diagnostic dataset for compositional language and elementary visual reasoning. In: Proceedings of the IEEE Conference on Computer Vision and Pattern Recognition (CVPR), pp. 2901–2910 (2017)
3. Krishna, R., et al.: Visual genome: connecting language and vision using crowdsourced dense image annotations. Int. J. Comput. Vision **123**(1), 32–73 (2017)
4. Wang, S., Zhang, L.L., Luo, X., et al.: RL-CSDia: representation learning of computer science diagrams. arXiv preprint arXiv:2103.05900 (2021)
5. Suhr, A., Lewis, M., Yeh, J., Artzi, Y.: A corpus of natural language for visual reasoning. In: Proceedings of the 55th Annual Meeting of the Association for Computational Linguistics (ACL), pp. 217–223 (2017)
6. EbrahimiKahou, S., Michalski, V., Atkinson, A., Kádár, Á., Trischler, A., Bengio, Y.: FigureQA: an annotated figure dataset for visual reasoning. arXiv preprint arXiv:1710.07300 (2017)
7. Kafle, K., Price, B., Cohen, S., Kanan, C.: DVQA: Understanding data visualizations via question answering. In: Proceedings of the IEEE Conference on Computer Vision and Pattern Recognition (CVPR), pp. 5648–5656 (2018)
8. Lu, P., et al.: Inter-GPS: Interpretable geometry problem solving with formal language and symbolic reasoning. In: The 59th Annual Meeting of the Association for Computational Linguistics (ACL) (2021)
9. Sachan, M., Dubey, K.A., Mitchell, T.M., Roth, D., Xing, E.P.: Learning pipelines with limited data and domain knowledge: a study in parsing physics problems. In: Advances in Neural Information Processing Systems (NeurIPS), pp. 140–151 (2018)
10. Lu, P., Qiu, L., Chen, J., et al.: IconQA: a new benchmark for abstract diagram understanding and visual language reasoning. arXiv preprint arXiv:2110.13214 (2021)
11. Cai, Z., Vasconcelos, N.: Cascade R-CNN: delving into high quality object detection. In: Proceedings of the IEEE Conference on Computer Vision and Pattern Recognition, pp. 6154–6162 (2018)
12. Vaswani, A., Shazeer, N., Parmar, N., et al.: Attention is all you need. In: Advances in Neural Information Processing Systems 30 (2017)
13. Devlin, J., Chang, M.W., Lee, K., et al.: BERT: pre-training of deep bidirectional transformers for language understanding. arXiv preprint arXiv:1810.04805 (2018)
14. He, K., Zhang, X., Ren, S., Sun, J.: Deep residual learning for image recognition. In: Proceedings of the IEEE Conference on Computer Vision and Pattern Recognition, pp. 770–778 (2016)
15. Cho, K., Van Merriënboer, B., Gulcehre, C., et al.: Learning phrase representations using RNN encoder-decoder for statistical machine translation. arXiv preprint arXiv:1406.1078 (2014)

Financial Event Extraction of NEC Dataset Based on Pointer Network

Keyu Pu[✉], Hongyi Liu, Yixiao Yang, Yaohan He, and Jinlong Li

China Merchants Bank Artificial Intelligence Laboratory, Shenzhen 518000, China
{pukeyu,lhy24,yangyixiao,heyh18,lucida}@cmbchina.com

Abstract. This paper presents a solution for the CCKS 2022 NEC Task: Financial Event Extraction. What is challenging in this task is detecting semantically ambiguous and complex event in short and low-context settings. Our team (CMB AI Lab) propose a ner method for event extraction: first, the dataset is split by the cause-and-effect list, and then a model based on biaffine layer/global pointer is built to predict span boundaries of specific category. The basic pre-trained models we choose are MacBERT and NEZHA-WWM. The evaluation result of our approach achieves an F1 score of 0.60738, which ranks the first on the final leader board.

Keywords: Event extraction · Financial news · Pointer network

1 Introduction

Event extraction is a crucial task of information extraction, which is able to extract some specific type of event (event type recognition) and identify the important components of the event (event element recognition) from unstructured information and presents the results in a structured form.

In the financial field, accurate event extraction is necessary to build a high-quality event graph, which can be applied to many business scenarios such as robot financing and risk management. However, the event types in the financial field are extremely diverse. Therefore, it requires high expertise and labor costs to define different schemas for different event types. Inspired by the idea of open-domain event extraction, CCKS 2022 NEC Task defines relatively standard event schemas and data annotations to achieve event extraction of rich financial event types.

The purpose of this task is to recognize cause-effect events from massive financial news, and extract specific elements of the events. As shown in Fig. 1, a piece of text T contains a cause event C and a result event E, the extract results of which includes not only the event but also the event element.

In this task, precision (P), recall (R), and F1 (F1-measure, F1) are used to evaluate the recognition effect of event elements. The P and R is calculated from all samples, regardless of the entity type, and the F1 value is calculated by the micro-average.

N. Zhang et al. (Eds.): CCKS 2022, CCIS 1711, pp. 87–97, 2022.
https://doi.org/10.1007/978-981-19-8300-9_10

Input:A piece of text that contains a cause event C and a result event E
Output:Event elements for cause and effect events
Sample:

input:{"text_id":"123456", "text": "恒大地产2012年拟裁员30%: 1月4日, 恒大地产（3333.HK）的一位副总裁向记者确认, 公司内部发文, 2012年将裁员30%。知情人士透露, 按步骤初期只裁10%, 因为2009年裁员的时候, 矛盾冲突比较激烈。该副总称裁员的原因主要是项目销售问题。", "cause_effect_mention":"裁员的原因主要是项目销售问题", "cause_effect_list": [{"id":"123456_0", "cause_mention":"项目销售问题","effect_mention":"裁员"}]}

Output:
{"text_id":"123456," "cause_effect_list":[{"id":"123456_0", "cause_mention":"项目销售问题", "cause_actor":["项目"], "cause_action":"销售问题", "cause_object":[""], "cause_region":[],"cause_industry":["地产"], "cause_organization":["恒大地产"], "cause_product":[], "effect_mention":["裁员"], "effect_actor":["恒大地产"], "effect_action":["裁员"], "effect_object":"", "effect_region":[], "effect_industry":["地产"], "effect_organization":["恒大地产"], "effect_product":[]}]}

Fig. 1. Example of causal event feature extraction in finance

The rest of the paper is organized as follows: Sect. 2 reviews some related works; Sect. 3 discusses our approach; Sect. 4 presents the experiment implementations and results; Sect. 5 concludes the paper and sketches directions for future work.

2 Related Work

Event extraction aims to predict the event category, event trigger word, corresponding element of the trigger word, and the arguments of the corresponding element for a given document [1]. Similar to the classification tasks, sequence annotation tasks and machine reading tasks [2], the event elements recognition can be equivalent to an NER (Named Entity Recognition) problem according to the word-level corresponding event type.

The most common approaches for event extraction are roughly divided into two categories: pattern matching technique and machine learning algorithms.

2.1 Pattern Matching Technique

Event extraction based on pattern matching mainly includes supervised pattern matching technique and weakly supervised pattern matching technique [3].

In 1995, the WordNet semantic dictionary was introduced to event extraction, and the semantic framework and phrase structure were implemented, proving the effectiveness of mining a large dictionary [4]. Developed by Ellen et al., the AutoSlog-ST system based on AutoSlog did not require the annotation of all event elements in the corpus, but the annotation of the event type, and was capable of automatically learning the event mode by a pre-classified corpus [5]. Proposed by Jifa, a domain general event pattern matching method IEPAM, divides event extraction patterns into three parts: semantic patterns, trigger patterns and extraction patterns, and achieved excellent results in flight accident event extraction in MUC-7 corpus [6].

2.2 Machine Learning Algorithms

In order to release the limitation of poor portability of the traditional pattern matching, machine learning algorithms (especially the deep learning neural networks) have become a major trend in event extraction [7–11], which can be migrated to many fields [12].

A two-way LSTM was employed by Nguyen et al. to extract semantic features in sentences, and the sentence structure features were combined to extract event trigger words and event elements at the same time [13]. Recently, Wang et al. proposed the confrontation-neural event model (AEM) based on a generative confrontation network to achieve event extraction [14]. In 2019, Zhang et al. also proposed a new neural network-based transformation model for predicting complex joint structures in a state-transition process by capturing structural dependencies among entities and event mentions [15].

Attention mechanism has been applied in various NLP tasks, such as NER, name tagging, sentence classification and question answering, showing great performance. Besides, the pointer network structure has also become a mainstream method in NER problem. However, in the general pointer networks, the start and end pointers are encoded together. Therefore, an attention mechanism that simultaneously considered the using a biaffine operation was proposed which achieved a better performance in NER tasks [16].

3 Approach

In this section, we will describe our approach in the competition. The processing flow of our approach is illustrated in Fig. 2 below.

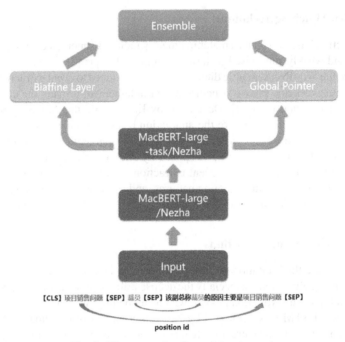

Fig. 2. The processing flow of the approach

We regard this cause-effect event extraction task as a NER task which extracts entities with defined cause event text and effect event text. Considering the numerous nested entities in the training dataset, the two pointer networks are selected to resolve the problem: biaffine layer and global pointer layer. Furthermore, other strategies such as continue pre-training, data cleaning and adding custom position id have also been tried.

3.1 Overall Model Structure

We built two boundary detection models which are both created by connecting the last hidden states of the pre-trained model to the pointer network to obtain the span boundaries. The two pointer networks are the biaffine network [17] and the global pointer network [18]. The output of the biaffine model is a span boundary matrix $s_\alpha(i, j)$ as illustrated in Fig. 3, which is similar to the global pointer model. All pairs of start-end tokens have corresponding scores indicating whether they are the spans we need. Figure 4 shows an example of a span boundary matrix. The reason why Jackie Chen and the museum are the entities in this sentence is that they are the two pairs of start-end tokens: the value 1 in the score matrix indicating that the text from index i to index j belongs to the category α.

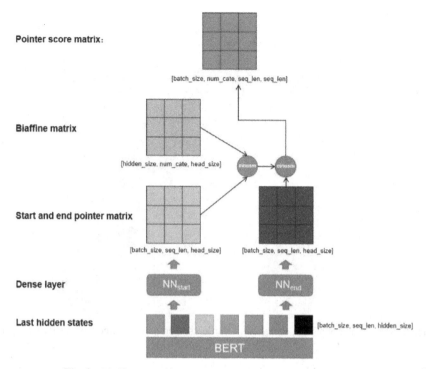

Fig. 3. Biaffine model: using start-end pointer to explore all span

In detail, we suppose that the text length is n. h_t represents the last hidden states output of the pre-trained model. NN_s and NN_e represents the pointer dense layer of head and tail. The output is expressed as:

$$h_s(t) = NN_s(h_t) \tag{1}$$

$$h_e(t) = NN_e(h_t) \tag{2}$$

Then, the $h_s(t)$ is applied to the biaffine matrix and then applied to the $h_e(t)$ to get the final output s(t), which can be computed as follows:

$$s(t) = h_s(\mathrm{t})^T U h_e(\mathrm{t}) + b \tag{3}$$

Since the task involved a variety of labels, we choose the multi-label soft-max cross-entropy as the loss function [19]:

$$Loss = \log\left(1 + \sum_{(i,j)\in P_\alpha} e^{-s_\alpha(i,j)}\right) + \log\left(1 + \sum_{(i,j)\in Q_\alpha} e^{s_\alpha(i,j)}\right) \tag{4}$$

P_α is the set of head-tail of category α, and Q_α is the set of head-tail of the rest:

$$P_\alpha = \left\{(i,j)\,|\, text\big[i:j\big] \text{ is the entity of categorie of } \alpha\right\} \tag{5}$$

$$Q_\alpha = \{(i,j)\,|\,1 \leq i \leq j \leq n\} - P_\alpha \tag{6}$$

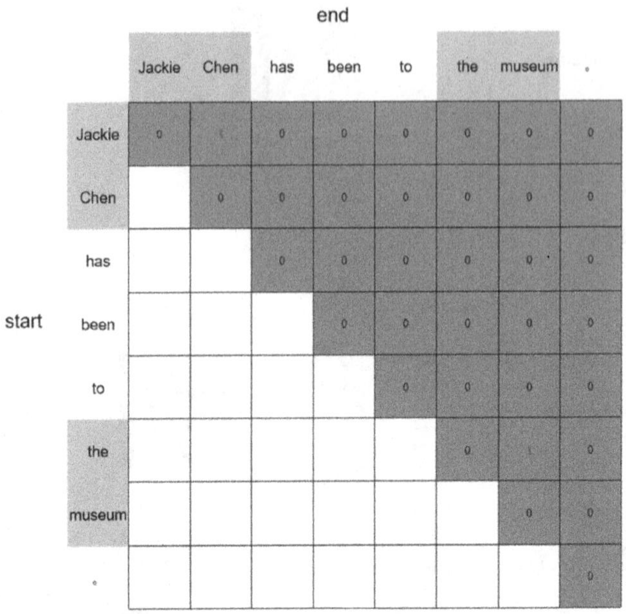

Fig. 4. Span boundary matrix: scores of all start-end token-pair for detecting boundary of span

3.2 Custom Position Id

Since we use [CLS] *cause mention* [SEP] *effect mention* [SEP] *original sentence* [SEP] as one input sentence to extract the specific entities, the position of cause mention text and effect mention text are of importance. We try to add the relative position information by using the custom position ids. The position ids of cause mentions and effect mentions are the same with these texts in sentence.

3.3 Adversarial Training

Model fusion adopts multi-model voting attenuation strategy and FGM adversarial training to improve the robustness of the model. In the process of adversarial training, the samples will be mixed with some small disturbances (the change is very small, but likely to cause misclassification), and then make the neural network adapt to this change, so as to be robust to the adversarial samples. In our experiment, the embedding parameter matrix is directly disturbed to obtain the diversity of samples.

3.4 Continue Pre-training

Multi-phase adaptive pre-training offers large gains in task performance [20]. We continue pre-training the unlabeled data of the task (task-adaptive pre-training) to see whether it is still helpful. Because of the small size of training dataset, there is almost no difference between the original pre-trained model and the pre-trained model after task-adaptive pre-training.

3.5 Model Voting

According to the idea of ensemble learning, the output results of different models will be voted by the bagging strategy. First, make statistics on all predictions and aggregate the prediction results of all predictions. For classification scenarios, the principle of the minority obeying the majority can be utilized to calculate the final results or calculate the average prediction probability of all categories. Then, make horizontal comparison in the direction of categories, and directly calculate the average in regression scenarios. Compared with the single model scenario, the integration mode can effectively reduce the deviation and variance. The structure of the multi-model voting strategy based on the ensemble learning is shown in the Fig. 5 below.

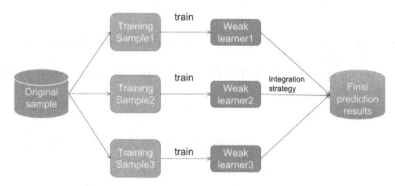

Fig. 5. The structure of the multi-model voting strategy

4 Experiment

This section introduces the dataset provided in the competition, and the experiments conducted to evaluate our approach.

4.1 Dataset

The dataset provided in the competition is from the financial news which contains id, contents, cause-text, effect-text, and their corresponding entities: cause_actor, cause_action, cause_object, cause_region, cause_industry, cause_organization, cause_product, effect_actor, effect_action, effect_object, effect_region, effect _industry, effect_organization, effect_product. The statistics of each type and its role is shown in Table 1.

However, there are numerous wrong tags among the dataset provided. In order to resolve this problem, we clean the dataset as shown in Fig. 6:

1. *Splitting them into 10-fold.*
2. *Predicting one-fold by the model trained with the rest 9 folds.*

Table 1. Statistics of dataset

Event-element	Total	Event-element	Total
cause_actor	2465	effect_actor	2888
cause_action	4062	effect_action	4096
cause_object	350	effect_object	324
cause_region	1130	effect_region	1030
cause_industry	560	effect_industry	779
cause_organization	623	effect_organization	767
cause_product	599	effect_product	872

3. *Concatenating the 10 folds to get the complete dataset and repeat the step 1 and 2 to get 25 datasets.*
4. *Add the entities which appear in all 25 datasets, delete the entities which not appear in any one dataset.*

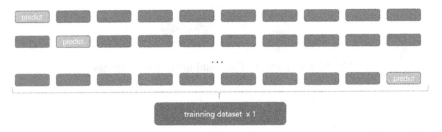

Fig. 6. The structure of the clean dataset

4.2 Implementation

Two pre-trained models are chosen in our method, one of which is the NEZHA-LARGE-WWM which includes functional relative positional encoding as an effective positional encoding scheme, whole word masking strategy, mixed precision training and the LAMB optimizer [13], the other of which is the MacBERT-LARGE which is a robustly optimized BERT pre-training model [14]. We apply Biaffine Layer/Global Pointer Layer to the output of the pre-trained model with the head set to 64. During the training process, we set the batch size as 4, the learning rate as $2e-5$ and the epoch number as 18. Furthermore, we apply adversarial training to improve robustness.

For our model ensemble strategy, 20 NEZH-LARGE-WWM based models and 20 MacBERT-LARGE based models have been trained, and these results are combined to obtain the final results.

4.3 Main Result

Since we can only get the score of the validation data on the leader board daily, we conduct experiments on the validation data. The F1-score on validation data is 0.61906 which is the highest score in the leader board daily of the competition. Finally, the F1-score of our approach on the final testing data is 0.60738 which ranks the first place.

4.4 Ablation Study

We conduct an ablation study during the competition where the results are shown in Table 2. We have two baseline models. One is built on NEZHA-LARGE-WWM. Another is built on MacBERT-LARGE. These two models use the content and the mention as the input, other event element as the label, which acquire the F1-score: 57.157% and 57.016%. We introduce the mention position after the content & mention, and acquire 1% improvement. We also find that there was some dirty data in the training data, such as the content without element texts. After cleaning the data and re-training the model, an improvement of about 1.5% is achieved. Finally, extra 2% improvement on the score of the final result is achieved by our model ensemble strategy.

Table 2. Results on the validation dataset

Method	F1 (%)
Baseline nezha	57.157
w/position	58.178
w/data clean	**59.850**
Baseline macbert	57.016
w/position	58.032
w/data clean	**59.315**
Ensemble strategy	**61.906**

5   Conclusion

The CCKS 2022 Financial Field Domain Event Element Extraction Task is a text extraction competition based on a financial corpus. We design a two-stage model that combine the state-of-the-art BERT-like based models pre-trained on Chinese corpus and the biaffine attention mechanism or global pointer to achieve event extraction. The model we built outperforms on the competition dataset with an F1-score of 0.60738 as the first-place ranking.

References

1. Sultana, S., Cavaletto, L.A., Bosu, A.: Identifying the prevalence of gender biases among the computing organizations. arXiv preprint arXiv:2107.00212 (2021)
2. Liu, J., et al.: Event extraction as machine reading comprehension. In: Proceedings of the 2020 Conference on Empirical Methods in Natural Language Processing (2020)
3. Chen, Y., et al.: Automatically labeled data generation for large scale event extraction. In: Proceedings of the 55th Annual Meeting of the Association for Computational Linguistics (2017)
4. Kim, J.-T., Moldovan, D.I.: Acquisition of linguistic patterns for knowledge-based information extraction. IEEE Trans. Knowl. Data Eng. **7**(5), 713–724 (1995)
5. Riloff, E., Shoen, J.: Automatically acquiring conceptual patterns without an annotated corpus. In: Third Workshop on Very Large Corpora (1995)
6. Jifa, J.: A method of obtaining event information extraction mode. Comput. Eng. (2005)
7. Sha, L., et al.: Jointly extracting event triggers and arguments by dependency bridge RNN and tensor-based argument interaction. In: Thirty-Second AAAI Conference on Artificial Intelligence (2018)
8. Huang, L., et al.: Zero-shot transfer learning for event extraction (2017)
9. Yang, S., et al.: Exploring pre-trained language models for event extraction and generation. In: Proceedings of the 57th Annual Meeting of the Association for Computational Linguistics (2019)
10. Zheng, S., et al.: Doc2EDAG: an end-to-end document-level framework for Chinese financial event extraction. arXiv preprint arXiv:1904.07535 (2019)
11. He, R.F., Duan, S.Y.: Joint Chinese event extraction based multi-task learning. J. Softw. **30**(4), 1015 (2019)
12. Jiang, M., et al.: A study of machine-learning-based approaches to extract clinical entities and their assertions from discharge summaries. J. Am. Med. Inform. Assoc. **18**(5), 601–606 (2011)
13. Nguyen, T.H., Cho, K., Grishman, R.: Joint event extraction via recurrent neural networks. In: Proceedings of the 2016 Conference of the North American Chapter of the Association for Computational Linguistics: Human Language Technologies (2016)
14. Wang, R., Zhou, D., He, Y.: Open event extraction from online text using a generative adversarial network. arXiv preprint arXiv:1908.09246 (2019)
15. Zhang, J., et al.: Extracting entities and events as a single task using a transition-based neural model. In: IJCAI (2019)
16. Dozat, T., Manning, C.D.: Deep biaffine attention for neural dependency parsing. arXiv preprint arXiv:1611.01734 (2016)
17. Yu, J., Bohnet, B., Poesio, M.: Named entity recognition as dependency parsing. arXiv preprint arXiv:2005.07150 (2020)
18. Su, J.: GlobalPointer: handle the nested and non-nested NER by a unified method. https://kexue.fm/archives/8373. Accessed 01 May 2021
19. Su, J.: Apply softmax cross-entropy loss function to multi-label classification. https://kexue.fm/archives/7359. Accessed 25 Apr 2020
20. Gururangan, S., et al.: Don't stop pretraining: adapt language models to domains and tasks. In: Proceedings of the 58th Annual Meeting of the Association for Computational Linguistics, pp 8342–8360. Association for Computational Linguistics (2020)
21. Deng, S., et al.: OntoED: low-resource event detection with ontology embedding. In: Proceedings of the 59th Annual Meeting of the Association for Computational Linguistics and the 11th International Joint Conference on Natural Language Processing (Volume 1: Long Papers), pp. 2828–2839, August 2021

22. Lou, D., Liao, Z., Deng, S., Zhang, N., Chen, H:. MLBiNet: a cross-sentence collective event detection network. In: Proceedings of the 59th Annual Meeting of the Association for Computational Linguistics and the 11th International Joint Conference on Natural Language Processing (Volume 1: Long Papers), pp. 4829–4839, August 2021
23. Deng, S., Zhang, N., Kang, J., Zhang, Y., Zhang, W., Chen, H.: Meta-learning with dynamic-memory-based prototypical network for few-shot event detection. In: Proceedings of the 13th International Conference on Web Search and Data Mining, pp. 151–159, 20 January 2020

High Quality Article Recognition Based on Ernie and Knowledge Mapping

Huihai Liu, Pingfei Cui[✉], and Lin Han

Research Institute of Advanced Information Technology, Zhongyuan Institute of Technology, Zhengzhou, Henan, China
cpf1975@qq.com, cpf1975@126.com

Abstract. Nowadays, with the explosive growth of we media articles, in the context of information distribution such as search and recommendation, how to identify high-quality articles and distribute them to users has important research significance and practical application value. The task of this competition is to introduce external Knowledge mapping, combined with the internal knowledge logic of the article, realizes high-quality article recognition on the basis of a deeper semantic understanding of the article. We mainly use Ernie pre training model and Article title - knowledge map - the modeling method of part of the article content, the use of pseudo label data sets and other ways to get the predicted value, and finally achieved the result of 0.82 in the B list.

Keywords: Knowledge map · Ernie · Pseudo tags

1 Introduction

With the rapid development of the Internet, the emergence of 4G, 5g, big data and artificial intelligence has brought us into the digital era. More and more people devote themselves to we media, which makes the number of we media articles present a straight upward trend. In the retrieval and recommendation system, how to identify high-quality articles and distribute them to our users has very important research significance and practical application value. Therefore, in response to this problem, CCKS 2022 officially released the task of identifying high-quality articles through knowledge mapping modeling. The data set provided in this task is Baidu Baijia, the domestic mainstream we media platform. There are 10000 + articles in the data set. Each article has a title, body, whether it is a high-quality article label and the corresponding knowledge map information, including 8000 + articles for the training set, 1000 + articles for the A-list test, and 1000 + articles for the B-list test; In the construction of the data set, we get all angles of the article by asking special labelers to rate the collected data in 7 dimensions. Finally, based on the seven dimensions of the article, 1000 pieces of data are labeled manually and fitted by decision tree (acc: 0.98), resulting in a complete dataset. Decision Tree Contribution: [Title: 0.172, Text quality: 0.076, Visual and understandable: 0.157, Multi-party/Multi-angle: 0.099, Background information: 0.130, Aging/Creative: 0.267, Positive and Optimistic: 0.099], as shown in Fig. 1. The format of the evaluation results required to be submitted is the

N. Zhang et al. (Eds.): CCKS 2022, CCIS 1711, pp. 98–106, 2022.
https://doi.org/10.1007/978-981-19-8300-9_11

label of the article link and whether the article is of high quality; Finally, the related papers of the data set are provided.

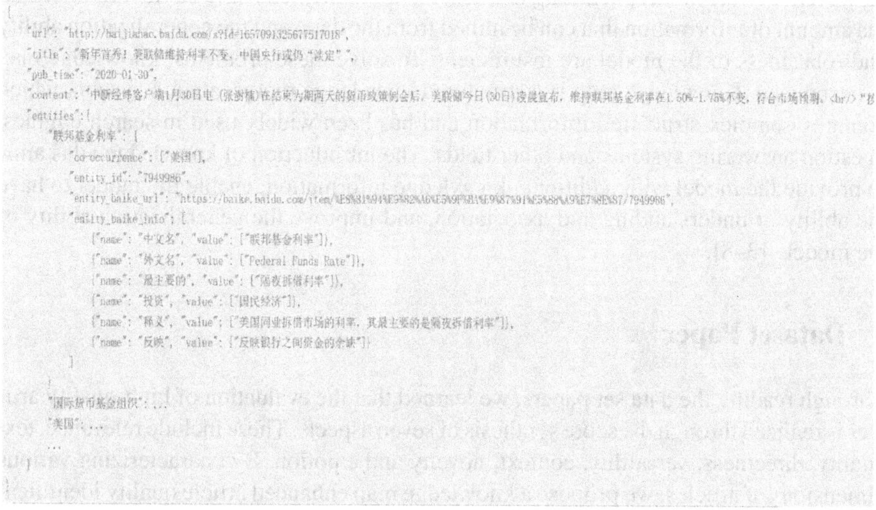

{
  "url": "http://baijiahao.baidu.com/s?id=1657091325677517018",
  "title": "新年首秀！要联储维持利率不变，中国央行或仍 "淡定" ",
  "pub_time": "2020-01-30",
  "content": "中新经纬客户端1月30日电（张澍楠）在结束为期两天的货币政策例会后，美联储今日（30日）凌晨宣布，维持联邦基金利率在1.50%-1.75%不变，符合市场预期。
 "转
  "entities": [
    "联邦基金利率": [
      "co-occurrence": ["美联储"],
      "entity_id": "7949986",
      "entity_baike_url": "https://baike.baidu.com/item/%E8%81%94%E9%82%A6%E5%9F%BA%E9%87%91%E5%88%A9%E7%8E%87/7949986",
      "entity_baike_info": [
        {"name": "中文名", "value": ["联邦基金利率"]},
        {"name": "外文名", "value": ["Federal Funds Rate"]},
        {"name": "最主要的", "value": ["隔夜拆借利率"]},
        {"name": "投资", "value": ["国民经济"]},
        {"name": "释义", "value": ["美国同业拆借市场的利率，其最主要的是隔夜拆借利率"]},
        {"name": "反映", "value": ["反映银行之间资金的余缺"]}
      ]
    }
    "国际货币基金组织": ...
    "美国": ...
}

Fig. 1. Data set

2 Related Work

Text classification plays an important role in natural language processing and text mining. Recognition and classification through continuous learning of text features are of great significance and value in all aspects of research [1].

The traditional text classification is based on machine learning methods [2], including support vector machines, decision trees, naive Bayes, etc., which solve the problems at the lexical level, but the model can not effectively learn and reflect the semantic correlation and deep semantic features between words [2].

In recent years, with the deep learning, remarkable achievements have been made in the field of computer vision and natural processing. The short text classification algorithm based on deep learning began to attract people's attention. Cnn [3, 4] model, rnn [5, 6] model, gnn [7] model, attention [8] and pre training model emerged. The powerful pre training language model makes many natural language processing tasks including text classification show good performance.

At present, relying on large-scale training data and the powerful computing power provided by high-performance GPU and TPU, the neural network model with BERT as the baseline shines brightly and has achieved better results in many application scenarios. However, the current deep learning text classification methods have some limitations on the amount of information that can be mined from the data, and the generalization ability and robustness of the model are insufficient. To solve these problems, knowledge map is introduced. Knowledge map is a structured knowledge representation system, which contains complex structured information and has been widely used in search engines, question answering systems and other fields. The introduction of knowledge atlas aims to provide the model with additional knowledge information, enable the model to have the ability of understanding and association, and improve the generalization ability of the model   [3–8].

3   Dataset Paper

Through reading the data set papers, we learned that the evaluation of high-quality articles is realized through the score synthesis of seven aspects. These include relevance, text quality, directness, versatility, context, novelty and emotion. By characterizing various dimensions of articles, we propose a knowledge map enhanced article quality identification dataset (kgea) [9]. Relevance refers to whether there is a high degree of consistency between the title and content of high-quality articles; Text quality refers to whether the spelling and grammar of high-quality sentences are standard; The remaining five aspects respectively refer to whether the expression of high-quality articles is accurate, concise and comprehensive, whether its logic is rigorous, whether its thinking is positive and so on. They also extract features through relevant tools and use the co-occurrence of entities between articles and Baidu Encyclopedia to build a knowledge map for each article [9].

In addition, the author of the data set obtained the relevant training data set according to the screening criteria, and carried out the relevant experimental verification by using the four baseline models of Bert, GCN, Ernie 1.0 and k-bert under the modeling method of knowledge map. In the final results, it was found that GCN (graph based text classification model) had the most outstanding effect - the F1 values of validation set and test set were 0.776 and 0.734, respectively.

4   Method

In recent years, a large number of studies have shown that large-scale corpus-based pre-training models (PTM) can learn common language representations, facilitate downstream NLP tasks, and avoid training models from scratch. With the development of computing ability, the emergence of depth model (i.e. Transformer) and the enhancement of training skills make PTM develop continuously from shallow to deep. ERNIE is a semantic understanding framework for continuous learning based on knowledge enhancement. This framework combines big data pre training with multi-source rich knowledge. Through continuous learning technology, ERNIE continuously absorbs vocabulary, structure, semantics and other knowledge from massive text data to achieve continuous evolution of model effects. Therefore, we use the pre-training model based on Transformer (mainly ERNIE) with fine-tuning mode, which is shown in the following Fig. 2.

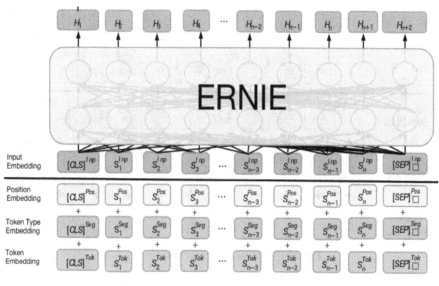

Fig. 2. ·Ernie model

The pretraining model ERNIE deals with Chinese data in words. PaddleNLP has built-in tokenizers for various pre-training models. Specify the name of the model you want to use to load the corresponding tokenizer.

The tokenizer is used to convert the original input text into a form of input data acceptable to the model. As shown in Fig. 3:

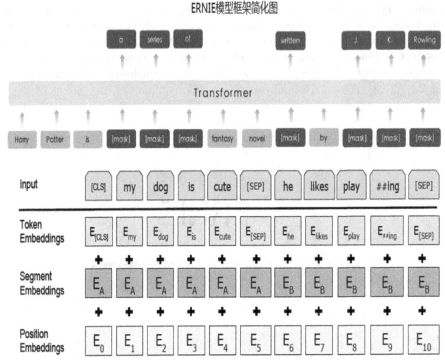

Fig. 3. ERNIE model framework diagram

4.1 Summary

First, we use content modeling to Roberta, Ernie and Nezha pre training models are used for training prediction, and then the prediction results are weighted and fused as pseudo tags into the training set. Finally, the Ernie pre training model is used for training by using the modeling method of Article Title Knowledge Map part of article content, and then the model with the lowest loss is selected for prediction. The final effect is very significant. Our method is shown in Fig. 4:

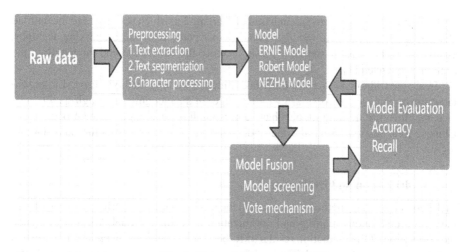

Fig. 4. Data modeling process

4.2 Text Preprocessing

After getting the training set and the verification set, we wrote the code and took out a piece of data from the training set. The format of the data set includes the link of the article, the article title, the article publishing time, the article content, and the entity set in the article. So we wrote code to extract the article content of the data set and remove the <br/> characters between paragraphs, article titles, entity sets and whether the article is of high quality.

Since the maximum length of text that Ernie and other pre training models can handle is 512, in order to make the model learn more features in the process of training, we chose the maximum segmentation after the combination of article content, knowledge map and article title. At the same time, the author also did some operations such as removing all punctuation marks in the article to make a solid foundation for the subsequent experiments.

4.3 Text Classification Model

Ernie [10] is a continuous learning semantic understanding framework based on knowledge enhancement. It discards Bert's word fragment mask mechanism and uses entity level and phrase level mask mechanisms, so that it absorbs a large amount of knowledge about the vocabulary, structure, semantics and other aspects of text data, and realizes the continuous evolution of model effect [10].

Nezha [12] is a transformer based pre training model. Its overall structure is similar to that of Bert, except that it adds a relative position coding function. The Bert model has absolute position coding, but most of the time the length of the data is too short to the maximum length of the model, so the position vector of the back position cannot be fully trained. The Nezha model considers the relative position relationship between the tokens, and can better learn the relationship between characters [12].

Roberta [11] is an improvement based on Bert model, which is adjusted to the optimal Bert model. It is mainly to modify Adam's super parameter, add the mixing accuracy, change the static mask to dynamic mask, increase the batch size, and the length of the training sequence [11].

In the pre training model, we used three kinds of training methods: ernie-1.0, nezha-large-wwm-chinese and roberta-wwm-ext-large. In the recognition of high-quality articles, the three pre training models have corresponding advantages in the processing of Chinese long text data sets and the understanding of semantic structure and internal logic.

4.4 Model Fusion and Evaluation

In different modeling methods, we selected the models with high performance and fused them after continuous training and optimization of a single model. We first evaluated the correlation of the prediction results of Roberta, Ernie and Nezha pre training models under the article content modeling, and found that Ernie's prediction results had better performance and lower correlation coefficient than the other two. Finally, we determined the weighted fusion of 1:2:1 and got a new prediction result.

In terms of model evaluation, we use the cross entropy function and the following evaluation indicators to evaluate every 300 steps of model training, print the relevant loss function, accuracy and recall rate, and save the existing weight model.

4.5 Evaluating Indicator

The evaluation index of this task adopts F1 value, that is, the harmonic average of precision (P) and recall (R). The accuracy rate is the ratio of the correct number of identified high-quality articles to the total number of identified articles. Recall rate is the ratio of the correct number of identified high-quality articles to the correct number of standard answers. When the label of the identified high-quality article is the same as that of the standard correct answer, it is recorded as correct identification. Written in mathematical formula, namely:

$$F1 = \frac{2PR}{P + R} \tag{1}$$

5 Experiment

After reading and understanding the dataset papers, we knew the screening rules of high-quality papers and the best results obtained by using knowledge map modeling. At the same time, after looking at the relevant requirements of the competition task and the dataset format, we first chose to reproduce some data results of the dataset papers, Then, the untreated and processed article content were modeled, and the article title - knowledge map - part of the article content modeling, multi-mode fusion and other experiments were carried out.

The relevant experimental data results based on the article title - knowledge map - part of the article content modeling are as follows:

Model	Precision	Recallr	F1
Ernie-1.0	0.795	0.812	0.803
Nezha large WwM Chinese	0.691	0.917	0.788
Roberta WwM ext large	0.747	0.846	0.794
Weighted fusion	0.785	0.859	0.82

The specific parameters of the model are configured as follows:

Model	Max_Seq_Length	Epochs	Learning_Rate	Evaluation steps
Ernie-1.0	512	3	2e−5	300

6 Conclusion

Based on a large number of experiments, it is found that the stability of the training model is poor without using knowledge map modeling (in the finals, we used the weighted fusion result of 0.779), and it is difficult to further improve the effect of the model only according to the effect of knowledge map modeling and prediction (compared with the dataset paper). So according to the relevance of the paper to judge the high-quality articles, we used the modeling method of Article Title Knowledge Map part of the article content in the data set processing, and the method of pseudo label data set using multi-mode fusion, which made the model result achieve good results.

Acknowledgment. We have done a lot of experiments to verify the performance of the modeling method, and finally achieved good results in the competition, so we are very excited and happy. At the same time, in the process of the competition, the teacher gave us hard and unremitting guidance; After the competition, the staff will review in the background and actively respond to relevant questions.

Therefore, we would like to express our gratitude to the staff of CCKS Organizing Committee, the sponsor of this contest, to the reviewers of this paper, and to the instructors for spending so much time and energy on this matter.

References

1. Minaee, S., Kalchbrenner, N., Cambria, E., Nikzad, N., Chenaghlu, M., Gao, J.: Deep learning based text classification: a comprehensive review. Corr, abs/2004.03705 (2020)
2. Cheng, J.: Research and implementation of Chinese long text classification algorithm based on deep learning. University of the Chinese Academy of Sciences (Institute of artificial intelligence, Chinese Academy of Sciences) (2020). https://doi.org/10.27824/d.cnkiGzkdx2020.000029
3. Wan, S., Lan, Y., Guo, J., Xu, J., Pang, L., Cheng, X.: A deep architecture for semantic matching with multiple positive sense representations. Corr, abs/1511.08277 (2015)

4. Wang, Z., Hamza, W., Florian, R.: Bilateral multi-perspective matching for natural language sentences. In: Procedures of the Twenty Sixth International Joint Conference on Artistic Intelligence, ijcai-17, pp. 4144–4150 (2017)
5. Le, H.T., Cerisara, C., Denis, A.: Do revolutionary networks need to be deep for text classification? Corr, abs/1707.04108 (2017)
6. Guo, B., Zhang, C., Liu, J., Ma, X.: Improving text classification with weighted word embeddings via a multi-channel textcnn model. Neurocomputing **363**, 366–374 (2019)
7. Yao, L., Mao, C., Luo, Y.: Graph revolutionary networks for text classification. Corr, abs/1809.05679 (2018)
8. Kim, S., Hong, J.H., Kang, I., Kwak, N.: Semantic sense matching with densely connected recurrent and co attentive information. Corr, abs/1805.11360 (2018)
9. Ai, C., Wang, D., Xu, Y., Xie, W., Cao, Z.: KGEA: a knowledge graph enhanced art quality identification dataset. arXiv:2206.07556 (2021)
10. Sun, Y., et al.: ERNIE: enhanced representation through knowledge integration. arXiv preprint arXiv:1904.09223 (2019)
11. Liu, Y., et al.: RoBERTa: a robust optimized BERT pre training approach. arXiv:abs/1907.11692 (2019)
12. Wei, J., et al.: NEZHA: neural contextualized representation for Chinese language understanding. arXiv:abs/1909.00204 (2019)
13. 丁辰晖,夏鸿斌,刘渊.融合知识图谱与注意力机制的短文本分类模型. 计算机工程**47**(01), 94–100 (2021). https://doi.org/10.19678/j.issn.1000-3428.0056734
14. 唐望径,许斌,仝美涵,韩美奂,王黎明,钟琦.知识图谱增强的科普文本分类模型. 计算机应用**42**(04), 1072–1078 (2022)
15. Chen, M., Ubul, K., Xu, X., Aysa, A., Muhammat, M.: Connecting text classification with image classification: a new preprocessing method for implicit sentiment text classification. Sensors **22**(5) (2022)
16. Chen, X, et al.: KnowPrompt: knowledge-aware prompt-tuning with synergistic optimization for relation extraction. In: Proceedings of the ACM Web Conference, April 25, pp. 2778–2788 (2022)
17. Chen, X., et al.: Decoupling knowledge from memorization: retrieval-augmented prompt learning. arXiv preprint arXiv:2205.14704, 29 May 2022

High-Quality Article Classification Based on Named Entities of Knowledge Graph and Multi-head Attention

Zhancheng Liang, Zhenkun He, and Peipei Jia[✉]

Shenzhen Institute for Advanced Study, University of Electronic Science and Technology of China, Shenzhen, China
{zhancheng_liang,202122280936}@std.uestc.edu.cn,
jiapeipei@uestc.edu.cn

Abstract. With the number of all kinds of self-media articles explosive growth, it is of great research significance and practical application value to recommend high-quality articles to users. This paper explores how to combine named entities of knowledge graph and multi-head attention mechanism with quality article identification, not only the contents of articles. For the article classification task of CCKS 2022, we proposed an incorporating named entity information approach based on the NEZHA model with continual pre-training combined, multi-head attention and BiGRU. Five-fold cross-validation solved the problem of less training data, warm-up strategy handled the problem of unstable effect at the beginning of training and focal loss treated the unbalanced samples. Then we selected the top three results in terms of F1 scores for voting fusion. Finally, data augmentation was applied in accordance with certain rules in the fusion results. Our method achieves F1 score of 86.51% on the test set of the task and ranks the second place in the competition.

Keywords: Multi-head attention · Named entity · Knowledge graph

1 Introduction

In the era of mobile Internet and big data, all kinds of We-media articles have witnessed explosive growth. In the information distribution scenarios such as search and recommendation, it is of great research significance and practical application value to screen out high-quality articles and distribute them to users. In addition to the writing quality of the article itself, high-quality articles should have the depth and novelty of the content. However, simply relying on the content of the article may not completely recognize high-quality articles. The CCKS 2022 identification of high-quality articles based on knowledge graph explores how to achieve high-quality article classification by using the external knowledge graph related to the article and combining the internal knowledge logic of the article based on a deeper semantic understanding of the article.

The dataset of this task comes from a mainstream we-media platform in China called Baidu Baijia. There are more than 10,000 articles in the dataset, and each article has title, body, label of whether it is a high-quality article and corresponding knowledge graph information [1]. Professional annotators scored the collected data in seven dimensions to get the main points of the article. The complete dataset was fitted by decision tree based on manually annotated data. Figure 1 gives an example of text classification for this task.

In this task, precision (P), recall (R) and F1-score are used to evaluate the classification effect of identification. And F1-score is the harmonic average of P and R:

$$F_1 = \frac{2 \cdot P \cdot R}{P + R} \tag{1}$$

Compared with the classification method of using the content of articles only, the problem is limited information cannot improve the accuracy of identifying high-quality articles because the content may not be related to requirements [1]. To solve this problem, we proposed a learning method based on attention mechanism model combined knowledge graph information.

Sample

Input:


```
{
  "url": "http://baijiahao.baidu.com/s?id=1657091325677517018",
  "title": " 新年首秀！美联储维持利率不变，中国央行或仍“ 淡定 ”",
  "pub_time": "2020-01-30",
  "content": " 中新经纬客户端 1 月 30 日电（张澍楠）在结束为期两天的货币政策例会后，美联储今日（30 日）凌晨宣布，维持联邦基金利率在 1.50%-1.75% 不变，符合市场预期。<br/>" 按兵不动 "成共识...",
  "entities":{
    " 联邦基金利率 ": {
      "co-occurrence": [" 美国 "],
      "entity_id": "7949986",
      "entity_baike_url": "https://baike.baidu.com/item/%E8%81%94%E9%82%A6%E5%9F%BA%E9%87%91%E5%88%A9%E7%8E%87/7949986",
      "entity_baike_info": [
        {"name": " 中文名 ", "value": [" 联邦基金利率 "]},
        {"name": " 外文名 ", "value": ["Federal Funds Rate"]},
        {"name": " 最主要的 ", "value": [" 隔夜拆借利率 "]},
        {"name": " 投资 ", "value": [" 国民经济 "]},
        {"name": " 释义 ", "value": [" 美国同业拆借市场的利率，其最主要的是隔夜拆借利率 "]},
        {"name": " 反映 ", "value": [" 反映银行之间资金的余缺 "]}
      ]
    }
    " 国际货币基金组织 ": ...
    " 美国 ": ...
    ...
  }
}
```


Output:


```
{
  "url": "http://baijiahao.baidu.com/s?id=1657091325677517018",
  "label": 0
}
```


Fig. 1. Example of high-quality article classification based on knowledge graph.

The rest of the paper is as follows: Sect. 2 describes our method; Sect. 3 presents the experiment implementations and results; Sect. 4 concludes the paper and discusses the future work.

2 Methods

We use the NEZHA model based on attention mechanism as the basic template to make full use of the context. To make the model understand the relationship between quality and article better, we add entities to every corresponding content text. To make the format of data conform entered style (label, text) of the model, we preprocess the original dataset firstly. Next, we added multi-head self-attention and BiGRU network after NEZHA pre-training model to get more context information. To enhance robustness, we train our model by partitioning the dataset with 5-fold cross-validation and then the prediction results of the model are fused by voting. Our scheme uses focal loss to effectively solve the model performance problem caused by data imbalance. Finally, the results with the top three F1 scores are used for voting fusion. Figure 2 shows the overview of our method.

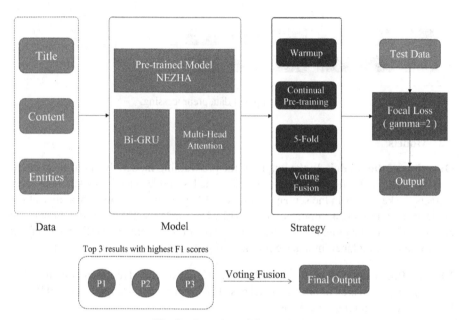

Fig. 2. Overview of the method.

2.1 Data Preprocessing

Firstly, we preprocess the text of the content part by replacing "<br>" and the extra space character with a space character. Then, we choose title and content as our basic text data and concatenate them by a special word "[SEP]" and then take the first 256 characters. The experiment proved that the first 256 characters of content can make better effect of identification than other text length.

Next, the entities are concatenated one by one at the end of the content and divided by "[SEP]". Moreover, the total text length is no longer than 512 characters long—to match our computing resources and model, 512 characters text length is set in our method. Figure 3 gives an example of data preprocessing.

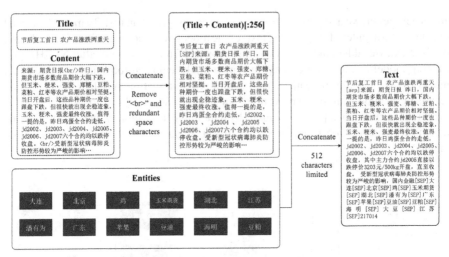

Fig. 3. Example of data preprocessing.

2.2 Models

Overview of the Model. In the output of the pre-training model, the multi-head attention layer and the BiGRU layer are added after the last hidden state. The Attention layer extracts the keywords in the sentence, and the GRU improves the memory ability of the model to achieve more accurate predictions [2]. Then we concatenate the output with the output of CLS embedding for classification, dropout for preventing overfitting and focal loss for alleviating label imbalance problem. Figure 4 shows our model framework.

NEZHA Pre-trained Model. NEZHA (NEural contextualiZed representation for CHinese lAnguage) [3] is an improved model based on the pre-trained language model BERT. It has the following improvements:

- Functional Relative Positional Encoding as an effective positional encoding scheme.
- Whole Word Masking (WWM) strategy.
- Mixed precision training.
- the LAMB Optimizer in training the models.

$$a_{ij}[2k] = \sin\left(\frac{j-i}{10000^{\frac{2\cdot k}{d_z}}}\right) \tag{2}$$

$$a_{ij}[2k+1] = \cos\left(\frac{j-i}{10000^{\frac{2\cdot k}{d_z}}}\right) \tag{3}$$

The BERT model uses absolute position encoding, but many times the length of the data exceeds the model's maximum length of 512, so the position vectors at the rear are not fully trained. The NEZHA model considers the relative positional relationship between tokens, which can better learn the mutual relationship between characters [2]. In the above equation, a_{ij} represents the relative position between position i and j, and d_z is equal to the hidden size per head of the self-attention in NEZHA model.

Our pre-training model is "NEZHA-base-wwm" with whole word masking, which masks the whole word during pre-training. WWM works better with Chinese sentences composed of words than with a single word. Based on the model, multi-head attention and BiGRU helps get more semantic information.

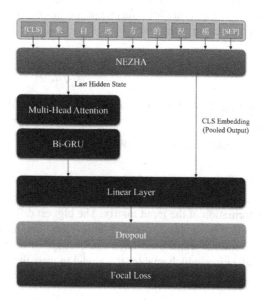

Fig. 4. Overview of the model framework.

BiGRU. GRU (Gate Recurrent Unit) [4] is a type of Recurrent Neural Network (RNN). Like LSTM (Long-Short Term Memory), it is also proposed to solve problems such as long-term memory and gradients in backpropagation. Compared to LSTM, GRU has fewer parameters with only the input and forget gate and is easier to converge. A Bidirectional GRU (BiGRU) [5] is a sequence processing model that consists of two GRUs.

$$\overrightarrow{h} = GRU\left(x_t, \overrightarrow{h_{t-1}}\right) \tag{4}$$

$$\overleftarrow{h} = GRU\left(x_t, \overleftarrow{h_{t-1}}\right) \tag{5}$$

$$h_t = w_t \overrightarrow{h_t} + v_t \overleftarrow{h}_t + b_t \tag{6}$$

In the equation above, one of the GRUs taking the input in a forward direction, and the other in a backwards direction, and finally take the weighted sum of their hidden states to get the final hidden state h_t. BiGRU is used to obtain the semantic features of a word in the text through the context information, which has the advantage of preserving the information of a word in the context as much as possible and improving the accuracy of classification. For this task, we take the last hidden state of the GRU output as one of the inputs of the linear layer.

Muti-head Attention. In the attention mechanism [6], the more similar the current input is to the target state, the greater the weight of the current input will be, indicating that the current output is more dependent on the current input. Multi-head attention can be treated as multiple attention in parallel to further refine the attention layer and improve the performance of the attention layer.

$$Attention(Q, K, V) = softmax\left(\frac{QK^T}{\sqrt{d_k}}\right)V \tag{7}$$

$$MultiHead(Q, K, V) = Concat(head_1, \ldots, head_h)W^O \tag{8}$$

$$head_i = Attention\left(QW_i^Q, KW_i^K, VW_i^V\right) \tag{9}$$

The above is the equation for the multi-head attention mechanism, where $\sqrt{d_k}$ is the length of the $\overrightarrow{k}$, W is for linear transformations, and the matrix Q, K, V come from the linear transformation of the input matrix. The biggest difference between self-attention and self-attention is the source of information input. The input of self-attention is unified, while the input of multi-head attention is mapped to different subspaces through random initialization, which enables the model to view the same problem from different perspectives and can get better results.

Focal Loss. The distribution of sample types is extremely unbalanced (shown in Fig. 5)—negative samples are almost twice as large as positive samples. The value of the loss function is mostly affected by the categories with large sample size, which leads to the result that the classification results of the model will favor the categories with large sample size.

To solve this problem, we use Focal Loss [7] instead of the cross-entropy loss function to solve this problem through class-weighted loss. And it can focus on adding weights to the loss corresponding to the sample according to the difficulty of distinguishing the sample. Specifically, the losses of those samples that are easier to distinguish are suppressed. Conversely, for more indistinguishable samples, the impact of the loss will be amplified

$$Loss(x, class) = -\alpha(1 - softmax(x)[class])^\gamma \cdot log(softmax(x)[class]) \tag{10}$$

where γ is a constant and α is a vector. According to the experience of the original paper, we set $\gamma = 2$. For this task, we set $class = 2, \alpha = (1, 1)$.

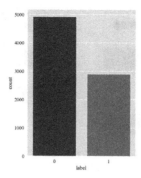

Fig. 5. The distribution of labels

2.3 Strategies

Warmup. Since the neural network is unstable at the beginning of training, the learning rate at the beginning should be set low to ensure that the network can have good convergence. However, a lower learning rate will make the training process very slow. Thus, the "warm-up" [8] stage of network training will be implemented by gradually increasing the learning rate from a lower learning rate to a higher learning rate.

$$\eta(t) = \eta_{wm} \cdot \left(\frac{\eta_0}{\eta_{wm}} \right)^{t/n_{wm}} \tag{11}$$

In the equation above, n_{wm} is the training step count of warmup stage, η_{wm} is the initial learning rate of beginning warmup, η_0 is the initial learning rate of the beginning model training, and $t(t \le n_{wm})$ is the global step of training. When $t = n_{wm}$, $lr = \eta_0$, the warmup stage is over. Next step is to gradually reduce the learning rate to 0 as the training progresses, the equation is as follows:

$$\eta(t) = \left(1 - \frac{t - n_{wm}}{n_{ttl} - n_{wm}} \right)^{p} \cdot \eta_0 \tag{12}$$

where n_{ttl} is the total training step count, and p controls the rate at which the learning rate decreases.

Continual Pre-training. To obtain the pre-trained model suitable for different industries fields and improve the effect of downstream classification tasks, we continue pre-training our model and introduce relevant knowledge according to the data set.

Each input text is manipulated with a 50% probability (shown in Fig. 6), and the rules are as follows:

- 80% replaced with [MASK].
- 10% replaced with another word in the vocabulary.
- 10% left unchanged.

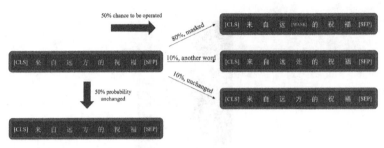

Fig. 6. MASK scheme for model pre-training.

We feed the processed data (include the mask-processed text) text into our model for continual pre-training. We also add multi-head attention layer and BiGRU layer to the model with cross-entropy loss.

5-Fold Cross-Validation & Voting Fusion. To solve the problem that the amount of data is not large enough, we use 5-fold cross validation method to train the model. Firstly,

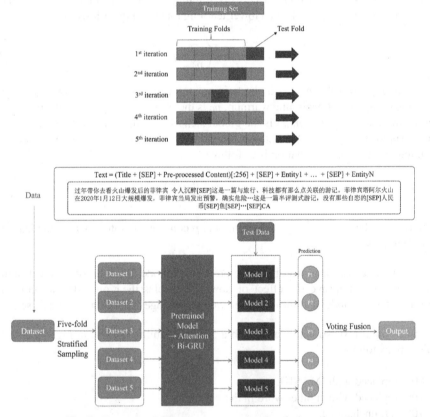

Fig. 7. Example of 5-Fold strategy and voting fusion of results.

the training set is divided into five sample subsets of equal size. The current subset is used as the validation set, and the remaining samples are used as the training set. Next, the test set data were predicted by each fold of the model successively, and finally the 5 prediction results were voted and fused (shown in Fig. 7).

2.4 Data Augmentation

Through the analysis of the training set, we find the number of entities can also play a role in identifying the quality of articles. Specifically, for articles, the number of entities larger than a certain value must be a high-quality article, and less than a certain value must not be a high-quality article. Experiments show that when the number of entities is greater than 50, positive class samples are far more than negative class samples (341 and 5, respectively). Similarly, when the number of entities is less than 12, positive class samples are far less than negative class samples (1911 and 20, respectively). The statistical results are shown in Table 1 and Table 2.

Table 1. The relationship between the minimum number of entities and sample number

Min entity num (≥)	Positive sample num	Negative sample num
30	1314	148
40	623	19
50	**341**	**5**
60	157	1
80	46	0

Table 2. The relationship between the maximum number of entities and sample number

Max entity num (≤)	Positive sample num	Negative sample num
11	0	1623
12	**20**	**1911**
13	60	2192
14	128	2466
15	196	2773

We manually set the results with the number of entities not less than 50 to the positive class and set the results with the number of entities not more than 12 to the negative class. This statistical information of the entities can be used as a data augmentation method to "correct" the results because the sample class needs to contain a small amount of noise to enhance generalization but not too much.

3 Experiment

This section introduces the dataset provided in the competition and conducts experiments to evaluate the model.

3.1 Dataset

The dataset used in this task comes from the articles of Baidu Baijia. It totally contains 7835 articles, and each article contains URL, title, publish time, content and between 2 and 196 entities. Moreover, the content length of each article is between 1073 and 27180, which is too long for model to extract valid information accurately. We processed the data according to the method in Sect. 2.1 to obtain a dataset with the length of each text no longer than 512. And the dataset is split into training, validation, and test sets as 8:1:1. More details for the subsets are listed in Table 3.

Table 3. The statistics of the preprocess subsets in the competition

Subset	Total number	Number of positive samples	Number of negative samples	Entity number
Train	6268	2337	3931	132896
Val	783	284	499	16867
Test	784	282	502	16827

3.2 Experimental Setups

Based on HUAWEI Noah's framework, we treat the "nezha-base-wwm" model with 12 layers and 768 of hidden layer size as our pre-trained language model. The initial learning rate for BertAdam is set to 3e−5 for training. We choose "warmup linear" as our warmup schedule and the warmup proportion is 0.1. The maximum sequence length of token is 512, batch size is 32. Seven epochs per fold are set in 5-fold cross-validation training.

We evaluated our model using for scores for training, validation and testing performance: precision, recall and F1 score. All scores presented in this paper are the average of 3 runs performed with different random seeds to mitigate the effect of training order. Finally, we selected the results with the top three F1 scores for voting fusion.

3.3 Results

The results are presented in Table 4 and show the performance on the preprocessed test data and all experiments are based on the warmup strategy. In Table 4, "NEZHA" represents "NEZHA-base-wwm" pre-trained model, "CEL" represents cross-entropy loss,

"FL" means focal loss, "CPT" means continual pre-training (trained for 27 epochs), "Attention" represents multi-head attention, and "GRU" represents BiGRU. The experiment shows that focal loss has a better discrimination ability for hard-to-distinguish samples than cross-entropy loss—F1 score 81.13% than 80.59%. While multi-head attention reduces precision score, it improves F1 score compared with BiGRU. Continual pre-training accelerates the convergence rate of the model and improves scores. Then we select the top three results (85.81%, 85.54% and 85.30%) of the F1 scores in Table 4 for voting fusion, and the result is shown in Table 5.

Table 4. Results of our methods with preprocessed data

Method	Precision	Recall	F1
NEZHA + CEL	84.17	77.30	80.59
NEZHA + FL	83.90	86.88	81.13
NEZHA + FL + GRU	84.51	85.11	84.81
NEZHA + FL + Attention	83.78	87.94	**85.81**
NEZHA + FL + Attention + GRU	81.03	89.36	84.99
NEZHA + FL + Attention + GRU + CPT	81.72	89.54	**85.54**
NEZHA + FL + Attention + GRU + CPT + 5-Fold	87.36	83.33	**85.30**

Table 5. Result of F1 score top 3 voting fusion

Precision	Recall	F1
83.84	88.30	**86.01**

We compare the results of data with and without entity features. The data without entity features only comes from the title and content, concatenated by "[SEP]", and the maximum sequence length is also 512. Table 6 shows the comparison of results preprocessed and un-preprocessed data based on "NEZHA + FL + Attention + GRU" model above with the same experimental setup as Sect. 3.2. In addition, "data1" represents the data with entity features and "data2" means the data without entity features. Based on Table 6, the method that data with entity features performers better than that without entity features. We conclude that no important information can be derived from truncated text that is too long. On the contrary, combining the data with entity features and short text has a better classification effect.

To show the effect of data augmentation, we performed data augmentation on the resulting data in Table 6. And Table 7 shows the comparison before and after data augmentation that after the data augmentation, the F1 score improved. And the highest

F1 score is 86.51% of top3 voting fusion method whose recall score is 88.65% and precision score is 84.46%.

Table 6. Result comparison of preprocessed and un-preprocessed data

Method	Precision	Recall	F1
Model with data1	**81.03**	**89.36**	**84.99**
Model with data2	71.58	70.57	71.07

Table 7. Data augmentation result comparison

Method	F1 (NO DA)	F1 (DA)
Model with data1	84.99	85.67 (+0.68)
Model with data2	71.07	75.71 (+4.64)
Top 3 voting fusion	86.01	**86.51 (+0.50)**

4   Conclusion

The CCKS 2022 identification of high-quality articles based on knowledge graph is a text classification task that not only focuses on the titles and contents of articles but also the more information about articles such as entities and so on. In this paper, we propose a deep learning method based on the integration of entities into the contents of articles. Combining warmup strategy, multi-head attention and BiGRU with NEZHA-WWM model and preprocessed data, we achieved a good classification effect for high-quality articles, and the F1 score reached 85.91% on the test set after voting fusion. Meanwhile, focusing on the problem of imbalanced sample, we used focal loss to increase the weight of the hard-to-distinguish samples, so that the classifier paid more attention to the hard-to-distinguish samples. We use continual pre-training to improve the effect of downstream classification tasks. 5-fold cross-validation and voting fusion are used to expand our training set, and the F1 score is 85.30%.

Furthermore, we also performed data augmentation on the results of the method "NEZHA + FL + Attention + GRU" and top 3 scores voting fusion. Finally, the "Top 3" voting fusion F1 score with the highest score increased from 86.01% to 86.51%. It shows that articles' quality is related to the number of named entities of the articles.

In future work, Boundary smoothing [9] and adversarial training methods such as FGM [10] and PGD [11] can be used to improve the robustness of the model. And the weighted voting fusion of multiple pre-trained models is also a method to improve the generalization ability of models.

References

1. Ai, C., Wang, D., Xu, Y., et al.: KGEA: a knowledge graph enhanced article quality identification dataset. arXiv preprint arXiv:2206.07556 (2022)
2. Han, D., Tohti, T., Hamdulla, A.: Attention-based transformer-BiGRU for question classification. Information **13**(5), 214 (2022)
3. Wei, J., Ren, X., Li, X., et al.: Nezha: neural contextualized representation for Chinese language understanding. arXiv preprint arXiv:1909.00204 (2019)
4. Cho, K., Van Merriënboer, B., Gulcehre, C., et al.: Learning phrase representations using RNN encoder-decoder for statistical machine translation. arXiv preprint arXiv:1406.1078 (2014)
5. Liu, J., Yang, Y., Lv, S., Wang, J., Chen, H.: Attention-based BiGRU-CNN for Chinese question classification. J. Ambient. Intell. Hum. Comput., 1–12 (2019)
6. Vaswani, A., Shazeer, N., Parmar, N., et al.: Attention is all you need. In: Advances in Neural Information Processing Systems, 30 (2017)
7. Lin, T.Y., Goyal, P., Girshick, R., et al.: Focal loss for dense object detection. In: Proceedings of the IEEE International Conference on Computer Vision, pp. 2980–2988 (2017)
8. He, K., Zhang, X., Ren, S., et al.: Deep residual learning for image recognition. In: Proceedings of the IEEE Conference on Computer Vision and Pattern Recognition, 770–778 (2016)
9. Zhu, E., Li, J.: Boundary smoothing for named entity recognition. arXiv preprint arXiv:2204.12031 (2022)
10. Dong, Y., Liao, F., Pang, T., et al.: Boosting adversarial attacks with momentum. In: Proceedings of the IEEE Conference on Computer Vision and Pattern Recognition, pp. 9185–9193 (2018)
11. Yang, C., Ochal, M., Storkey, A., et al.: Prediction-guided distillation for dense object detection. arXiv preprint arXiv:2203.05469 (2022)

Implementation and Optimization of Graph Computing Algorithms Based on Graph Database

Jiaqi Wei, Shuang Wu, Jinkang Jia, and Ziqian Liu[✉]

China Telecom Cybersecurity Technology Co., Ltd., Beijing, China
{weijq3,jiajk,liuzq}@chinatelecom.cn

Abstract. Data mining and knowledge inferring over knowledge graph has gained particular attention and been widely applied in industry over the past years. These works can be generalized to graph computing and graph analysis tasks, such as shortest path search, hop-constrained reachability, PageRank, triangle counting, and closeness centrality computation. However, existing graph database query language (SPARQL, Gremlin, etc.) dose not implement these algorithms. Therefore, CCKS 2022 holds a benchmark of graph computing algorithm based on graph database. We implemented all these five algorithms mentioned above based on graph database and made many optimizations to improve computation efficiency. On the final leaderboard, we took the first place, which shows extremely high practicality and efficiency.

Keywords: Graph computing · Graph data management · Graph data analysis

1 Introduction

RDF data is enjoying an increasing popularity since the launching of knowledge graph (KG) by Google in 2012. However, the explosion in the volume of RDF data has brought many challenges to data querying and analysis tasks, which requires efficient systems to store and query these data. Recently, lots of works utilize graph database techniques (such as a structure-aware index and a graph matching algorithm) to address RDF data management, such as gStore [1].

Data mining and knowledge inferring over knowledge graph has gained particular attention and widely applied in industry over the past years, such as route planning over large graphs, friend recommendation over social networks, and risk forecast over event graphs. These works mentioned above can be generalized to graph computing and graph analysis tasks, such as, relation discovery, community detection, and node influence assessment. Breadth-first search (BFS) and depth-first search (DFS) are at the heart of most classical graph algorithms. Based on BFS and DFS, a series of graph algorithms and their variants have been designed for different needs, such as shortest path search, hop-constrained reachability, PageRank [2], triangle counting, and closeness centrality computation. However, existing graph database query language (SPARQL,

N. Zhang et al. (Eds.): CCKS 2022, CCIS 1711, pp. 120–126, 2022.
https://doi.org/10.1007/978-981-19-8300-9_13

Gremlin, etc.) dose not implement these algorithms. Therefore, the 2022 China conference on knowledge graph and semantic computing (CCKS) holds a benchmark of graph computing algorithm based on graph database gStore. We implemented all these five mentioned algorithms based on gStore and made many optimizations to improve computation efficiency. On the final leaderboard, we took the first place in the competition, which shows extremely high practicality and efficiency.

2 Preliminaries

2.1 Background

A knowledge graph is modeled as a multi-relational graph, denoted as $G = (V, P, E)$, where V consists of vertexes (entities), P is the set of relations (predicates), and $E \in V \times P \times V$ is composed of labeled edges representing knowledge assertions (triples). A labeled and directed edge $(s, p, o) \in E$ naturally forms a triple, of which $s, o \in V$ are subject and object respectively, $p \in P$ is the predicate indicating some specific relation between them.

Store Format of Knowledge Graph. We use n, m and l for representing the number of vertices ($|V|$), the number of edges ($|E|$) and the number of predicates ($|P|$). Each vertex in the graph can be uniquely identified by a number between 1 and $n - 1$ and each predicate can be identified by a number between 1 and $l - 1$. . Compressed sparse row (CSR) format is adopted to store knowledge graph data on gStore. As shown in Fig. 1, we maintain an offset list and an adjacency list for each predicate. The size of the offset list and adjacency list is n and m. The adjacency lists of all vertexes are concatenated and reshaped to $(1, m)$, and each element in the offset list indicates the index of the adjacency list where each vertex starts and ends.

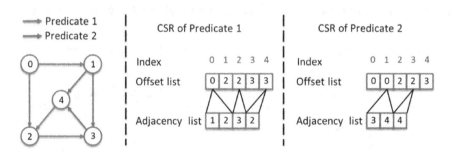

Fig. 1. The store format of knowledge graph on gStore.

2.2 Task Statement

This task belongs to knowledge fusion and knowledge graph storage management. Given a specific graph query or analysis algorithm, the participants should implement the algorithm through designing the atomic and user-defined function on the experimental platform, and verifies the accuracy and efficiency of the algorithm with the help of the experimental platform. The following is the graph computing algorithm specified to be implemented:

(1) **Path search algorithms**: shortest path searching, hop-constrained reachability.
(2) **Importance analysis algorithms**: closeness centrality computation, top-k personalized PageRank.
(3) **Community discovery algorithm**: triangle counting.

The knowledge graph dataset used in this evaluation task is the simulated social network data generated by LDBC SNB Datagen, and the influence factor of the dataset is SF1.

3 Methodology

In this section, we present our solutions of these graph computing algorithms mentioned above.

3.1 Shortest Path Searching

The shortest path problem aims to find the shortest path between two vertices in a graph. Actually, a breadth-first search (BFS) starting from source vertex, which is defined as *forward search*, can be easily applied to answer shortest path query. However, we find that a *bi-directional search* (a BFS process both starting from source vertex and target vertex) is more efficient than *single-directional search* when the edges in the graph are in uniform distribution. AS shown in Fig. 2, for the graph on the top panel, the number of traversal vertices with forward search and bi-directional search is 6 and 4, respectively.

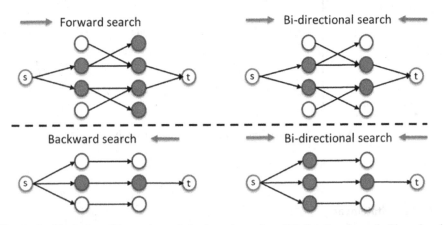

Fig. 2. An illustration of forward search, backward search and bi-directional search. The colored vertices in the graph indicate visited vertices in the BFS traversal process.

For most cases, bi-directional search can prune some invalid traversal. However, for the graph on the bottom panel, *backward search* is much more efficient than bi-directional search because the degree of target vertex is much smaller than the source vertex.

Based on the analysis discussed above, we designed an adaptive traversal algorithm with respect to different data distribution. Given a source vertex s and a target vertex t, the degree of s and t is denoted by $deg(s)$ and $deg(t)$. When $deg(s) < 0.5 * deg(t)$, a forward search is adopted. And when $deg(t) < 0.5 * deg(s)$, a backward search is adopted. Otherwise, a bi-directional search would be chosen.

3.2 Hop-Constrained Reachability

Paths formed by linking multiple edges with shared vertices can be regarded as representing more complex relations between its source and target vertices. Actually, many path-finding algorithms originate from the basic problem of finding the relation between two vertices. Most of these algorithms are designed to determine the existence of a relation between two vertices (i.e., reachability), or to find a relation between two vertices satisfying specific characteristics (such as the shortest path and Top-k path enumeration). In this task, we solve the problem of efficiently searching a list of paths that represent the relation between a source and a destination vertex. Given a hop constraint k, we search all paths from source vertex s to destination vertex t within k hops, which is referred to as the k-hop $s - t$ path set. Intuitively, a DFS that starting from source vertex can easily tackle this problem. However, the algorithm computes the k-hop $s - t$ path set with $O(n^k)$ worst time complexity due to reduplicated traversal as shown in Fig. 3. Since the graph is almost fully connected, there are totally $(\frac{n}{k})^k$ paths from s. To improve the efficiency of our algorithm, we should reduce these reduplicated and invalid traversals in the algorithm implementation.

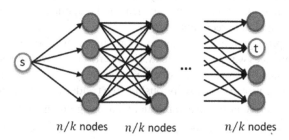

n/k nodes n/k nodes n/k nodes

Fig. 3. Worst case graph for DFS.

To address the efficiency problem, we propose a two-stage algorithm that applies both BFS and DFS. First, we conduct a k-hop BFS followed by out-going edges to record $dist(s, v)$ for each reachable vertex v from source vertex s, which indicates the distance between s and v. Second, we similarly compute the distance from target vertex t to reachable vertex v (denoted by $dist(v, t)$) by a k-hop BFS followed by in-going edges. Finally, we conduct a DFS that starting from source vertex to search all k-hop paths. Based on the distance information obtained by k-hop BFS, we can prune most reduplicated and invalid traversals. Specifically, we conduct a k-hop DFS starting from source vertex. As shown in Fig. 4, for each traversal edge $(u, p, v) \in E$, we check $dist(s, u) + 1 + dist(v, t) \leq k$. If the inequality mentioned above holds, we can sure path $p = (p_s(s, u), (u, v), p_s(v, t))$ is a k-hop path, where $p_s(s, u)$ (resp. From)denotes one shortest path from s to t. Otherwise, we stop the traversal starting from v. Since we can guarantee each vertex is visited only once and each edge is checked only once, the complexity is asymptotically linear of the graph size.

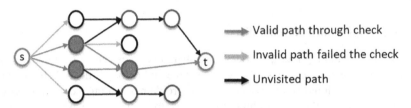

For each $(u, v) \in E$, check $dist(s, u) + 1 + dist(v, t) \leq k$

Fig. 4. An illustration of k-hop DFS with distance information.

3.3 Top-k Personalized PageRank

Given a graph $G = (V, P, E)$, a source vertex $s \in V$, and a jump factor α, a random walk starts from s to traverse the graph, and at each step, the walker either terminates at current vertex with probability α, or jumps to a out-neighbors of current vertex. We define the Personalized PageRank (PPR) [3] score $\pi(s, v)$ as the probability that a random walk starting from s terminates at v. Intuitively, the PPR score of v indicates its relevance from the perspective of source vertex s, which can be applied in many areas, such as influence analysis and item recommendation.

The residue propagation method is an approximate method to compute the PPR scores of all the vertices w.r.t source vertex s. Each vertex v has two values, a approximate value $\vec{p}$ and a residue $\vec{r}$, with initial value $\vec{r} = 1$ and $\vec{p} = 0$. With a preset threshold r_{max}, residue propagation process keeps pushing the residues of the vertices v satisfying $\frac{\vec{r}(v)}{d_{out}(v)} > r_{max}$ to their approximate value and their out-going neighbors' residues. The relation among approximate value $\vec{p}$, residue $\vec{r}$ and exact value $\vec{\pi}$ is defined as follows:

$$\vec{p} + \vec{r} = \vec{\pi} \tag{1}$$

Obviously, as long as we keep reducing the residue $\vec{r}$, we can make the approximate value $\vec{p}$ approach the exact value $\vec{\pi}$. This approximation process is a forward push process, which can be denoted by the following equation:

$$\begin{cases} \vec{p}(u) = \vec{p}(u) + (1 - \alpha)\vec{r}(u) \\ \vec{r}(v) = \vec{r}(v) + \alpha\vec{r}(u)/d_{out}(u) \end{cases} \tag{2}$$

In This Process, a Part of the Residue $\overrightarrow{r}$ of a Vertex u is Converted into the Approximate Value $\overrightarrow{p}$, and the Other Part is Propagated to the Neighbor $v \in N(u)$, Until the Residues of All Vertices Are Less Than a Certain Threshold r_{max}.

3.4 Closeness Centrality Computation

Closeness centrality is a way of searching vertices that are able to spread information very efficiently through a graph. The closeness centrality of a vertex is defined as the average inverse distances from a vertex to all other reachable vertices, which measures the cost that information is transmitted from this vertex to other vertices. Vertices with a high closeness score have the shortest distances to all other vertices in the graph. The closeness centrality of a vertex v_i is computed using the following formula:

$$C_c(v_i) = \sum_{v_i \neq v_j} \frac{1}{dist(v_i, v_j)} \tag{3}$$

where $dist(v_i, v_j)$ denotes the shortest distance between v_i and v_j.

To compute the closeness centrality of a given vertex v_i, we conduct a BFS to record the shortest distance to every reachable vertices from source vertex v_i. Then we can obtain the closeness centrality value by Eq. 3.

3.5 Triangle Counting

A triangle is a special topological structure that is commonly used for computing important measures in a graph, including clustering coefficients and transitivity. Searching all triangles in a graph is a computationally expensive task, especially for large graphs.

Triangle counting algorithm can be categorized into two branches: point iteration [4] and edge iteration [5]. The point iteration algorithm traverses every vertex in the graph, and checks whether each pair of its neighbors of is connected by edges. If any, it forms a triangle. The edge iteration algorithm traverses each edge, and takes the intersection of the neighbor lists of its two endpoints. The number of elements in the intersection is the number of the triangle containing the current edge. In addition, there is an edge iteration algorithm [6], which is a pruning version of the edge iteration algorithm: by using the ID value of vertices, only counting the edges with large IDs to small IDS can improve the performance to a certain extent.

In our final implementation, we design a edge iteration method. As shown in Fig. 5., compressed sparse row (CSR) format is adopted to store the graph. For each edge (u, v), we firstly obtain the adjacency lists $adj\_list(u)$ and $adj\_list(v)$ of u and v, respectively. Then we compute the number of intersections between these two adjacency lists through bitmap.

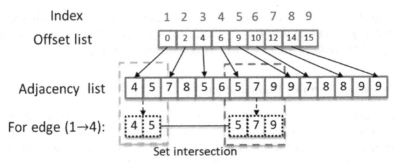

Fig. 5. An illustration of triangle counting algorithm based on edge iteration.

4 Conclusion

In this paper, we have proposed our optimized design of five graph computing algorithms over the graph database gStore. On the final testing data, we ranked first in shortest path search, top-k personalized PageRank and triangle counting, and ranked second in the rest of tasks. In the final leaderboard, we took the first place, which verifies the performance of our methods.

References

1. Zou, L., Mo, J., Chen, L., Özsu, M.T., Zhao, D.: gStore answering SPARQL queries via subgraph matching. Proc. VLDB **4**(8), 482–493 (2011)
2. Page, L., et al.: The PageRank citation ranking: bringing order to the web. Stanford InfoLab (1999)
3. Jeh, G., Widom, J.: Scaling personalized web search. In: WWW, pp. 271–279 (2003)
4. Alon, N., Yuster, R., Zwick, U.: Finding and counting given length cycles. Algorithmica **17**(3), 209–223 (1997)
5. Batagelj, V., Mrvar, A.: A subquadratic triad census algorithm for large sparse networks with small maximum degree. Soc. Networks **23**(3), 237–243 (2001)
6. Schank, T., Wagner, D.: Finding, counting and listing all triangles in large graphs, an experimental study. In: Nikoletseas, S.E. (ed.) WEA 2005. LNCS, vol. 3503, pp. 606–609. Springer, Heidelberg (2005). https://doi.org/10.1007/11427186_54

Knowledge Graph Construction for Foreign Military Unmanned Systems

Yilin Chen, Jingting Wang, Shutong Zhu, Yuang Gu, Haoyu Dai, Jingyi Xu, Yipeng Zhu, and Tianxing Wu[✉]

School of Computer Science and Engineering, Southeast University, Nanjing, China
tianxingwu@seu.edu.cn

Abstract. Unmanned systems have become a significant component of modern military forces and play a more and more important role in various military operations. It mainly consists of four major domains which are unmanned aerial system (UAS), unmanned ground vehicle (UGV), unmanned underwater vehicle (UUV), and unmanned surface vessel (USV). This paper focuses on the construction of a high-quality knowledge graph on foreign unmanned systems and proposes an effective method to complete the construction. The method first analyses the data provided by CCKS2022 evaluation organizers and builds a schema. Then not only data provided are used to construct the knowledge graph but also external data are crawled and extracted as triples under constraints of the schema. After that, entities are aligned and logic rules are also utilized to knowledge graph completion. Finally, the knowledge graph constructed is stored and visualized in the Neo4j database and evaluated by the question-answering tasks. This paper presents our technics for the 13th task of CCKS2022 evaluation (i.e. knowledge graph construction and evaluation on foreign military unmanned systems) and our team win the 3rd place in this task.

Keywords: Unmanned systems · Knowledge extraction · Knowledge graph · Knowledge graph completion

1 Introduction

As the product of military technologies, unmanned systems can continuously perform missions, be competent with various mission scenarios, and avoid casualties to a large extent. Unmanned systems have significant advantages in battlefield awareness, high-risk project management, and critical target protection. With such superiorities, unmanned systems have become an indispensable part of modern military operations.

The concept of knowledge graphs was first proposed by Google in 2012 and knowledge graphs such as WordNet [1], Freebase [2], and Yago [3] have been leveraged in many AI applications. Knowledge graphs are composed of factual triples, for example, a factual triple can be represented as (h, r, t) where h and t are head and tail entities respectively, and r is the relation between h and t. In the graph, h and t are represented as nodes, and r is represented as the directed edge which connects from h to t.

© The Author(s), under exclusive license to Springer Nature Singapore Pte Ltd. 2022
N. Zhang et al. (Eds.): CCKS 2022, CCIS 1711, pp. 127–137, 2022.
https://doi.org/10.1007/978-981-19-8300-9_14

The knowledge graph on unmanned systems which can give a better analysis of those systems and promote the development of related technologies. Various downstream tasks such as information retrieval and question answering can be well supported with knowledge graph. However, compared with general knowledge graphs or knowledge graphs on popular domains such as medicine and e-commerce, there are few knowledge graphs on unmanned systems currently. There are two main challenges of the construction, one is how to extract structured knowledge from large amounts of unstructured text and the other is how to perform continuous knowledge graph completion based on the initially built knowledge graph.

To solve the problems above, this paper proposes an effective method and constructs a high-quality knowledge graph on foreign unmanned systems. There are three stages of the whole construction, namely schema construction, data crawling and knowledge extraction, entity alignment and knowledge graph completion. The knowledge graph is stored and visualized in the Neo4j database. In the stage of data crawling and knowledge extraction, the joint extraction model SpERT (Span-based Entity and Relation Transformer) [4] is used to extract triples from unstructured text. RNNLogic (Learning Logic Rules for Reasoning on Knowledge Graphs) [5] also helps infer new relations between existing entities in the knowledge graph completion.

2   Related Work

2.1   Knowledge Graph Construction

Knowledge graph construction is an iterative process with many methods and tools need to be applied. [6] summarizes techniques of constructing Chinese knowledge graphs. [7] proposes a framework which focuses on knowledge extraction and knowledge linking to construct knowledge graphs from multiple online encyclopedias. Methods for the construction can be roughly divided into two categories, one is top-down and the other is bottom-up [8]. In top-down methods, the schema of data is usually first summarized, then data should be filled into the knowledge graph under the constraints of the schema. On the contrary, there is no explicit knowledge architecture in the bottom-up methods, in which entities, concepts, hypernym–hyponym relations, and even schema should be learned from massive data automatically.

In this paper, the domain of the knowledge graph is specified and the schema is relatively simple, so a top-down method is used.

2.2   Knowledge Extraction

Knowledge extraction aims at extracting knowledge (i.e. factual triples) from various source data which can be structured, semi-structured, or unstructured. Extraction methods vary according to different types of data.

In this task, unstructured data (i.e. text) accounts for the majority so the main work in extraction is relation extraction (RE) which aims at extracting entities with predefined relations. There are two main types of methods for RE: rule-based methods and statistic-based methods. Compared with statistic-based methods, rule-based methods need predefined rules which require comprehensive knowledge of the domain [9]. Statistic-based methods can be divided into five categories: unsupervised, semi-supervised, supervised, distant supervision, and neural network. However, in the first four methods, high-quality extracted features derived from natural language processing tools are needed [9]. As a result, neural network methods become the best choice for this task. There are two types of neural network models: pipeline models and joint extraction models. Pipeline models first extract entities and then classify relations, while joint models extract entities and relations at the same time. However, pipeline methods tend to propagate errors from entity extraction to relation classification, and joint extraction models can avoid such errors [10].

Various joint extraction methods were proposed. Kate et al. [11] proposed a "card-pyramid" graph encoding all possible entities and relations in a sentence to accelerate the joint extraction. Miwa et al. [12] introduced a table representation of entities and relations which is simple and flexible to extract entities and relations in a sentence. Bekoulis et al. [13, 14] used the adversarial training to improve the performance of joint extraction tasks and modeled the joint extraction task as a multi-head selection problem. Tan et al. [15] proposed a joint extraction model with the translation mechanism that can adaptively discover multiple triples simultaneously in a sentence. Sun et al. [16] performed joint inference on entity and relation types with an entity-relation bipartite graph. Fu et al. [17] proposed a method which can jointly learn named entities and relations with the graph convolutional network. Dai et al. [18] directly tagged entity and relation labels to extract overlapping triplets with the unified joint extraction model proposed. Eberts et al. [4] proposed an attention model called SpERT which is based on BERT [19] embeddings for joint entity and relation extraction, and it is easy-to-use with good performance. In this paper, we take SpERT as the knowledge extraction model.

2.3 Knowledge Graph Completion

Knowledge graphs are always incomplete because many implicit entities and relationships are undiscovered [20]. Traditional methods include rule-based reasoning methods, probability graph model methods, and graph computing methods. With the development of deep learning, methods based on representation learning have emerged in recent years. The most commonly used methods are rule-based reasoning methods and representation learning methods. However, rule-based methods depend on the search for candidate entities and relations and as the scale of knowledge graphs increases, the searching space becomes too large to search efficiently. Although representation learning methods can reason faster with embedding vectors, the lack of interpretability is a significant drawback. To solve the problems above, some methods combined rules and representation learning. Omran et al. [21] and Meilicke et al. [22] utilized embeddings to reduce the search space of candidate rules. Wu et al. [23] proposed a semi-supervised method integrating rules to learn relations from both Chinese and English social Web sites. Qu et al. [5] proposed a model called RNNLogic which consists of a rule-generator for suggesting high-quality rules and a reasoning predictor predicting missing information. We use RNNLogic in this paper for knowledge graph completion.

3   Knowledge Graph Construction

The construction of the unmanned system knowledge graph consists of three stages, including schema construction, data crawling and knowledge extraction, and entity alignment and graph completion. The whole process is shown in Fig. 1. In schema construction, source data are analyzed and the schema is preliminarily constructed. Under the constraints of the schema, new data are crawled and used to improve the schema. In knowledge extraction, structured data are extracted automatically by designed patterns and unstructured data are processed by SpERT [4]. In the last stage, after the entities are aligned manually, both rules built manually and learned by RNNLogic [5] are used to complete the knowledge graph.

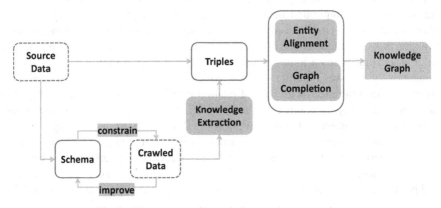

Fig. 1. The process of knowledge graph construction.

The knowledge graph on foreign military unmanned system is constructed, and finally stored and visualized in the Neo4j database.

3.1   Schema Construction

The schema is constructed mainly based on the data provided by the CCKS2022 evaluation organizer and continuously improved according to crawled data. We extract triples from the provided data manually because part of the data is well structured, for example, there are many tables and descriptions in key-value format, and the workload is also acceptable to deal with textual data. The schema is shown in Fig. 2. Due to limited sizes, there is only part of the schema in this figure.

The entities are divided into eleven categories which are foreign unmanned system, communication method, institution, military branch, system equipped, system component, technology, application, sensor, control unit, and weapon. Further, foreign unmanned systems consist of unmanned aerial systems (UAV), unmanned ground systems (UGV), and unmanned marine systems (UMS). After the classes of entities are determined, we also summarize the relations between them. With the work above, the architecture of the schema is built, then attributes of these classes are filled into corresponding classes to finish the construction.

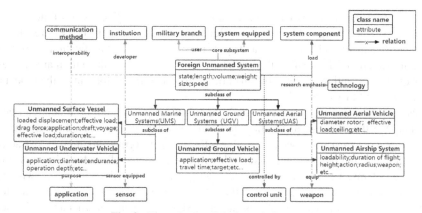

Fig. 2. The schema of the knowledge graph.

It is worth noting that the schema will be modified according to the data crawled after the preliminary construction because the structure of knowledge is not fixed and we need to get a schema up-to-date.

3.2 Data Crawling and Knowledge Extraction

Data Crawling. In this task, entities can only be extracted from the data provided by the CCKS2022 evaluations organizer. To get more entity relations and attributes, we crawl data about unmanned systems from the Web as an extension.

Online encyclopedias include Baidu Baike (https://baike.baidu.com/), Chinese Wikipedia (http://zh.wikipedia.org/), and news site Ifone (https://www.ifeng.com/) are crawled with python crawlers. At first, we simply concatenate the entity name and URL to search and download as much related HTML information as possible, but in this way, lots of unrelated information would pollute our data. For example, when we request the URL for 'MQ-9', many entries not only 'MQ-9', 'MQ-9 Reaper' but also 'Transformers (Movie)' (which is unrelated) are returned. To solve this problem, we built a table to record the mapping of entities and entries, then we only crawl entries that appeared in this table to ensure that all data crawled are useful.

Knowledge Extraction. Infobox data in the above online encyclopedias can be directly extracted as fact triples and stored in the knowledge graph. Figure 3 is an example of infobox data for the Baidu Baike entry '系留气球雷达系统', and we can get the triple (系留气球雷达系统, 外文名, TARS).

中文名	系留气球雷达系统		主要特点	预警、探测、监视持续时间长
外文名	TARS		主要组成	气球、光电系留缆绳

Fig. 3. An example of infobox data.

In addition to infobox data, there is a lot of unstructured textual data which is hard to extract manually, so SpERT [4] is used to jointly extract triples from textual data due to its good performance and ease of use. As shown in Fig. 4, SpERT consists of three parts: Span Classification, Span Filtering, and Relation Classification. Instances are filtered and identified in span classification and span filtering. Relation classification is used for relation extraction. The input of the model are tokens of text and the output are entities, types of entities, and relations between entities. To get better performance, the model is trained on a military corpus before use.

We first tokenize textual data to split them into corpus which the model can take as input. We then feed data into the model and get candidate triples. For automated extraction, there are usually two issues. One is that useful information cannot be extracted completely and the other is that false triples will be extracted. To reduce the impact of the two problems, we first manually select high-quality triples which are in line with the original meaning of extracted text, and then we label the triples which are not extracted from the text. With the selected triples and labeled text, we can construct a new dataset. We repeat the dataset construction and training several times, the performance of the model can get much better.

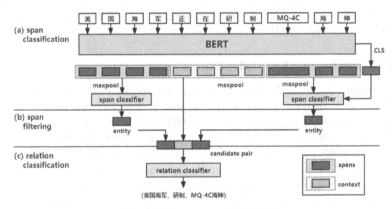

Fig. 4. The structure of SpERT.

3.3   Entity Alignment and Knowledge Graph Completion

Entity Alignment. There are many entities whose names are different but refer to the same object, such as 'MQ-9' and 'MQ-9 predator'. We analyze entities that have the issue above and find the number of such entities is small, and that is mostly because the entities are fixed for that they all come from the data provided. As a result, we align entities manually by adding 'synonymous' relations among them. This work is necessary because it will improve the quality of the knowledge graph and benefit to the question-answering task in the evaluation.

Knowledge Graph Completion. Knowledge graphs are always incomplete and lots of implicit relations are neglected in the construction process. The easiest method to complete the knowledge graph is to design rules and perform reasoning with them. For example, according to the transitivity, we get a rule: (A, is-a, B) ∧ (B, is-a, C) → (A, is-a, C) and that means, once we get the first two triples in the rule (i.e. (A, is-a, B) and (B, is-a, C)), then we can get a new triple (A, is-a, C). Some relations are also symmetrical, for example, for the relation 'cooperate_with', (A, cooperate_with, B) and (B, cooperate_with, A) both can be true once one of them is true and that means once we have one triple of them we can infer the other.

Besides the work above, we also use RNNLogic [5] to learn rules and complete the knowledge graph automatically. As shown in Fig. 5, the RNNLogic consists of a rule generator and a reasoning predictor. It takes queries, for example, q = (h, r, ?), where q is a triple, h and r mean the head entity and relation in the triple respectively, ? means the missing tail entity queried, as input. According to the query, rule generator generates rules which are fed to the reasoning predictor to knowledge graph reasoning, and we can get the candidate answers t. In the optimization stage, the high-quality rules which can generate the right answers are identified and used to update the rule generator. The model is optimized in the loop of the above process. We convert the format of our data, put them into the model and get some triples. Then, we filter the triples inferred by the model and filled them into the knowledge graph for completion.

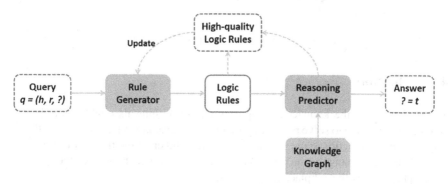

Fig. 5. The overview of RNNLogic.

3.4 Visualization

The knowledge graph is stored and visualized in the Neo4j database. It is a graph database and support searching for sub-graphs with high efficiency. A sub-graph about the navigational system (导航系统) searched in the database is shown in Fig. 6.

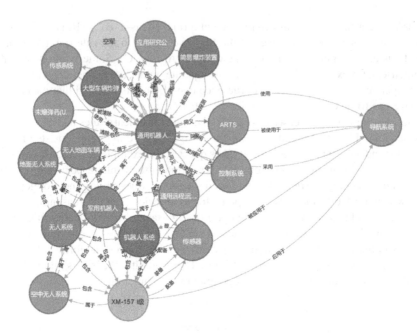

Fig. 6. A sub-graph about navigational system.

4   Evaluation

The evaluation of the knowledge graph aims at examining its quality and checking whether it is capable to solve practical problems. The evaluation has two stages, the first stage is the construction stage which checks the number of entities and triples of the graph. The second stage is the question answering stage which assesses the quality of the graph. We took the 3rd place in both stages.

Construction Evaluation. In this stage, the evaluation focuses on the number of entities and triples in the graph. The score in this stage is calculated by the formula

$$Score = N + R \tag{1}$$

where N stands for the number of entities which has relations with other entities and R stands for the number of all triples including relation triples and attribute triples. That means we need to extract as many entities and triples as possible. Finally, the score of our team in this stage is 80602.

Question Answering Evaluation. In this stage, the ability to solve practical problems was evaluated. Three questions were given by organizers and we need to get answers from the knowledge graph. In general, to answer these questions, we searched for the entities and relations related to the question and filtered the results from the knowledge graph, then we ran Cypher queries in the database to get visualized answers. The answers were judged by experts from the different neighborhoods and we won the 3rd place in this evaluation. Specifically, we took the 2nd and 1st places in the evaluation of the first and second questions, respectively.

The first question is finding the usage of lasers, finding all relations between unmanned aerial vehicles (UAV) which use lasers and the Hellfire missile, finding out which UAV found above has the highest service ceiling, and what tasks it can perform. For this question, we first searched for 'laser' in the knowledge graph and got 26 triples containing related entities, entity types, and attributes. Then we summarized the usage of lasers according to the triples we got as the answer. To find relations between UAVs using lasers and the Hellfire missile, we identified UAV entities related to lasers based on triples we got before and took them as head entities in the query to search for their relations with Hellfire missiles. In this query, we found that the Hellfire missile has another name in our knowledge graph, we also took this name as the tail entity. Then we got the subgraph (shown in Fig. 7) as the answer, and it contains 6 target relations in total. To find the highest service ceiling we only need to search for those entities one by one and it turns out that the answer is MQ-9 Reaper, which has a 50000 feet ceiling. At last, we need to find the task that MQ-9 can perform. First, we got all its alias and searched for their relations and attributes related to tasks they can perform. Finally, we get 11 triples which were taken as the answer.

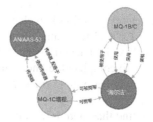

Fig. 7. The relations between UAV used lasers and the Hellfire missile.

The second question is extracting all nodes related to navigation services and all their relations in two hops. To answer this question, we searched for all entities and attributes related to navigation services. There are 34 entities that meet the conditions. Then, we searched for all their relations in two hops and got 34 subgraphs. The subgraph shown in Fig. 8 is one of them.

The last question is extracting all information about anti-access (A2), area-denial (AD), and overcoming the threat of intervention. This question was not answered well by our knowledge graph. We searched in the whole knowledge graph and got nothing related to those keywords in the question. As a remedy, we checked the source data provided and found that this question is related to autonomy, so we searched for the information about autonomy as an alternative. At last, we got 20 triples as the answer.

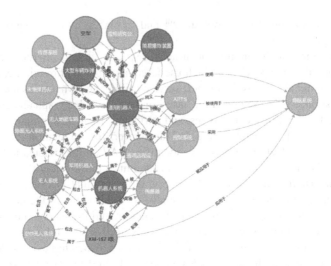

Fig. 8. The relations in two hops of the navigation system.

5   Conclusion

In this paper, we propose a framework to build a knowledge graph on foreign unmanned systems. The data is provided by CCKS2022 evaluation organizers. To get more knowledge about this domain, we crawl external data from the Web. The SpERT model is used to extract information from text. To complete the knowledge graph, rules are designed and the RNNLogic model is used to learn more rules. Finally, we get the 3rd place in this evaluation task.

During the construction, we find that there is a lot of work to be done before using deep learning models in practical tasks. For example, data preprocessing, candidate answers filtering and fine-tuning.

Acknowledgement. This work is supported by the NSFC (Grant No. 62006040), the Project for the Doctor of Entrepreneurship and Innovation in Jiangsu Province (Grant No. JSSCBS20210126), the Fundamental Research Funds for the Central Universities, and ZhiShan Young Scholar Program of Southeast University.

References

1. Miller, G.A.: WordNet: a lexical database for English. Commun. ACM **38**(11), 39–41 (1995)
2. Bollacker, K., Evans, C., Paritosh, P., Sturge, T., Taylor, J.: Freebase: a collaboratively created graph database for structuring human knowledge. In: Proceedings of the ACM SIGMOD International Conference on Management of data, pp. 1247–1250 (2008)
3. Fabian, M., Gjergji, K., Gerhard, W.: Yago: a core of semantic knowledge unifying wordnet and Wikipedia. In: Proceedings of the International Conference on World Wide Web, pp. 697–706 (2007)
4. Eberts, M., Ulges, A.: Span-based joint entity and relation extraction with transformer pre-training. arXiv preprint arXiv:1909.07755 (2019)

5. Qu, M., Chen, J., Xhonneux, L.P., Bengio, Y., Tang, J.: RNNLogic: learning logic rules for reasoning on knowledge graphs. arXiv preprint arXiv:2010.04029 (2020)
6. Wu, T., Qi, G., Li, C., Wang, M.: A survey of techniques for constructing Chinese knowledge graphs and their applications. Sustainability **10**(9), 3245 (2018)
7. Wu, T., et al.: Knowledge graph construction from multiple online encyclopedias. World Wide Web **23**(5), 2671–2698 (2019). https://doi.org/10.1007/s11280-019-00719-4
8. Zhao, Z., Han, S.K., So, I.M.: Architecture of knowledge graph construction techniques. Int. J. Pure Appl. Math. **118**(19), 1869–1883 (2018)
9. Cui, M., Li, L., Wang, Z., You, M.: A survey on relation extraction. In: Proceedings of China Conference on Knowledge Graph and Semantic Computing, pp. 50–58 (2017)
10. Pawar, S., Palshikar, G.K., Bhattacharyya, P.: Relation extraction: a survey. arXiv preprint arXiv:1712.05191 (2017)
11. Kate, R., Mooney, R.: Joint entity and relation extraction using card-pyramid parsing. In: Proceedings of the Conference on Computational Natural Language Learning, pp. 203–212 (2010)
12. Miwa, M., Sasaki, Y.: Modeling joint entity and relation extraction with table representation. In: Proceedings of the Conference on Empirical Methods in Natural Language Processing, pp. 1858–1869 (2014)
13. Bekoulis, G., Deleu, J., Demeester, T., Develder, C.: Adversarial training for multi-context joint entity and relation extraction. arXiv preprint arXiv:1808.06876 (2018)
14. Bekoulis, G., Deleu, J., Demeester, T., Develder, C.: Joint entity recognition and relation extraction as a multi-head selection problem. Expert Syst. Appl. **114**, 34–45 (2018)
15. Tan, Z., Zhao, X., Wang, W., Xiao, W.: Jointly extracting multiple triplets with multilayer translation constraints. In: Proceedings of the AAAI Conference on Artificial Intelligence, pp. 7080–7087 (2019)
16. Sun, C., Gong, Y., Wu, Y., Gong, M.: Joint type inference on entities and relations via graph convolutional networks. In: Proceedings of the Annual Meeting of the Association for Computational Linguistics, pp. 1361–1370 (2019)
17. FuTJ, L., GraphRel, M.Y.: Modeling text as relational graphs for joint entity and relation extraction. In: Proceedings of the Annual Meeting of the Association for Computational Linguistics, pp. 1409–1418 (2019)
18. Dai, D., Xiao, X., Lyu, Y., Dou, S., She, Q., Wang, H.: Joint extraction of entities and overlapping relations using position-attentive sequence labeling. In: Proceedings of the AAAI Conference on Artificial Intelligence, pp. 6300–6308 (2019)
19. Devlin, J., Chang, M.W., Lee, K., Toutanova, K.: Bert: Pre-training of deep bidirectional transformers for language understanding. arXiv preprint arXiv:1810.04805 (2018)
20. Chen, Z., Wang, Y., Zhao, B., Cheng, J., Zhao, X., Duan, Z.: Knowledge graph completion: a review. IEEE Access **8**, 192435–192456 (2020)
21. Omran, P.G., Wang, K., Wang, Z.: Scalable rule learning via learning representation. In: Proceedings of the International Joint Conference on Artificial Intelligence, pp. 2149–2155 (2018)
22. Meilicke, C., Chekol, M.W., Fink, M., Stuckenschmidt, H.: Reinforced anytime bottom up rule learning for knowledge graph completion. arXiv preprint arXiv:2004.04412 (2020)
23. Wu, T., Wang, H., Qi, G., Zhu, J., Ruan, T.: On building and publishing Linked Open Schema from social web sites. J. Web Semant. **51**, 39–50 (2018)

Knowledge-Enhanced Classification: A Scheme for Identification of High-Quality Articles

Yanmao Zhou[1], Yunni Xia[1(✉)], and Yongbo Wang[2]

[1] School of Computer Science, Chongqing University, Chongqing 400044, China
xiayunni@hotmail.com
[2] Ant Group, Hangzhou 316123, China
wyb269207@antgroup.com

Abstract. How to find high-quality articles from many articles is the topic of this competition and also the problem that many enterprises want to solve. In this classification problem, from TF-IDF to word2vec, then to RNN and LSTM, and now to transformer-based models, such as Bert, have achieved great improvement in NLU tasks. However, for many specific problems, such as recognition of high-quality article, directly inputting the text content into the transformer model cannot get the optimal solution, and many other optimizations are needed. In this paper, we try to add statistical features of articles and knowledge graphs, and add entities name of knowledge graph into Bert-based model, specific methods are in Sect. 2 and Sect. 3. Finally, our model achieved 83.6 F1-score in the official test set and ranked first among all teams in task 2 of CCKS-2022. This paper is divided into four parts: 1) The introduction of our task; 2) Main ideas of our model; 3) Other innovation strategies; 4) Experiments and result.

Keywords: Text Classification · Statistic features · Knowledge Graph

1 Introduction

1.1 Task Definition

In the era of Artificial Intelligence and Big Data, various of media articles are growing explosively. In search, recommendation and other scenarios, identifying and sending high-quality articles to users has important research significance and practical application value. In addition to the writing quality of the article itself, high-quality articles should have the depth and novelty of the content. Therefore, relying solely on the content of the article itself cannot completely identify high-quality articles. This task will introduce the external knowledge graph related to the article, combine the internal knowledge logic of the article, and realize high-quality article recognition on the basis of deeper semantic understanding of the article.

N. Zhang et al. (Eds.): CCKS 2022, CCIS 1711, pp. 138–147, 2022.
https://doi.org/10.1007/978-981-19-8300-9_15

Input data: Includes the article url, title, release time, content, knowledge graph and other information. The knowledge graph's information includes: entity name, related entities, entity ID, Baidu Encyclopedia link of the entity, Baidu Encyclopedia information of the entity (Table 1).

Table 1. Fields of input data

Field	Information
URL	*The URL of article*
PUB_TIME	*The publish time of article*
TITLE	*The title of article*
CONTENT	*The content of article*
ENTITIES	*The important entities of article*

Aim: Use the above information to identify whether the article is a high-quality article.

1.2 Main Challenges and Solutions

Obviously, this is a text classification problem. In the text classification task, the more traditional algorithms include TF-IDF, BM25 and word2vec [1]. However, the common approach to solve such problems today is generally based on the transformer model of the fine tuning pre training paradigm. This task is different from other text classification tasks in that: 1) in addition to the text information, the organizer of the competition also provided the information of the knowledge graph. How to integrate this information into the model is a challenge; 2) The sample size of the training data set is too small, and the sample label is unbalanced.

For challenge 1, Perozzi et al. proposed DeepWalk [2] by corresponding vertices to words. DeepWalk performs random walks to generate vertex sequences and trains Skip-Gram model to obtain vertex representations. Derived from Skip-Gram, DeepWalk has been extensively verified on various network analysis tasks. Defferrard et al. use Convolutional Neural Networks (CNN) to extract the features of knowledge graph [3]. It makes full use of CNN's Strictly localized filters, Low computational complexity, Efficient pooling and other advantages. Because the advantages of Bert and other pre training models in text processing are usually greater than CNN, Liu et al. proposed K-BERT [4] to fuse the information of knowledge graph to the Bert network, which solved the problem of insufficient receptive field of CNN.

For challenge 2, The common idea in the academic community is to construct a zero-shot model, so that the model can be trained well when the sample size is insufficient to make the model converge. Schick et al. introduce Pattern-Exploiting Training (PET) [5], a semi-supervised training procedure that reformulates input examples as cloze-style phrases to help language models understand a given task. This method can make the fine-tuning task consistent with the MLM pre-training task, and has good effects on zero-shot and few-shot. However, the disadvantages are obvious. The input templates are all manually constructed, and the results depend on the quality of the templates, with great uncertainty. Li et al. propose prefix-tuning [6], a lightweight alternative to fine-tuning for natural language generation tasks, which keeps language model parameters frozen, but optimizes a small continuous task-specific vector (called the prefix), it based on the idea that we may not necessarily have to build discrete tokens type prompt that people can understand, and it is also possible to build continuous vector type prompt that the model can accept.

2 Our Method

2.1 Overview of Basic Model Structure

First, we choose NEZHA [7] model and XLNet [8] model as backbone of our model, which is a kind of pretrained model based on transformer. It has some advantages. Introduction and details are in Sect. 2.2.

Second, we constructed multiple input types for NEZHA and XLNet, details are in Sect. 2.3.

Third, traditional method for classification is choose the CLS part of last layer. Our method is to choose the mean value of last layer, and input to a pooler function. Introduction and details are in Sect. 2.4.

Overview of our model is shown in Fig. 1.

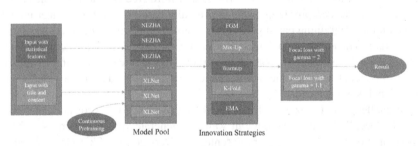

Fig. 1. Overview of our model

2.2 Model Backbone

After the publication of *Attention is All Your Need* [9], the model based on Transformer's pre training fine tuning paradigm became popular. For NLU tasks, models such as Bert, Roberta and XLNet that use the encoder part of transformer can achieve good results. In this paper, we mainly use NEZHA and XLNet models as our backbones. This is mainly because NEZHA performs well in Chinese classification tasks, while XLNet is good at handling long texts. The following is a brief introduction to these two models.

NEZHA:

1) Functional relative position encoder

$$a_{ij}[2k] = \sin\left(\frac{j-i}{10000^{\frac{2k}{dz}}}\right)$$

$$a_{ij}[2k+1] = \cos\left(\frac{j-i}{10000^{\frac{2k}{dz}}}\right)$$

where a_{ij} describe the value of relative position of position i and position j, and dz means the hidden size of each head in self-attention. The advantage of this is that the relative positional relationship between different positions can be obtained.

2) Whole word masking.

NEZHA uses Jieba as Chinese word segmentation tool to segment the text, and then performs [mask] operation on whole word.

3) Mixed precision training.

The mixed precision training can improve the training efficiency by 2–3 times and reduce the space occupied by the model, so that a larger batch size can be used.

4) Lamb optimizer

A large batch size is an effective method to accelerate training. However, if the learning rate is not carefully adjusted, when the batch size exceeds a threshold, the performance will be greatly damaged. The lamb optimizer adopts a general adaptive strategy to provide convergent insights (i.e. moving in the direction of convergence) through theoretical analysis. It can accelerate the training without affecting the performance when the maximum batch size is 30K, thus reducing the pre training time from 3 days to 76 min.

XLNet:

1) The AR model is combined with the AE model for pre training, and the self-supervised pretraining is carried out by predicting the next word in a disordered order to replace the MLM task of Bert and other models.

Formula.

2) XLNet integrates a previous work of Google: Transformer XLNet is difficult to process too long text due to the calculation amount of transformer. Transformer XL uses the idea of RNN for reference. For long text, first segment the text, make sequential attention on each text, and at the same time, attach the last few tokens of the previous text and the first few tokens of the current text, so as to obtain the association between text segments.

2.3   Input with Diversity

As mentioned above, in order to effectively reduce variance in model fusion, we need to construct some inputs with large differences.

In this competition, the most important and innovative input is the input with statistical characteristics.

First idea is Conditional Layer Normalization [10]. As we all know, Bert-based model's normalization method is Layer Normalization. We divide statistical information into multiple conditions by manual or neural network. Then different groups of gamma and beta affine transformation parameters of layer normalization is used according to different conditions. And the second idea is directly input the statistical features into the transformer (including the self-attention module) model in some form to fit. Finally, we use the second method in the competition.

In DSIN [11], the relationship between sequence features is mined by self-attention. Therefore, the second idea is directly input the statistical characteristics into the Bert-based model in some way.

Cause the input of the Bert-based model is a list of the indexes of each word in the sentence in the word dictionary, we treat the statistical information as the index of the embedding matrix, and treat it as the text feature. At the same time, because the statistical information of this competition is too discrete, we decided to take the logarithm, so that the statistical features with close values will be mapped to the same row of the embedding matrix. The specific input format is shown in Fig. 2:

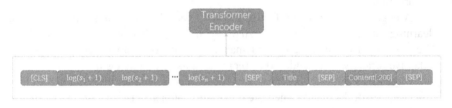

Fig. 2.   Input with statistical features

At the same time, we also explored how to integrate into the entity. In the integration of knowledge graph, Tsinghua's Ernie [12] of and Tencent's K-BERT both gave effective methods. K-BERT uses soft position and masked matrix encoding methods instead of Ernie's method of using transform. However, because the original text of the entities is too long, we cannot input the full text, many entities cannot be spliced with the original text in the form of soft position. Therefore, in this competition, we use the second idea mentioned above.

2.4   Change Model Structure

We do experiments on the output structure of the model. The traditional Bert-based model uses the CLS part of the last layer as the output of the model, many parameters in last layer are not used. Therefore, we transformed the model and made a comparison.

The three transformed methods are: 1) taking the mean pool of the last layer; 2) Input the last layer into Bi-LSTM [13]. 3) The CLS part is connected with the output of Bi-LSTM as a residual. It may be the reason that the training set has too few samples. If a more complex model is used, it will lead to overfitting. Thus, we choose the first method as our final method. Figure 3 clearly describes the output form of our mean pool method.

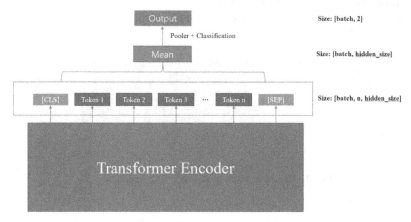

Fig. 3. Mean pooling of last layer

3 Innovation Strategies

3.1 Adversarial Training

The meaning of the adversarial training is to move the input along the direction of the gradient, so that the model loss rises at the fastest speed, thereby forming an attack. In order to fight against such an attack, the model needs to learn such adversarial examples and look for more robust parameters in the optimization process.

The most commonly used adversarial training methods are FGM [14] and PGD [15]. The difference between the two is PGD will iterate several times with smaller amplitude during each back propagation to find the optimal disturbance slowly, but it will also lead to a significant increase in training time. We adopted FGM for adversarial training. The idea of FGM is straightforward. Increasing the loss is to increase the gradient so that we can take:

$$r_{adv} = \epsilon \cdot \frac{g}{\|g\|_2}$$

$$g = \nabla_x L(\theta, x, y)$$

$$loss = \min_\theta \mathbb{E}_{(x,y)\sim D} L(\theta, x + r_{adv}, y)$$

3.2 K-Fold Cross-Fusion

We use the idea of k-fold cross-fusion to divide the training set into k different data sets. Each data set has a different valid set, and the distribution of their entity labels is different. We use the same model to train k models on the k datasets, then use the k models to predict on the test dataset, and perform hard fusion on the prediction results to obtain the fusion result of the k models.

Figure 4 shows an example of k-fold cross-fusion when k = 5.

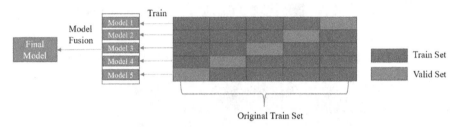

Fig. 4. Example graph of K-Fold cross-fusion, k = 5

3.3 Continued Pre-training

We know that the transformer model has a good performance in NLU task and NLG task, not only because of the self-attention mechanism, but also because it is a pretrained model with various unlabeled text in pretraining stage.

In order to make the language model more adaptable to the fields of cancer and imaging, we used all the text data in the train set and test set to conduct the self-supervised training of the MLM task (one of pretraining task of bert). We perform 10-epoch mask language model pre-training on those text.

3.4 EMA

EMA, the full name is empirical moving average, also known as weighted moving average, is an average method that gives higher weights to recent model parameters.

In the optimization process of deep learning, it is the model weights at time t and the shadow weights at time t. In the process of gradient descent, the shadow weight will always be maintained, but the shadow weight will not participate in the training. Only in prediction part, we use the shadow weight to predict.

$$V_t = \alpha \cdot V_{t-1} + (1 - \alpha) \cdot \theta_t$$

Generally, the value of α is between 0.9 and 0.999. In this competition, we set $\alpha = 0.9$ cause the amount of data in the training set is small.

3.5 Focal Loss

Because of the imbalance between positive and negative samples, the cross entropy loss function is used directly, and the result is not good. Focal loss [16] is used in those datasets with unbalanced samples.

$$FL(p) = -\alpha(1-p)^{\gamma}\log(p)$$

When it is small (the sample is difficult to be divided, no matter whether the score is correct or not), the adjustment factor approaches 1, and the weight of the sample in the loss function is not affected; When it is very large (the sample is easy to be divided, no matter whether the score is correct or not), the adjustment factor approaches 0, and the weight of the sample in the loss function decreases a lot.

The focus parameter can adjust the reduction degree of the weight of easy to classify samples. The greater the weight, the greater the reduction degree. In addition to the label imbalance, focal loss function can accelerate training and achieve better results in small sample data set such as this competition.

4 Experiments

4.1 Dataset

The CCKS 2022 High Quality Article Recognition Based on Knowledge Graph Competition provides 7,835 labeled data as a training set. It contains 2,903 data with positive label and 4,932 data with negative label. In train set, the average length of title is 24.51, the average length of content is 3,704.94, the average number of entities is 21.26. The final test set has 1,106 data without label. In final test set, the average length of title is 24.36, the average length of content is 3,704.61, the average number of entities is 21.04.

4.2 Implementation

We use NEZHA-CN-BASE and CHINESE-XLNET-BASE as our models. We ap- ply Dropout to the output of the pre-trained model with the rate set to 0.2 for each model. During the training process, we set the batch size as 8 and the learning rate as 2e-5. Furthermore, for other parameters, we use multi-group parameters to build a model pool with huge differences, in order to reduce the variance of the prediction results. And we randomly divided the original train set into 10 folds, took one fold as the dev set, and the remaining data as new train set for this experiment.

4.3 Result

BASE model means we just use title and content as our input data. And BASE + ENTITIES means we add name of entities into input, and BASE + STATISTIC means we add statistical features into input. In our model pool, we use the method BASE + ENTITIES to train 4 NEZHA models, and for BASE + STATISTIC, we finetuned 5 NEZHA models and 2 XLNet models. Cause there are many models in our model pool, we can get a lower variance by voting, so as to get a better result.

The results of Experiment are shown in Table 2.

Table 2. Result of the experiment

Model	Optimization steps	F1-Score (dev set)
BASE	Original model ^{0}	0.7073
	0 + Continued pre-training ^{1}	0.7089
	1 + Mean pooling ^{2}	0.7123
	2 + EMA ^{3}	0.7155
	3 + Focal loss ^{4}	0.7168
	4 + Adversarial training ^{5}	0.7176
BASE + ENTITIES	*Add name of entities into input*	0.8324
BASE + STATISTIC	*Add statistical features into input*	0.8279
VOTING	*Voting by models from model pool*	0.8376

References

1. Mikolov, T., Chen, K., Corrado, G., Dean, J.: Efficient estimation of word representations in vector space. In: ICLR Workshop (2013)
2. Perozzi, B., Al-Rfou, R., Skiena, S.: DeepWalk: online learning of social representations. ACM (2014)
3. Defferrard, M., Bresson, X., Vandergheynst, P.: Convolutional neural networks on graphs with fast localized spectral filtering. arXiv:1606.09375 (2016)
4. Liu, W., Zhou, P., Zhao, Z., et al.: K-BERT: Enabling language representation with knowledge graph (2019)
5. Schick, T., Schütze, H.: Exploiting cloze questions for few shot text classification and natural language inference. arXiv:2001.07676 (2020)
6. Li, X.L., Liang, P.: Prefix-tuning: optimizing continuous prompts for generation (2021)
7. Wei, J., Ren, X., Li, X., et al.: NEZHA: neural contextualized representation for chinese language understanding. arXiv:1909.00204v3 (2019)
8. Yang, Z., Dai, Z., Yang, Y., et al.: XLNet: generalized autoregressive pretraining for language understanding. arXiv:1906.08237 (2019)
9. Vaswani, A., Shazeer, N., Parmar, N., et al.: Attention is all you need. arXiv:1706.03762 (2017)
10. Su, J.: Conditional layer normalization. https://spaces.ac.cn/archives/8337/comment- page-2
11. Feng, Y., Lv, F., Shen, W., et al.: Deep session interest network for click-through rate prediction. arXiv:1905.06482 (2019)
12. Zhang, Z., Han, X., Liu, Z., et al.: ERNIE: enhanced language representation with informative entities. arXiv:1905.07129 (2019)
13. Peng, Z., Wei, S., Tian, J., et al.: Attention-based bidirectional long short-term memory networks for relation classification. In: Proceedings of the 54th Annual Meeting of the Association for Computational Linguistics (Vol. 2: Short Papers) (2016)

14. Miyato, T., Dai, A.M., Goodfellow, I.: Adversarial training methods for semi-supervised text classification. arXiv:1605.07725 (2016)
15. Madry, A,. Makelov, A., Schmidt, L., et al.: Towards deep learning models resistant to adversarial attacks. arXiv:1706.06083 (2017)
16. Lin, T.Y., Goyal, P., Girshick, R., et al.: Focal loss for dense object detection. IEEE Trans. Pattern Anal. Mach. Intell. **PP**(99), 2999–3007 (2017). arXiv:1708.02002

Learning Seq2Seq Model with Dynamic Schema Linking for NL2SQL

Xingxing Ning[1], Yupeng Zhao[2,1], and Jie liu[1,3(✉)]

[1] Cloopen Research, Beijing, China
ningxx@yuntongxun.com
[2] College of Mathematics and Statistics, Huazhong University of Science and Technology, Wuhan, China
zhaoyupeng@hust.edu.cn
[3] College of Artificial Intelligence, Nankai University, Tianjin, China
jliu@nankai.edu.cn

Abstract. NL2SQL (Natural Language to SQL) is a cutting-edge problem in the field of semantic parsing and TableQA. "CCKS2022: Financial NL2SQL Evaluation" raises a challenging scenario for building NL2SQL systems in the financial domain. To deal with the problem of small-scale data and the requirement of adapting to financial scenarios, we propose an NL2SQL approach to automatically converts natural language questions into SQL queries to achieve accurate table question answering. We use cross-validation and schema linking method that fuses table-column-value information to make full use of all the training data. Then we train a Transformer-based Seq2Seq semantic parsing model with T5 as pre-training model to understand common questions in the financial field and parse the database's tables, attributes, foreign keys and other complex relationships, and finally generate SQL queries. Experiments are conducted to test the effectiveness of our strategy. Our best ensemble model achieves EM score of 0.287 on testing set and ranks 2nd in the competition.

Keywords: Semantic parsing · Natural language to SQL · Schema linking · Seq2Seq model

1 Introduction

NL2SQL (Natural Language to SQL) [1] is a cutting-edge problem in the field of semantic parsing and TableQA. It plays a vital role in natural language processing since it can convert human natural language questions into Structured Query Language (SQL), which enables seamless interaction between humans and databases and improves the efficiency of database analysis.

In the real-world systems, most of the data is stored in relational databases, especially in the fields of financial services, healthcare, and sales industries. Despite the rapid increase in popularity of relational databases, the ability to retrieve information

---

X. Ning and Y. Zhao—The first two authors contributed equally to the work.

N. Zhang et al. (Eds.): CCKS 2022, CCIS 1711, pp. 148–153, 2022.
https://doi.org/10.1007/978-981-19-8300-9_16

from these databases remains limited, in part because users need to understand complex query languages. Moreover, traditional string matching methods are difficult to meet the requirements in terms of coverage, accuracy, and transferability. Therefore, we need to provide a natural language interface for relational databases, through which users can communicate directly with the database using natural language.

"CCKS2022: Financial NL2SQL Evaluation" raises a challenging scenario for building NL2SQL systems in the financial domain. Specifically, the first challenge is that the existing NL2SQL data and methods mainly focus on the setting of specified database/table in closed scenarios, which is difficult to meet the needs of dynamic development of the business scope; the second challenge is that from the perspective of domain characteristics, financial data are mostly time series, including daily market quotations, quarterly financial reports, annual GDP, irregular stock pledge release, etc., which will undoubtedly increase the difficulty of converting natural language questions to SQL.

In this work, we propose an NL2SQL approach to tackle these two challenges. We use cross-validation and schema linking method that fuses table-column-value information to make full use of all the training data. We train a Transformer-based Seq2Seq semantic parsing model with T5 as pre-training model to understand common questions in the financial field and parse the database's tables, attributes, foreign keys and other complex relationships, and finally generate SQL statements.

Experiments are conducted to test the effectiveness of our strategy and an ensemble model is finally implemented on the testing set to accomplish the CCKS-2022 Shared Task and the effectiveness of our approach has been proved accordingly.

2 Related Work

2.1 NL2SQL Task Classification and Common Datasets

Many representative datasets [2, 3] in Chinese and English in the NL2SQL field have been proposed, such as WikiSQL, Spider, CSpider, DuSQL, etc. In general, the NL2SQL task classification and common datasets can be divided according to whether it is cross-domain, whether it is cross-table, and whether it is multi-round.

2.2 The Development of NL2SQL

Figure 1 shows some representative works in the field of NL2SQL in academia in the form of a timeline. Whether it is the database research level or the natural language processing technology research level, the research work on NL2SQL has been evolving for decades.

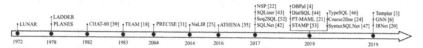

Fig. 1. A brief history of natural language interface to relational databases.

Early NL2SQ methods were mainly based on intermediate logical representations or rule-based semantic parsing methods, which were very dependent on artificially constructed mapping rules, so they had certain limitations.

In recent years, with the rise of big data technology and the rapid improvement of computing power, deep-learning-based methods have been widely used in various basic tasks in the field of natural language processing. And the introduction of deep learning enables NL2SQL to more effectively utilize database schema information and the knowledge representation capabilities of large-scale pre-training models, thus making the implementation of NL2SQL possible. Many SOTA achievements have been achieved, such as X-SQL [4], SeaD [5], IRNet [6], RATSQL [7], etc.

3   Approach

According to the characteristics of the dataset, such as "cross-domain database", "more connected table query" and "large number of table columns", we designed a Seq2Seq semantic parsing model based on the Transformer-based Encoder-Decoder architecture that integrates table-column-value information to complete the end-to-end NL2SQL task.

3.1   Map the Column in SQL to the Form of "Table. Column"

First, we normalize the SQL query of the dataset, and then map the column names in the SQL query to the form of "table name.column name" through schema linking [8], which is used to enhance the correspondence between table and columns. In addition, after experimental verification, the experiment result is better than English when the "table name.column name" is in Chinese expression style, so we use SQL with "table name.column name" in Chinese for model training.

3.2   Dynamic Schema Linking

For the NL2SQL task, how to link the input natural language question with database information is very critical, which is called schema linking [9]. For the End2End translation model we used in this competition, the traditional schema linking technology is not applicable. Therefore, we adopt a information generation technology based on string matching to dynamically enhance the input of the model. With dynamically integrating schema information and DB Content information, we build a simple and effective schema linking mechanism, which makes natural language questions more semantically related to target tables and columns in the database.

First, in order to associate natural language questions with the schema of the database, we need to normalize the table names and column names in the database (for example, unreasonable naming, ambiguous naming, English naming, etc., reorganize according to the business).

Then, for all normalized table names and column names, we score the similarity with natural language questions by fuzzy matching, and perform string splicing of table column names according to the scores from large to small, in the following form:

$$"\{Table\ name1 : Column1|Column2|...\}|\{...\}..." \tag{1}$$

As shown in Eq. (1), we aggregate the information of different tables with "{ }" and then separate them by "|". Different columns in the same table are separated by "|". Both the sorting of the information between the tables and the sorting of the information in the table are performed according to the string fuzzy matching score.

We generate such dynamic schema information for each natural language question before the model input, and then splicing it into the original natural language question as the new input of the model. Similarly, our dynamic schema generation technology can also be used for information splicing of DB Content.

3.3 Seq2Seq Pre-trained Model

T5(Text-to-Text Transfer Transformer) [10] is an end-to-end multi-task Encoder-Decoder translation framework that retains most of the architecture of the original Transformer [11], but highlights some key aspects. In addition, some minor changes have been made to vocabulary and functionality. As shown in Fig. 2, Every task considered in T5(including translation, question answering, and classification) is cast as feeding model text as input and training it to generate some target text. This allows us to use the same model, loss function, hyperparameters, etc. across diverse set of tasks.

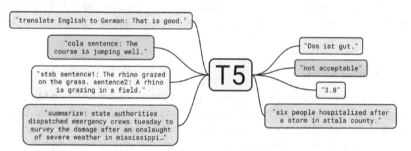

Fig. 2. A diagram of T5 text-to-text framework.

Some of the main concepts of T5 mode are listed below:

1. The encoder and decoder remain in the model.
2. Self-attention is order-independent. It explores the relationship between each word and other words in a sequence. A positional encoding is added to the word's embedding before doing the dot product.
3. The original Transformer uses sine and cosine to learn location embeddings. Whereas T5 uses relative position embedding.
4. The positional encoding is shared and re-evaluated simultaneously in all layers of the model.

The T5 model training data consists of two parts: the input source text and the output target text. The source text is composed of prefix and the original input text and is spliced with ":". Prefix is a label used to distinguish multiple tasks. In particular, in this task it is "translation". We store the prefix, natural language question and SQL query in the form of a list, and input it into the model. It is worth emphasizing that in the actual training process, the natural language question refers to natural language question with schema string added.

4   Evaluation

In this section, we outline the experimental setup, our baselines for the task, and the influences of our strategies applied on our baseline model. Our final model performance beats most of the teams on the CCKS-2022 Leaderboard and ranks the 2nd place among all the teams.

4.1   Dataset

The dataset of "CCKS2022: financial NL2SQL evaluation" competition comes from the real corpus in the financial field. The training set and the validation set respectively contain 3966 and 1000 financial scenario question-SQL statement pairs, involving funds, stocks, bonds and other data objects; the test set contains 2000 frequently used query questions in the financial field, including different ways of asking the same type of questions. In addition to labeled data, it also includes basic database information, database tables, domain knowledge, etc. The preliminary leaderboard measures the performance on the validation set, while the final leaderboard measures the performance on the test set.

4.2   Evaluation Metric

The final evaluation metric of this evaluation task is the accuracy of Exact Match (EM): the accuracy of the exact match of SQL in the prediction structure. It is considered that the prediction result of the sample is correct only when all elements (from, select, where, groupBy, having, orderBy, limit) are matched. It is also correct to disrupt the internal order without affecting the execution result.

4.3   Experimental Setup

We use T5-base-Chinese [12] as the pre-trained model. For NL2SQL model, the max sequence length is 512, the batch size is 7, the learning rate is 1e-4 and the optimizer is Adafactor.

4.4   Postprocess

We integrated the NL2SQL model to further improve the performance of our model. Specifically, due to the small scale of the dataset, we re-divided the dataset by ten-fold cross-validation in order to make full use of the training set, and merged the output of the model through voting to obtain Chinese SQL queries. By identifying the Chinese SQL queries that cannot be mapped to English and parsed into SQL, we compare it with the database and correct it, realize the repair of table name, column name and other rules, and convert SQL into AST (Abstract Syntax Tree) according to ASDL (Abstract Syntax Description Language) to get the final submission result.

5   Conclusion

In this work, we propose a simple and easy-to-implement NL2SQL method to automatically convert natural language questions into SQL queries to achieve accurate data question answering. Our dynamic schema linking method on Seq2Seq model is a novel solution to NL2SQL in financial scenarios, the key to which is that we propose a dynamic schema linking technology and build a transformer-based Seq2Seq model that incorporates table column value information. We conduct experiments to test the effect of the strategy and implement an ensemble model on the test set to further improve the performance of the competition. The final submission of our model ranks the 2nd place among all team submissions on the CCKS-2022 leaderboard.

In the future, we will further improve the prediction accuracy of the model by improving the encoder of the model, and try to migrate to more complex scenarios, such as cross-domain, complex nesting, etc.

References

1. Hyeonji, K., et al.: Natural language to SQL: where are we today? In: Proceedings of the VLDB Endowment, vol. 13.10, pp. 1737–1750 (2020)
2. Zhong, V., Xiong, C., Socher, R.: Seq2sql: generating structured queries from natural language using reinforcement learning. In: CoRR, abs/1709.00103 (2017)
3. Yu, T., et al.: Spider: a large-scale human-labeled dataset for complex and cross-domain semantic parsing and text-to-sql task. In: EMNLP, pp. 3911–3921 (2018)
4. He, P., Mao, Y., Chakrabarti, K., et al.: X-SQL: reinforce schema representation with context. arXiv:1908.08113 (2019)
5. Xuan, K., Wang, Y., Wang, Y., et al.: Sead: end-to-end text-to-sql generation with schema-aware denoising. arXiv:2105.07911 (2021)
6. Guo, J., et al.: Towards complex text-to-sql in cross-domain database with intermediate representation. In: ACL, pp. 4524–4535 (2019)
7. Wang, B., Shin, R., Liu, X., et al.: RAT-SQL: relation-aware schema encoding and linking for text-to-SQL parsers. In: ACL (2020)
8. Dou, L., Gao, Y., Pan, M., et al.: UniSAr: A Unified Structure-Aware Autoregressive Language Model for Text-to-SQL. arXiv:2203.07781 (2022)
9. Hui, B., Shi, X., Geng, R., et al.: Improving text-to-sql with schema dependency learning. arXiv:2103.04399 (2021)
10. Raffel, C., Shazeer, N., Roberts, A., et al.: Exploring the limits of transfer learning with a unified text-to-text transformer. J. Mach. Learn. Res. 21(140), 1–67 (2020)
11. Vaswani, A., et al.: Attention is all you need. In: Proceedings of the 31st International Conference on Neural Information Processing Systems (NIPS'17), pp. 6000–6010. Curran Associates Inc., Red Hook, NY, USA (2017)
12. t5-base-Chinese. https://huggingface.co/lemon234071/t5-base-Chinese. Accessed 2021

Learning to Answer Complex Visual Questions from Multi-View Analysis

Minjun Zhu[1,2], Yixuan Weng[1], Shizhu He[1,2(✉)], Kang Liu[1,2], and Jun Zhao[1,2]

[1] National Laboratory of Pattern Recognition, Institute of Automation, CAS, Beijing, China
`zhuminjun2020@ia.ac.cn`, {`shizhu.he,kliu,jzhao`}`@nlpr.ia.ac.cn`
[2] School of Artificial Intelligence, University of Chinese Academy of Sciences, Beijing, China

Abstract. Visual Question Answering (VQA) has received increasing attention in NLP research. Most VQA images focus on natural scenes. However, some images widely used in textbooks such as diagrams often contain complicated and abstract information (e.g. constructed graphs with logic and concepts). Therefore, Diagram Question answering (DQA) is a challenging but significant task, which is also helpful for machines to understand human cognitive behaviors and learning habits. On DQA task, we propose a multi-perspective understanding based visual question-answering method, which constructs a variety of different self-monitoring tasks in the form of prompts to help the model learn deeper information. For the first time, we propose a decoding method of "Cross Entropy constraint Decoding", which can effectively constrain the content generated by the text when performing multiple selection tasks. This method has obtained SOTA in the evaluation task of CCKS-2022, which fully proves the effectiveness of the method.

Keywords: Diagram question answering · Visual question answering · Computer science

1 Introduction

Question Answering (QA) systems have long pursued the ability to understand human cognitive behaviors and learning habits. Diagram Question Answering (DQA) task requires dynamic and complex reasoning of knowledge representation, which helps to improve the understanding of abstract images by computers. Generally, Diagram is manually constructed with abstract meanings and widely used in pre-defined scenarios, such as textbooks and dictionaries, which requires fully understand the abstract schematic information according to questions. DQA is still a challenge task because the complicate expression and the lack of data.

CSDQA is a novel visual question answering dataset which contains 1294 different diagram such as circle, rectangle and triangle. CSDQA is a multiple-choice dataset that is mainly collected from textbooks. Each sample contains the

---

M. Zhu and Y. Weng—Contributed equally to this work.

© The Author(s), under exclusive license to Springer Nature Singapore Pte Ltd. 2022
N. Zhang et al. (Eds.): CCKS 2022, CCIS 1711, pp. 154–162, 2022.
https://doi.org/10.1007/978-981-19-8300-9_17

question, diagram, choice, and answer. It divides datasets questions into simple reasoning and complex reasoning. Complex reasoning requires two-step reasoning on the image to get the answer, and the proportion of complex reasoning is 22.98% in all questions.

Pre-trained models have promoted the progress of natural language processing and even multimodality. In previous studies, sequence-to-sequence models have been widely used for a large number of downstream tasks. CLIP uses a large number of text and text pairs in order to narrow them in the same embedding space; Vl-bert takes both visual and textual features as input. VLMo jointly learns a dual encoder and a fusion encoder with a modular Transformer network. However, multi-modal neural network model shows poor performance on diagram question answering task. Because existing multi-modal models are pre-trained on a large number of natural scenes images, which lack the ability to understand abstract information of diagram such as concept and logical relationship within different graphics. Moreover, the scarcity of diagram resources also limits the large corpus training of DQA task models.

We propose a Multi-View Analysis (MVA) method to enhance model's understanding of schematic abstract information. MVA are constructed with five different task forms and unified in Text2Text form. We take OFA model as backbone, and then introduce MVA to enhance the abstract understanding ability. In order to avoid the invalid generation in Decoding phase, we introduce Cross Entropy constraint Decoding, which restricts the results to achieves higher inference accuracy.

2   Main Methods

2.1   Multi-View Training

Existing multi-modal pre-trained models have strong ability to extract information from natural scene images, but it is still difficult for model to directly understand the abstract diagram information in low-resource Diagram Question Answering (DQA) task. Therefore, we introduce multi-View multi-task training to help model deeply understand the diagram. As depicted in Fig. 1. We constructed five different task forms based on Prompt and unified five different objectives as Seq2Seq form for training. Five tasks are respectively shown as follows:

- 1. Original task: the original data, including images, questions and answers.
- 2. Answer Judge task: ask model to answer whether the statement combined with the question, answer and judgement is correct.
- 3. Image Description task: require model to describe the image with details.
- 4. Ask Question task: require model to ask a question based on the input image and answer.
- 5. Image Text Match task: change some image-question pairs, and ask model to judge whether the description is grounding with the input image.

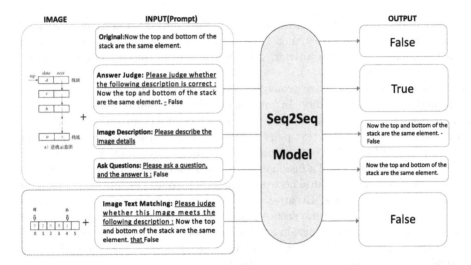

Fig. 1. The Multi-View Training by different tasks. We take origin as the initial sample and realize multi-view training by changing the position of its questions/answers/diagram.

2.2 Step Training

In order to alleviate the catastrophic forgetting problem caused by overtraining of the pre-trained model in Multi-View Training. We implemented the step learning based on Child-tuning [24] method. The Child-tuning method is used to fine-tune the backbone model in our method, where the parameters of the Child network are updated with the gradients mask. For the DQA task, the task-independent algorithm is used for child-tuning. When fine-tuning, the gradient masks are obtained by Bernoulli Distribution [2] sampling from in each step of iterative update, which is equivalent to randomly dividing a part of the network parameters when updating. The equation of the above steps is shown as follows

$$w_{t+1} = w_t - \eta \frac{\partial \mathcal{L}(w_t)}{\partial w_t} \odot B_t \tag{1}$$

$$B_t \sim \text{Bernoulli}(p_F) \tag{2}$$

where the notation $\odot$ represents the dot production, p_F is the partial network parameter.

3   Experiments

In this section, we will introduce the experimental settings and evaluation indicators. Then we compare MVA with the existing VQA technology and ablation experiments to prove the effectiveness of our method (Fig. 2).

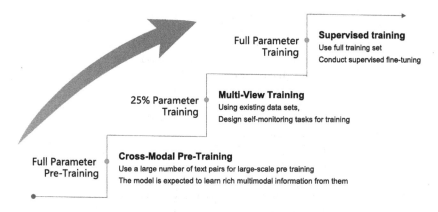

Fig. 2. In the training stage, we use step-by-step training to gradually make the model learn the image features of the schematic diagram.

3.1 Evaluation Metrics

Following prior work [1,4,13,19]. We use the accuracy rate as the evaluation metrics. We assume that the total quantity is n and the predicted correct quantity is C, then the calculation of concurrency is as follows:

$$\textbf{Accuracy} = \frac{\textbf{C}}{\textbf{n}} \times 100\% \tag{3}$$

3.2 Implementation Details

In order to compare the functions of the system more fairly. In recent years, natural language processing significant progress has been achieved [5,17] due to the introduction of Pre-trained Language Model [3,15,18]. Therefore, more and more methods begin to introduce the pre-trained language model in the VQA task [8,10,11,16,22].

For all methods, we use the same size model for finetuning. And we all use the large-size model for testing. We follow the original code for the remaining settings. We train the model using the Pytorch[1] [14] on the NVIDIA RTX3090 GPU and use the hugging-face[2] [23] framework. We use the AdamW [12] as the optimizer and the learning rate is set to 1e-5 with the warm-up [7]. The batch size is 8. We set the maximum length of 512, and delete the excess. We use the linear decay of the learning rate and gradient clipping of 1e-6. The dropout [20] of 0.1 is applied to prevent overfitting. The detailed experimental settings are shown in Table 1.

---

[1] https://pytorch.org.

[2] https://github.com/huggingface/transformers.

Table 1. Hyper-parameter settings.

Hyper-parameter	Value
Image Encoder	ResNet152 [6]
Encoder Hidden Size	4096
Encoder Num Layers	12
Encoder Attention Heads	16
Decoder Hidden Size	4096
Decoder Num Layers	12
Decoder Attention Heads	16
Dropout	0.1
Max Token Length	512
Language Model Loss Function	Cross Entropy
Learning Rate	1e–5
Batch size	8
Num Epochs	20
Weight Decay	1e–4
FP16	True
Gradient Accumulation	1
Beam Search	5

Table 2. Performance comparison of the variants methods on Computer Science Diagrams dataset. We highlight the best score ineach column in **bold**, and the second best score with underline. We will also show the improvement between first place and second place.

Metric	Accuracy			
Learning Rate	1e–5	2e–5	3e–5	Avg.
Random Mode	/	/	/	35.84
LayoutLMv3$_{Base}$ [9] (2022)	38.25	35.52	36.89	36.89
LayoutLMv3$_{Large}$ [9] (2022)	40.21	36.89	37.04	38.05
OFA$_{Base}$ [21] (2022)	52.86	53.31	52.25	52.80
OFA$_{Large}$ [21] (2022)	54.06	53.37	53.61	53.68
MVA	**58.89(4.83↑)**	**58.58(5.21↑)**	**57.23(3.62↑)**	**58.23 (4.55↑)**

All hyperparameters are optimized on the Valid set. In all our experiments, at the end of each training phase, we will test the effective data set and select the highest model (mainly depending on Accuracy) in the test data set for prediction. We report the results in the test data set. We repeated the experiment three times and reported the average score.

3.3   Comparison with State-of-the-Art Methods

In the CSDia dataset, we compared the baseline scheme with the existing dialogue generation.

Table 3. Performance comparison of the variants methods on Computer Science Diagrams dataset. We conducted some control experiments and tried to train the model using full data and showed its scores.

Metric	Accuracy			
Learning Rate	1e–5	2e–5	3e–5	Avg.
OFA$_{Large}$ [21]	54.06	53.37	53.61	53.68
W/O MV	56.93	56.63	55.57	56.38
W/O Step training	58.13	58.58	56.93	57.88
W/O CE Decode	58.28	57.98	57.23	57.83
MVA	58.89	58.58	57.23	58.23
+Full Data	60.24	59.49	59.19	59.64

The $LayoutLM_{v3}$ [9] is based on $LayoutLM_{v2}$ [26] and $LayoutLM_{v1}$ [25], and it uses unified text and image mask modeling objectives to pre train the multimodal model, which simplifies the model design. It requires that the hidden words in the text be restored according to the uncovered text and layout information in the document data set, and the masked image block data be restored at the same time. The $LayoutLM_{v3}$ achieved better results in form tasks than previous work.

The OFA [21] model realizes the unification of modes, tasks and structures, unifies the multi-modal and single-modal understanding and generation tasks into a simple seq2seq generative framework, and performs pre training and fine-tuning using task instructions. The OFA has achieved SOTA in four cross modal tasks: image capture, VQA, visual entailment and referring expression synthesis.

3.4   Experimental Result

We report the performance of the model in Table 2. We compared several models in different forms and sizes and selected $LayoutLM_{v3}$ and OFA respectively. We show the improvement of our method compared with the baseline model.

Among them, the performance of $LayoutLM_{v3}$ is weak. The $LayoutLM_{v3}$ has learned a large number of abstract characters and symbols in the pre-training process, it is difficult to learn the relevant features in the question and answer of complex schematic diagrams due to the lack of understanding of the overall graph and the task of the pre-training phase is mainly mask recovery rather than visual question and answer, which leads to difficulty in finetuning. In addition, we have directly fine-tuned the OFA model. It is not difficult for us to find that the OFA model can have strong performance on the visual question and answer the task, and the performance of the *Base* size and the *Large* size are relatively close, which indicates that the additional knowledge brought by the pre-training for the model has reached the limit. For the abstract schematic question and answer task, the OFA model still has a large room for improvement.

When we use the MVA, the baseline model can further learn more relevant knowledge. In Table 2, MVA exceeds the baseline model in three different learn-

Table 4. Online performance of CCKS-2022 in DQA task.

	A			B	
Rank	Team	Score	Rank	Team	Score
1	灵境_CASIA	55.57	1	灵境_CASIA	60.19
2	maoada	54.22	2	key7	58.09
3	福气boy	53.61	3	Cube	55.02
4	国足10号	53.01	4	福气boy	54.53
5	qddy	52.56	5	maoada	54.53
6	northsky	51.81	6	国足10号	53.39

ing rate settings, and its average score exceeds the baseline by 4.55%, which fully proves the reliability of our method.

3.5   Ablation Study

In Table 3, we can see some performance comparisons. We further carry out care learning in OFA [21], which is the best pre-trained model in Diagram Question Answering task. It can fully show the effect differences brought by different methods.

First, we try to cancel the Multi-View, which means that we no longer require the model to pretrain multi-view task in Diagram Question Answering. This may lead to the lack of understanding of the diagram so that the generated answer lacks the modeling of the diagram.

After canceling the Step Training, we directly train the model in one step. However, the experimental results show that compared with the Step Training, the performance will be reduced. We believe that this is because after the introduction of MV, the training tasks may deviate from DQA, resulting in the focus of the model learning is no longer DQA tasks. Therefore, using two-stage training and fixing parameters in the MV stage can help the model mitigate catastrophic forgetting and bring higher performance. Finally, if the CE decode is cancelled, there will be more than 2% of the answers, and it will be difficult to answer because it cannot be matched.

Since the task provides the target of the verification set, we additionally use full data for training and test in test, which brings us additional performance improvement.

3.6   Online Result

In Table 4, We showed the online results of two different lists, and we all got the results of SOTA, which reflects the superior performance of the method.

4   Conclusions

In this paper, we propose a new method to solve complex text questi answering. We provide multimodal and multi-perspective learning for the pre-training language generation model. By constructing a large number of different learning tasks, we can make the pre-training model play a more effective role in the low resource Abstract schematic scenario. Our MVA module is very flexible. We have built a unified task framework for multitasking learning, which can support almost all multimodal seq2seq models. In addition, we introduce CE decode decoding to constrain the generation results, which enhances the controlonslability of the multi-modal generation model and improves the performance. In the DQA task of CCKS-2022, our method won first place, which provides a powerful solution for the complex visual question and answers task.

References

1. Antol, S., et al.: Visual question answering. In: International Conference on Computer Vision, VQA (2015)
2. Chen, S.X., Liu, J.S.: Statistical applications of the poisson-binomial and conditional Bernoulli distributions. Statistica Sinica **7**, 875–892 (1997)
3. Devlin, J., Chang, M.-W., Lee, K., Toutanova, K.: BERT: pre-training of deep bidirectional transformers for language understanding. In: Proceedings of the 2019 Conference of the North American Chapter of the Association for Computational Linguistics: Human Language Technologies, vol. 1 (Long and Short Papers) (Minneapolis, Minnesota, June 2019), Association for Computational Linguistics, pp. 4171–4186
4. Goyal, Y., Khot, T., Agrawal, A., Summers-Stay, D., Batra, D., Parikh, D.: Making the V in VQA matter: elevating the role of image understanding in visual question answering. Int. J. Comput. Vis. **127**(4), 398–414 (2018). https://doi.org/10.1007/s11263-018-1116-0
5. Han, X., et al.: Pre-trained models: past, present and future. AI Open **2**, 225–250 (2021)
6. He, K., Zhang, X., Ren, S., Sun, J.: Deep residual learning for image recognition. arXiv:1512.03385 Computer Vision and Pattern Recognition (2015)
7. He, K., Zhang, X., Ren, S., Sun, J.: Deep residual learning for image recognition. In: 2016 IEEE Conference on Computer Vision and Pattern Recognition (CVPR), pp. 770–778 (2016)
8. Hu, R., Singh, A.: Unit: multimodal multitask learning with a unified transformer. In: International Conference on Computer Vision (2021)
9. Huang, Y., Lv, T., Cui, L., Lu, Y., Wei, F.: Layoutlmv3: pre-training for document AI with unified text and image masking
10. Li, B., Weng, Y., Sun, B., Li, S.: Towards visual-prompt temporal answering grounding in medical instructional video. arXiv preprint arXiv:2203.06667 (2022)
11. Li, W., et al.: UNIMO: towards unified-modal understanding and generation via cross-modal contrastive learning. In: Meeting of the Association for Computational Linguistics (2020)
12. Loshchilov, I., Hutter, F.: Decoupled weight decay regularization. In: International Conference on Learning Representations (2018)

13. Malinowski, M., Fritz, M.: A multi-world approach to question answering about real-world scenes based on uncertain input. In: Neural Information Processing Systems (2014)
14. Paszke, A., et al.: PyTorch: an imperative style, high-performance deep learning library. In: Wallach, H., Larochelle, H., Beygelzimer, A., d' Alché-Buc, F., Fox, E., Garnett, R. (eds.) Advances in Neural Information Processing Systems, vol. 32, Curran Associates Inc. (2019)
15. Peters, M.E., et al.: Deep contextualized word representations. In: North American Chapter of the Association for Computational Linguistics (2018)
16. Qi, D., Su, L., Song, J., Cui, E., Bharti, T., Sacheti, A.: ImageBERT: cross-modal pre-training with large-scale weak-supervised image-text data
17. Qiu, X.P., Sun, T.X., Xu, Y.G., Shao, Y.F., Dai, N., Huang, X.J.: Pre-trained models for natural language processing: a survey. Sci. China Technol. Sci. **63**(10), 1872–1897 (2020). https://doi.org/10.1007/s11431-020-1647-3
18. Radford, A., Narasimhan, K.: Improving language understanding by generative pre-training
19. Ren, M., Kiros, R., Zemel, R.S.: Exploring models and data for image question answering. In: Neural Information Processing Systems (2015)
20. Srivastava, N., Hinton, G.E., Krizhevsky, A., Sutskever, I., Salakhutdinov, R.: Dropout: a simple way to prevent neural networks from overfitting. J. Mach. Learn. Res. **15**, 1929–1958 (2014)
21. Wang, P., et al.: Unifying architectures, tasks, and modalities through a simple sequence-to-sequence learning framework
22. Wang, W., Bao, H., Dong, L., Wei, F.: VLMo: unified vision-language pre-training with mixture-of-modality-experts. arXiv: 2111.02358 Computer Vision and Pattern Recognition (2021)
23. Wolf, T., et al.: Transformers: state-of-the-art natural language processing. In: Proceedings of the 2020 Conference on Empirical Methods in Natural Language Processing: System Demonstrations Association for Computational Linguistics, pp. 38–45 (2020)
24. Xu, R., et al.: Raise a child in large language model: towards effective and generalizable fine-tuning. In: Proceedings of the 2021 Conference on Empirical Methods in Natural Language Processing, pp. 9514–9528 (2021)
25. Xu, Y., Li, M., Cui, L., Huang, S., Wei, F., Zhou, M.: LayoutLM: pre-training of text and layout for document image understanding. knowledge discovery and data mining (2019)
26. Xu, Y., et al.: LayoutLMv2: multi-modal pre-training for visually-rich document understanding. In: Meeting of the Association for Computational Linguistics (2020)

A Prompt-Based UIE Framework

Fubang Zhao, Yexiang Wang, and YangYang Kang[✉]

Alibaba Group, Hangzhou, China
{fubang.zfb,wangyexiang.wyx,yangyang.kangyy}@alibaba-inc.com

Abstract. Information extraction is the automated retrieval of specific information related to a selected topic from a body of unstructured text. Generally, many NLP tasks can be categorized as information extraction tasks, such as named entity extraction (NER), relation extraction (RE), event extraction (EE), etc. To dealing with different IE tasks of different situation, we propose a prompt-based universal information extraction framework which is friendly to both research and industry scenarios.

Keywords: Universal information extraction · Prompt learning

1 Introduction

Over the years, with the continuous development of pre-trained models, the generalization and transfer capabilities of deep learning have been significantly improved. This ability is not only reflected in the data in different fields of the same task, but also in the unified solution ability of the model to different tasks.

Information extraction is the automated retrieval of specific information related to a selected topic from a body of unstructured text. Generally, many NLP tasks can be categorized as information extraction tasks, such as named entity extraction (NER), relation extraction (RE), event extraction (EE), etc. Considering the complexity of information extraction tasks, different models are often used to handle different tasks, even if there are many similarities between these tasks. To alleviate this pain point, Y Lu [1] proposed a unified text-to-structure generation framework, namely UIE, based on a pretrained mechanism and prompt learning. The experiments showed that UIE achieved the SOTA on both supervised and low-resource scenarios.

The seq2seq scheme is a model with a high degree of freedom, and theoretically all NLP problems can be solved with this scheme. However, this degree of freedom also leads to some unexpected output results of the decoder in practical applications. To enhance the usability of UIE, another version of UIE [2] was proposed based on prompt-learning and machine reading comprehension. According to our experiments, we found that this version of UIE does have stronger zero-shot learning ability, but at the same time it also brings an increase in inference time cost.

Inspiring by the above work, we propose a prompt-based UIE framework which does not rely on a one-size-fits-all model but uses the same set of thought frameworks to solve the different tasks in different situations.

N. Zhang et al. (Eds.): CCKS 2022, CCIS 1711, pp. 163–171, 2022.
https://doi.org/10.1007/978-981-19-8300-9_18

2   Related Work

Information extraction is a long-term research field, which includes many classic tasks such as named entity extraction (NER), relation extraction (RE) and event extraction (EE).

The first work on NER using neural models can be traced back to 2003, when Hammerton [3] tried to address the problem by LSTMs [4]. Lample [5] introduce two neural architectures, one of which is the bidirectional LSTMs combined with CRFs. Recent state-of-the-art methods are generally based on a pre-trained language model, such as BERT [6]. In this line of work, Li et al. [4] formulate NER as a machine reading comprehension (MRC) task and propose a unified span-based framework which can handle both flat and nested NER tasks. Cui et al. [7] propose a template-based method for NER, which treat NER as a language model ranking problem in a sequence-to-sequence framework. Chen et al. [8] proposes a lightweight named recognition model with pluggable prompting. Recently, W^2NER [9] models the unified NER as word-word relation classification.

RE is usually performed with NER to mitigate error propagation and understand the interrelationship between tasks [10]. SpERT [11] uses a span classification module to detect token spans corresponding to entities, and followed by a relation classification module to obtain the relations. Ye et al. [12] and Zhang et al. [13] uses a generation-based approach with contrastive learning for relational triple extraction.

In recent year, joint models have beed proposed for EE to mitigate the effect of error propagation [14]. Yang et al. [15] performs joint inference on events, entities and relations by modeling the structural dependencies between them. Zhang et al. [16] propose a neural trainsitin-based extraction framework, which requires specially designed transition actions to incrementally predict complex joint structures in a state-transition process. Lou et al. [17] proposes a multi-layer bidirectional network (MLBiNet) to capture the document-level association of events and semantic information simultaneously.

In addition to the previous IE methods, Lu et al. [1] propose a unified text-to-structure generation framework to universally model various IE tasks, which achieved the state-of-the-art performance on 4 IE tasks, 13 datasets.

3   Task Description

This competition is not limited to the traditional evaluation of single task information extraction, but expresses a variety of different information extraction tasks in a unified general framework. It focuses on examining the adaptability and migration capabilities of related technical methods in the face of new and unknown information extraction tasks and paradigms, so as to meet the actual needs of rapid iteration and rapid migration in the current information extraction field, and be closer to practical business applications.

The evaluation data consists of the following two parts.

Six See Schemas. The track mainly evaluates the ability of existing technologies to build models based on the tag data, which consists of the following six fields:

- Life Information: extract (relationship type, subject span, object span) relationship triples and (entity span, entity type) entity tuples.
- Organization Information: extract (relationship type, subject span, object span) relationship triples and (entity span, entity type) entity tuples.
- Financial Information: extract (event type, argument role, argument span) event triples.
- Sports Competition: extract (event type, argument role, argument span) event triples.
- Movie and Television Emotion: extract (emotional polarity, opinion object span, emotional expression span) emotional triples.
- Disaster Accident: extract (event type, argument role, argument span) event triples.

Four Unseen Schemas. The track mainly evaluates the migration ability of the existing technology to the new extraction demand, which consists of the following four fields:

- Financial Public Opinion: extract (event type, argument role, argument span) event triples.
- Financial Supervision: extract (relationship type, subject span, object span) relationship triples.
- Doctor Patient Dialogue: extract (relationship type, subject span, object span) relationship triples and (entity span, entity type) entity tuples.
- Flow Information: extract (event type, argument role, argument span) event triples.

4 Methods

4.1 Three Sub-modules of Our Framework

In order to solve different IE problems more flexibly, we split the model required by IE tasks into three modules, including extraction, classification and combination.

Extraction Module. The most commonly used span extraction method is the sequence tagging model based on BIO schema and CRF. The advantage of this solution is that it can make good use of the dependencies between tags, but the viterbi decoding of CRF is relatively time-consuming and cannot solve the nested problem. Therefore, we choose the pointer network method to solve the span extraction problem, which can not only solve the nested problem, but also dynamically adjust the threshold according to the distribution of the data to balance precision and recall (Fig. 1).

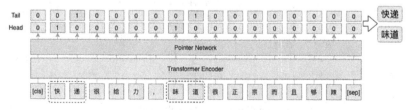

Fig. 1. The extraction module used in our framework

Classification Module. Our framework includes two classification methods: conventional classification and matching-based classification. In the case of sufficient supervised data, we will use the conventional classification method, while in the case of low resources, we will use the matching-based method to better utilize the transfer ability of the pre-trained model (Fig. 2).

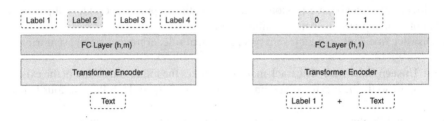

Conventional Classification   Matching-based Classification

Fig. 2. The illustration of two methods of classification, in which h means the hidden size of the encoder and m means the number of labels.

Combination Module. For complex IE tasks, the most important thing is how to combine the set of extraction and classification modules. In our framework, we realize the combination between each sub-module based on prompt and multi-task learing.

Explicitly concating the result of the previous step with the original text, namely, the method of prompt learning, is the most universal combination scheme. It can basically be used in the combination of all IE subtasks, and can better leverage the encoding ability of the pretrained model as well.

In addition, in order to reduce the space-consuming of the model, we use multi-task learning, which can also balance the various sub-tasks and prevent overfitting. The parameters of encoders are shared during the training and inference phase (Fig. 3).

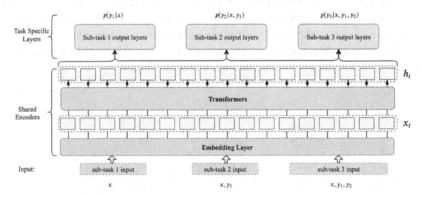

Fig. 3. The illustration of combination module

4.2 Our Models

In this section, we will introduce how we combine our submodules based on our framework to solve different IE problems in practice.

Named Entity Extraction Task. NER is a relatively simple task among IE tasks. First, we use a pretrained model as our encoder. Then, for each type of entity, we use a corresponding pointer network to extract spans, so as to alleviate the problem of nested entities (Fig. 4).

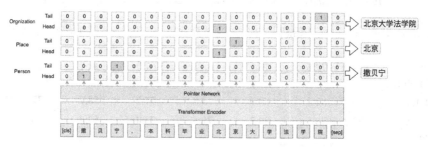

Fig. 4. The model oriented to NER Task based on our framework

Relation Extraction Task. We split the relationship extraction characters into three sub-modules, subject extraction, object extraction, and relationship classification, which correspond to two extraction modules and a conventional classification module in our framework respectively. Specifically, the input sentence is firstly fed into the subject extraction module to extract all subjects. Then each extracted subject is concatenated with the sentence, and fed into the object extraction module to extract all objects, which can form a set of subject-object pairs. Finally, the subject-object pair is concatenated with sentence, and fed into the relation classification module to get the relations between them [18].

Event Role Extraction Task. According to the evaluation metrics applied in this benchmark, we simply convert this task into a NER problem by concatenating the type of event and role ($[L_e, L_r, T_r]$ to $[L_e - L_r, T_r]$), in which L_e represents the type of event, L_r represents the type of role and T_r represents the text of role. The model framework is the same as that used in the NER task.

Low-Resources Task. On the four unseen schemas, we test two versions universal information extraction models, one based on a unified text-to-structure generation framework [1] and the other based on prompt-learning and machine reading comprehension (MRC) [2]. Experiments show that the model based on MRC has stronger adaptability and stability on the low-resources tasks, which is a span-based model and formulate the various IE tasks as a entity extraction task by constructing input samples.

5 Experiments

5.1 Experiment for Seen Schemas

We followed the method described in the section above to conduct experiments and achieved the state-of-the-art in Leaderboard A. The results are in Table 1, where "Official Baseline" is based on UIE method [1] and "ReLink" is the second team of the leaderboard.

Tabel 1. Comparison between models on seen schemas (Leaderboard A)

Leaderboard A	Score	人生信息	机构信息	体育竞赛	灾害意外	影视情感	金融信息
Official Baseline	67.2	72.5	76.2	66.4	67.7	48.7	71.8
ReLink	75.1	82.1	80.9	**73.8**	77.2	**58.7**	**77.9**
Our Method (Single)	72.3	78.5	80.7	71.5	73.4	53.4	76.4
Our Method (Ensemble)	**75.3**	**82.7**	**81.6**	**73.8**	**78.8**	57.2	**77.9**

5.2 Experiment for Unseen Schemas

Comparison of Two UIE Models

Unseen schemas mainly examines the ability of the model to perform few-shot learning. As introduced in Sect. 4.2, we compare two different two universal information extraction models and the experimental results are shown in Table 2.

Tabel 2. Results for two UIE models on Unseen Schemas

	金融舆情	金融监管	医患对话	流调信息
Generation-based UIE [1]	58.0	65.0	34.2	49.8
Span-based UIE [2]	76.1	88.2	56.0	69.3

Due to the limitation of upload times in the competition, we did not test the performance of a single model, and the results in the table are the results of model ensembles. According to the comparison of experimental results, we can find that the performance of span-based UIE is significantly better than that of generation-based UIE. Therefore, we mainly optimize the span-based UIE next.

Generate Data for Pretraining

We used the 157,220 pieces of training data (duuie.zip) given by the competition to generate 1,700,011 pieces of training data in the form of reading comprehension according to the corresponding schema to train the model.

A Sample of Train Data. {"id":   "dbc65bad4c60890b48d6397314b78f5a", "question": "李中斐的毕业院校", "context": "李中斐, 毕业于黑龙江大学, 现任市经济合作促进局党组成员、副局长", "answers": [{"answer_start": 7, "text": "黑龙江大学"}]}.

In this Competition, is Pre-training Necessary for UIE?

As described in the website, uie-base has been trained with a large amount of data and can support zero-shot scenarios. Considering that the open UIE model is only the base version, we believe that there is still a lot of room for improvement. Therefore, we tested with other pretrained models, and the results are shown in Table 3.

Tabel 3. Results on Unseen Schemas.TBSS means trained by Seen Schema data.

	金融舆情	金融监管	医患对话	流调信息
Generation-based UIE [1]	58.0	65.0	34.2	49.8
Span-based UIE [2]	76.1	88.2	56.0	69.2
Span-based UIE + TBSS	81.6	88.3	56.7	71.0
macbert-large + TBSS	78.6	88.0	56.9	72.1
roberta-large + TBSS	79.8	88.3	55.3	70.4
Span-based UIE + TBSS + circle loss + R-drop	80.8	89.5	56.9	73.8
Ensemble	**83.7**	**91.0**	**60.3**	**75.3**

Experiments show that although macbert and roberta are not pre-trained like uie-base, they are quite competitive with uie-base on unseen schemas after they are trained on seen schema dataset.

Some Optimization Methods

Due to the constraints of competition time and number of submissions, we did not have the opportunity to try many optimization strategies. We only tried to use circle loss [19] and R-drop [20] to optimize the model performance, and the results are shown in Table 2.

Ensemble

Considering that each pre-training language model will have different cognitive biases due to different pre-training corpora, in this competition, we have carried out an ensemble of heterogeneous models. The basic pre-trained language models involved include uie-base, macbert-large, roberta-large, and structbert-large. Each model is first trained on seen schema dataset, and then trained with all the data in unseen schemas, and finally the results are obtained by voting.

6   Conclusion

On the whole, this competition involves a lot of schemas, and includes NER, RE and EE tasks. Due to the tight schedule for B-list evaluation, it would be difficult to complete this task without an universal information extraction model. In this paper, we introduce the method used to accomplish the task, which is a prompt-based universal information extraction framework that is similar to a machine reading comprehension model. Experiments show that this model has strong rapid adaptability and achieves the state-of-the-art results on unssen schemas, but at the same time it also brings an increase in inference time cost, which needs to generate corresponding samples for each entity, relationship and event to predict. For future work, it is necessary to optimize its inference efficiency for application in practical scenarios.

References

1. Lu, Y., Liu, Q., Dai, D., et al.: Unified Structure Generation for Universal Information Extraction. arXiv preprint arXiv:2203.12277 (2022)
2. https://github.com/PaddlePaddle/PaddleNLP/tree/develop/model_zoo/uie
3. Hammerton, J.: Named entity recognition with long short-term memory. In: Proceedings of the seventh conference on Natural language learning at HLT-NAACL 2003, pp. 72–175 (2003)
4. Li, X., Feng, J., Meng, Y., et al.: A unified MRC framework for named entity recognition. arXiv preprint arXiv:1910.11476 (2019)
5. Lample, G., Ballesteros, M., Subramanian, S., et al.: Neural architectures for named entity recognition. arXiv preprint arXiv:1603.01360 (2016)
6. Devlin, J., Chang, M.W., Lee, K., et al.: Bert: pre-training of deep bidirectional transformers for language understanding. arXiv preprint arXiv:1810.04805 (2018)
7. Cui, L., Wu, Y., Liu, J., et al.: Template-based named entity recognition using BART. arXiv preprint arXiv:2106.01760 (2021)
8. Chen, X., et al.: LightNER: a lightweight tuning paradigm for low-resource NER via plug-gable prompting. In: Proceedings of the 29th International Conference on Computational Linguistics, pp. 2374–2387 (2022)
9. Li, J., Fei, H., Liu, J., et al.: Unified named entity recognition as word-word relation classification. In: Proceedings of the AAAI Conference on Artificial Intelligence, vol. 36, issur 20, pp. 10965–10973 (2022)
10. Ren, L., Sun, C., Ji, H., et al.: HySPA: Hybrid span generation for scalable text-to-graph extraction. arXiv preprint arXiv:2106.15838 (2021)
11. Eberts, M., Ulges, A.: Span-based joint entity and relation extraction with transformer pre-training. arXiv preprint arXiv:1909.07755 (2019)
12. Ye, H., et al.: Contrastive triple extraction with generative transformer. In: Proceedings of the AAAI Conference on Artificial Intelligence 2021 May 18, vol. 35, No. 16, pp. 14257–14265 (2021)

13. Zhang, N., et al.: Contrastive information extraction with generative transformer. IEEE/ACM Trans. Audio Speech Lang. Process. **14**(29), 3077–3088 (2021)
14. Du, X., Cardie, C.: Event extraction by answering (almost) natural questions. arXiv preprint arXiv:2004.13625 (2020)
15. Yang, B., Mitchell, T.: Joint extraction of events and entities within a document context. arXiv preprint arXiv:1609.03632 (2016)
16. Zhang, J., Qin, Y., Zhang, Y., et al.: Extracting Entities and Events as a Single Task Using a Transition-Based Neural Model. In: IJCAI, pp. 5422–5428 (2019)
17. Lou, D., Liao, Z., Deng, S., Zhang, N., Chen, H.: MLBiNet: a cross-sentence collective event detection network. In: Proceedings of the 59th Annual Meeting of the Association for Computational Linguistics and the 11th International Joint Conference on Natural Language Processing (Volume 1: Long Papers) 2021 Aug, pp. 4829–4839 (2021)
18. Zhao, F., et al.: Adjacency List Oriented Relational Fact Extraction via Adaptive Multi-task Learning. arXiv preprint arXiv:2106.01559 (2021)
19. Sun, Y., Cheng, C., Zhang, Y., et al.: Circle loss: a unified perspective of pair similarity optimization. In: Proceedings of the IEEE/CVF Conference on Computer Vision and Pattern Recognition. pp. 6398–6407 (2020)
20. Wu, L., Li, J., Wang, Y., et al.: R-drop: Regularized dropout for neural networks. Adv. Neural. Inf. Process. Syst. **34**, 10890–10905 (2021)

Multi-modal Representation Learning with Self-adaptive Threshold for Commodity Verification

Chenchen Han$^{(\boxtimes)}$ and Heng Jia

Zhejiang University, Zhejiang, China
hanchenchen@zju.edu.cn

Abstract. In this paper, we propose a method to identify identical commodities. In e-commerce scenarios, commodities are usually described by both images and text. By definition, identical commodities are those that have identical key attributes and are cognitively identical to consumers. There are two main challenges: 1) The extraction and fusion of multi-modal representation. 2) The ability to verify identical commodities by comparing the similarity between representations and a threshold. To address the above problems, we propose an end-to-end multimodal representation learning method with self-adaptive threshold. We use a dual-stream network to extract multi-modal commodity embeddings and threshold embeddings separately and then concatenate them to obtain commodity representation. Our method is able to adaptively adjust the threshold according to different commodities while maintaining the indexability of the commodity representation space. We experimentally validate the advantages of self-adaptive threshold and the effectiveness of multimodal representation fusion. Besides, our method achieves third place with an F1 score of 0.8936 on the second task of the CCKS-2022 Knowledge Graph Evaluation for Digital Commerce Competition. Code and pretrained models are available at https://github.com/hanchenchen/CCKS2022-track2-solution.

Keywords: Multi-modal representation · Self-adaptive threshold · CCKS-2022 competition

1 Introduction

We aims to identify identical commodities based on representation learning. Given a pair of commodities, we extract their representations and calculate the similarity between representations. Then we judge whether the pair is identical by comparing the similarity and threshold. In the second task of the CCKS-2022 Knowledge Graph Evaluation for Digital Commerce Competition, the commodity pair data is from the recall results of actual online models and manually labeled, where most of the negative pairs are similar but some key attributes do not match.

C. Han and H. Jia—Equal contribution. Listing order is random.

The traditional identical commodity verification methods usually adopt manually adjusted thresholds. There are some disadvantages of such a method.

1) **Inter-dataset adaptation problem.** Since data distribution usually varies between datasets, the corresponding representation distribution will be different as well. The threshold determined on one dataset may be hard to achieve comparable results on another, which affects the generalization of the model. It is necessary to manually adjust the threshold, which is laborious and burdensome.

2) **Intra-dataset adaptation problem.** Since the commodity pairs are usually similar, there representations often crowded together in the representation space. A slight fluctuation of the threshold may affect the performance much. Moreover, it is unwise to use the same threshold for different kinds of commodities.

3) **Model optimization problem.** Due to the high similarity of commodities, their similarity scores are usually higher than 0. However, the existing loss functions (e.g., binary cross entropy loss) are usually centered at 0. Consequently, the model is difficult to be optimized. Besides, it may destroy the representation space to force pushing the representations of similar but non-identical commodities away.

To mitigate the above problems, we propose an end-to-end multi-modal representation learning method with Self-Adaptive Threshold (SAT). We use a dual-stream network to extract multi-modal commodity embeddings and threshold embeddings separately and then concatenate them to obtain commodity representation. Our method can adaptively adjust the threshold according to different commodities, thus reducing the burden and drawbacks of manually adjusting the threshold. The dual-stream network optimizes the commodity representation distribution bidirectionally by either the commodity stream or the threshold stream, which results in a better distribution of representations. Therefore, it is less likely to force pushing away the representations of similar but different commodities. Moreover, with our self-adaptive threshold, the similarity of representations is basically centered at 0. While maintaining the indexability of the commodity representation space, the model is easier to be optimized and the representations are more robust (more details in Sect. 3.3).

Our main contributions are as follows:

1) We analyze the possible problems in the traditional commodity verification approach and then propose a multi-modal representation approach with SAT to learn the threshold adaptively. Our approach reduces the burden of adjusting thresholds and enhances the generalization and robustness of the representations.

2) We do not do special processing for the inputs (e.g. no detector), and the whole network is trained end-to-end so that other methods can be easily integrated.

3) We experimentally validate the advantages of the self-adaptive threshold and the effectiveness of our multi-modal representation fusion. Our method achieves an F1 score of 0.8936 and takes third place on the second task of the CCKS-2022 Knowledge Graph Evaluation for Digital Commerce Competition.

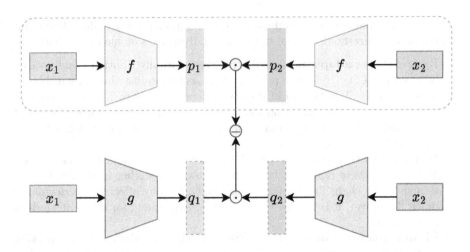

Fig. 1. Multimodal representation learning with self-adaptive threshold. The area in the red box is the traditional method of calculating the similarity of a commodity pair. The score is obtained by subtracting the pre-defined threshold from the similarity. When the score is greater than zero, the commodity pair is predicted to be identical, and vice versa. The higher score, the greater probability of being an identical commodity pair. We add a threshold stream to learn self-adaptive threshold embeddings and regard the difference between the inner product of commodity embeddings and threshold embeddings as the score. (Color figure online)

2   Method

In this section, we present SAT, a novel multi-modal representation learning method with self-adaptive threshold for commodity verification. We first detail the self-adaptive threshold in Sect. 2.1, then introduce the model architecture in Sect. 2.2 and the loss function in Sect. 2.3 finally. Figure 1 shows the overview of the proposed method.

2.1   Self-adaptive Threshold

Dual-Stream Embedding. We propose to use a dual-stream network to extract the commodity embedding and threshold embedding. Given a commodity x, we feed it to the commodity-stream f, and extract commodity embedding:

$$p = f(x) \tag{1}$$

where $p \in \mathbb{R}^{d1}$ is the commodity embedding; $d1$ is the commodity embedding dimension. Correspondingly, we have a threshold-stream g to extract the threshold embedding:

$$q = g(x) \tag{2}$$

where $q \in \mathbb{R}^{d2}$ is the threshold embedding; $d2$ is the threshold embedding dimension. Then we can acquire the complete embedding of commodity x by concatenation:

$$z = [p, q] \tag{3}$$

where $z \in \mathbb{R}^{d1+d2}$ is the complete embedding; $d1 + d2$ is the embedding dimension; $[\cdot, \cdot]$ represents concatenation.

Score Calculation. As our method is based on representation learning, we do not have to tackle a commodity pair simultaneously. Given a commodity pair (x_1, x_2), we extract their embeddings separately:

$$\begin{aligned} z_1 &= [p_1, q_1] \\ z_2 &= [p_2, q_2] \end{aligned} \tag{4}$$

The similarity s is obtained by the inner product between commodity embeddings p_1 and p_2:

$$s = p_1 \cdot p_2 \tag{5}$$

where $\cdot$ represents the inner product between vectors. Correspondingly, we can get the self-adaptive threshold by the inner product between threshold embeddings q_1 and q_2:

$$t = q_1 \cdot q_2 \tag{6}$$

The final score is the difference between similarity s and threshold t:

$$SCORE = s - t \tag{7}$$

If the score is greater than 0, it is a pair of identical commodities, otherwise not. The higher score, the greater probability of being an identical commodity pair.

2.2   Model Architecture

We use the identical architecture for both streams, but in fact we can design different architectures. Taking threshold stream as example, we have a RoBERTa [4] to encode textual feature q^u from text u and a Swin Transformer [5] to encode visual feature q^v from image v. Then we concatenate them and project the concatenated embedding into a common embedding space by a linear layer h:

$$q = h([q^u, q^v]) \tag{8}$$

Similarly, we can choose other backbones to encode single-modality features.

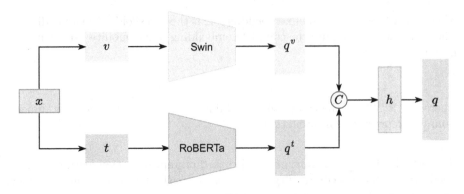

Fig. 2. Self-adaptive threshold network. We use Swin Transformer [5] and RoBERTa [4] to encode image features and text features respectively. The features of different modalities are fused by a linear layer.

2.3 Loss Function

We use cross entropy loss [2] to train the model:

$$\mathcal{L} = -\log \frac{y \exp(p_1 \cdot p_2) + (1 - y) \exp(q_1 \cdot q_2)}{\exp(p_1 \cdot p_2) + \exp(q_1 \cdot q_2)} \tag{9}$$

where $y \in \{0, 1\}$ is the ground-truth.

3 Experiments

3.1 Experimental Setup

Datasets. The official dataset contains about 50,000 commodity pairs for training and about 20,000 commodity pairs for test[1]. The training is only conducted on the official training set. We do not use unlabeled data or external dataset during training. When dividing the training and validation sets, we remove the items that appear in the training set to ensure that the training set and validation set do not overlap. The ratio of the final training set and validation set is about 5.6:1. We resize all images to 384×384. For text, we take the title and the 10 most frequent attributes as input. We do not apply augmentations on either image or text data.

Implementation Details. Our implementation is based on PyTorch [6] and HuggingFace [7]. We initialize the image encoder with Swin Transformer [5], pre-trained on ImageNet [1]. Text encoders are initialized from pre-trained RoBERTa [4]. We train SAT in an end-to-end manner. For all experiments, we use Adam optimizer [3] with betas [0.9, 0.999]. We train SAT for 100K steps

---

[1] https://tianchi.aliyun.com/competition/entrance/531956/information.

on 2 NVIDIA A100 GPUs with a total batch size of 8, which takes about 20 h. The initial learning rate and weight decay are 2e-6 and 1e-6 respectively. We use cosine annealing learning rate decay without warmup.

3.2 Ablation

In the ablation study, we validate the effectiveness of our method and analyze the impact of input modalities and pre-trained models. If not mentioned, hyper-parameters other than the ablated factor are the same.

Effectiveness of SAT. We first build a simple baseline as plotted in the red box of Fig. 1, which only have a commodity encoder. Besides, we add a Learnable Threshold (LT) to it. The threshold is learnable and the same for all commodities. As shown in Table 1, our SAT outperforms baseline methods by a large margin, indicating the effectiveness of SAT. Specifically, SAT brings significant F1-score improvements (i.e. +0.0620 higher than LT).

Table 1. Results of different methods on the validation set.

Method	F1-score	Precision	Recall	Accuracy
Baseline	0.7250	0.6097	**0.8940**	0.6432
LT	0.8204	0.8139	0.8270	0.8096
SAT	**0.8824**	**0.8795**	0.8853	**0.8759**

Impact of Modality. We further analyze the input modalities. Table 2 shows the detailed comparisons. Image-only SAT achieves better performance than text-only, with a lead of 0.0612 on F1 score. Taking text and images together as input can further improve the performance. We believe that SAT can be further enhanced with other modality inputs, which is worth exploring in the future study.

Table 2. Results of SAT with different input modalities.

Text	Image	F1-score	Precision	Recall	Accuracy
✓		0.7888	0.7555	0.8251	0.7676
	✓	0.8500	0.8599	0.8403	0.8440
✓	✓	**0.8824**	**0.8795**	**0.8853**	**0.8759**

Table 3. Ablation study of pre-trained models

Pre-trained	F1-score	Precision	Recall	Accuracy
✗	0.7815	0.7606	0.8037	0.7637
✓	**0.8824**	**0.8795**	**0.8853**	**0.8759**

Impact of Pre-trained Models. We also study the impact of pre-trained models. As mentioned above, we use Swin Transformer [5] pre-trained on ImageNet-1k and ImageNet-22k and pre-trained RoBERTa [4]. In this ablation, we random initialize the Swin Transformer [5] and RoBERTa [4]. As shown in Tab. 3, we observe significant performance improvement with pre-trained models, which indicates the importance of pre-trained models.

3.3   Score Distribution

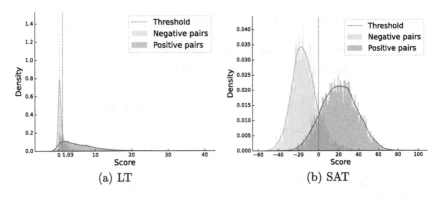

(a) LT   (b) SAT

Fig. 3. Visualization of score distribution. We show histograms of scores of LT and SAT. The density of the score is estimated by kernel density estimation. Compared to LT, the peak density of SAT is lower and farther away from the threshold.

Figure 3 shows the score distribution of LT and SAT. As shown in Fig. 3(a), the density peak of negative pairs is high with LT. In the meanwhile, the density peak of both positive and negative pairs is near the threshold, which means there are quantities of pairs around the threshold. The higher density peak and the closer density peak to the threshold, the more susceptible to threshold changes. A slight fluctuation of the threshold may affect the performance much. In addition, LT heavily depends on the training data distribution, not conducive to model generalization. By contrast, the density curve of SAT is much smoother and much easier to more distinctive than LT as shown in Fig. 3(a). It can be seen that the density peak of SAT is lower and farther away from the threshold. This indicates that default threshold 0 is virtually an optimum. Therefore without manually adjusting the threshold, we can distinguish positive and negative pairs by the default threshold of 0.

4 Conclusion

In this paper, we first analyzed the potential problems of traditional representation learning in the commodity verification task. Then we proposed SAT and demonstrated its effectiveness and advantages by quantitative experiments and score distribution visualization. With SAT, we obtained a representative and discriminative commodity representation space and achieved excellent performance. As future work, we would like to extend SAT to other multimodal representation learning tasks.

References

1. Deng, J., Dong, W., Socher, R., Li, L.J., Li, K., Fei-Fei, L.: ImageNet: a large-scale hierarchical image database. In: 2009 IEEE Conference on Computer Vision and Pattern Recognition, pp. 248–255 IEEE (2009)
2. Goodfellow, I., Bengio, Y., Courville, A.: Deep learning. MIT press (2016)
3. Kingma, D.P., Ba, J.: Adam: a method for stochastic optimization. arXiv preprint arXiv:1412.6980 (2014)
4. Liu, Y., et al.: RoBERTa: a robustly optimized BERT pretraining approach. arXiv preprint arXiv:1907.11692 (2019)
5. Liu, Z., et al.: Swin transformer: hierarchical vision transformer using shifted windows. In: Proceedings of the IEEE/CVF International Conference on Computer Vision, pp. 10012–10022 (2021)
6. Paszke, A., et al.: PyTorch: an imperative style, high-performance deep learning library. In: Advances in Neural Information Processing Systems 32, pp. 8024–8035. Curran Associates, Inc. (2019). http://papers.neurips.cc/paper/9015-pytorch-an-imperative-style-high-performance-deep-learning-library.pdf
7. Wolf, T., et al.: Transformers: state-of-the-art natural language processing. In: Proceedings of the 2020 Conference on Empirical Methods in Natural Language Processing: System Demonstrations, pp. 38–45. Association for Computational Linguistics (2020). https://www.aclweb.org/anthology/2020.emnlp-demos.6

Multimodal Representation Learning-Based Product Matching

Changkai Feng, Wei Chen, Chao Chen, Tong Xu$^{(\boxtimes)}$, and Enhong Chen

School of Data Science, University of Science and Technology of China, Hefei, China
{changkaifeng,chenweicw,chenchao11}@mail.ustc.edu.cn,
{tongxu,cheneh}@ustc.edu.cn

Abstract. This paper describes our methodology for the identical product mining task organized by the China Conference on Knowledge Graph and Semantic Computing (CCKS) 2022. This identical product mining task has two main challenges: 1) How to perform text representation to refine product representation. 2) How to more effectively combine text representation and image representation. For the first challenge, we propose the K-Gram Exponential Decay scheme in the text representation module to aggregate the information of surrounding words. For the second challenge, we apply conventional multimodal representation learning to combine text representation and image representation to generate the item representation. We view the identical product mining task as a binary classification task for product pairs, for which we adopt sample pair-based contrastive learning. Extensive experiments have demonstrated the effectiveness of our method. We won first place in the competition by utilizing model ensemble and post-processing.

Keywords: Multimodal representation learning · Product matching · Contrastive learning

1 Introduction

Knowledge Graphs are a significant component of enterprise data infrastructure and a core element of upper-layer applications [1]. In January 2022, Alibaba released AliOpenKG, the first Open Knowledge Graph for digital commerce. The process of creating e-commerce product relationships is a crucial step in the creation of the Knowledge Graph for digital commerce. However, the personalization of merchants' published product information has caused inadequate standardization and structuring of product, and different categories of product have various unique and important attributes, making it challenging to align fine-grained similar product.

Existing techniques [2] for fine-grained product alignment are mostly based on representation learning due to the large number of product on e-commerce platforms. Specifically, the item representation is obtained by characterizing the item with unstructured and structured information of the item. The same item is then obtained via vector retrieval. However, this identical product mining task

N. Zhang et al. (Eds.): CCKS 2022, CCIS 1711, pp. 180–190, 2022.
https://doi.org/10.1007/978-981-19-8300-9_20

views product alignment as a binary classification task based on product pairs, and employing vector-based retrieval is too complicated. For identical product mining, we employ sample pair-based contrastive learning. We first create separate textual and visual representations of the product using representation learning, then concatenate the two to create the final product representation. Finally, we utilize CoSENT[1] to gradually refine the product representation. In representation learning of text, since the traditional text representation method cannot highlight the local continuous token information, we propose the K-Gram exponential decay scheme, inspired by N-gram, for capturing and aggregating the surrounding continuous token information, which in turn refines the text representation. Additionally, inspired by Circle Loss [3] and Curricular Loss [4], we improved CoSENT further to create Circle-CoSENT and Curricular-CoSENT to promote contrastive learning between sample pairs.

In summary, this paper makes the following contributions:

- We propose the K-Gram Exponential Decay scheme refine text representation.
- We apply CoSENT for contrastive learning of sample pairs and further improve it to create Circle-CoSENT and Curricular-CoSENT.
- We adopt model ensemble for multimodal representation learning. It contains two sub-models for image representation and two for text representation.

2   Related Works

2.1   Product Matching

Product matching is generally based on representation learning. Tracz et al. [5] proposed category hard batch construction strategy and applied Triple Loss for product matching. Li et al. [6] utilized product titles and attributes to match product across platforms. Li et al. [7] proposed the Path-based Deep Network, which combines diversity and personalization to enhance matching performance. Peeters et al. [8] proposed the application of supervised contrastive learning for product matching.

2.2   Multimodal Representation Learning

Existing methods for multimodal information fusion generally use simple operations (e.g., concatenation, weighted summation) or attention-based methods. We utilize concatenation for fusion. Bi et al. [9] proposed characterizing three different types of news textual information (e.g., title, topic category, and entities) separately and obtaining news embedding by attention mechanism. Yu et al. [10] applied Cross-Modal Attention Mechanism to obtain textual representation of fused images and image representation of fused text and connect them for multimodal interaction.

---

[1] https://kexue.fm/archives/8847.

3   Methodology

3.1   Text Representation Module

In our text module, we choose RoBERTa [11] as encoder and feed the embedding of final layer into the following two sub-modules.

Conventional Method. First, we obtain the last layer of hidden layer features from the output of RoBERTa and perform the average pooling operation. Then, we use the dropout strategy to enhance the robustness. Finally, the final text representation is obtained by a layer of MLP.

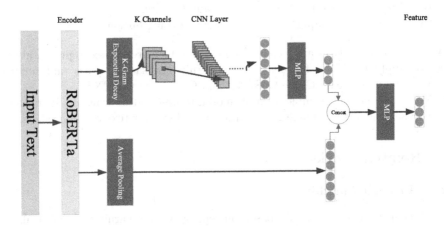

Fig. 1. Text representation module with K-Gram Exponential Decay and CNN

K-Gram Exponential Decay. We consider that text representation can be categorized into token representation, word representation, phrase representation, etc. The conventional text representation method can only highlight the global token information gained by the attention mechanism, not the local continuous token information that is crucial for forming word representation and phrase representation. Considering that the associated words generally occur consecutively, we are inspired by N-Gram and propose K-Gram Exponential Decay, a sliding window-like mechanism to capture phrase expressions of K consecutive tokens. We employ the K-Gram Exponential Decay scheme to process the token embedding output by RoBERTa to obtain multi-channel embedding, which is then enriched with the hidden information extracted by CNN [12]. Finally, the obtained embedding are concatenated with the embedding from the average pooling module and passed through an MLP layer to obtain the final text representation of the product. The general framework of the module is shown in Fig. 1. The K-Gram Exponential Decay scheme is described in the following.

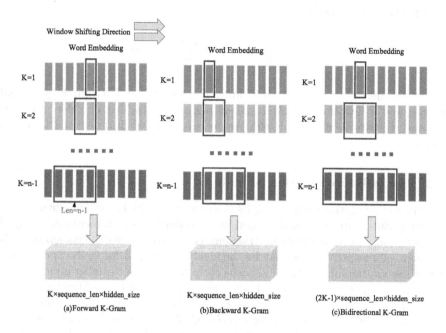

Fig. 2. K-Gram Exponential Decay

The K-Gram exponential decay scheme refines word embedding by aggregating information from surrounding token embedding. To reduce the computational cost, we parallelize the computation using a circular shift operation to improve computational efficiency and reduce running time. In addition, inspired by the decay factor of MDP in reinforcement learning, we exponentially decay the weights of the token embedding within the window to highlight the effect of relative position on the token embedding. The exponential decay weight α is a hyper-parameter, and we fix it to **0.8** in experiments. Given that token embedding fusion involves directionality, we consider forward K-Gram, backward K-Gram, and their combined form as choices for our downstream processing. The specific forms of the three K-Grams are shown in Fig. 2, and the formulas are as follows:

Forward K-Gram:

$$w_i^k = \sum_{j=0}^{k} e_{i-j} \times \alpha^j \tag{1}$$

Backward K-Gram:

$$w_i^k = \sum_{j=0}^{k} e_{i+j} \times \alpha^j \tag{2}$$

Bidirectional K-Gram:

$$w_i^k = \sum_{j=0}^{k} e_{i-j} \times \alpha^j + \sum_{j=1}^{k} e_{i+j} \times \alpha^j \tag{3}$$

where w_i^k denotes the word embedding obtained after K-Gram Exponential Decay, and e denotes the token embedding output by text encoder. j stands for the relative distance, and the greater the relative distance, the lower its weight.

3.2   Image Representation Module

We employ Swin-Transformer [13] as the image encoder in the era when Transformer architectures were widely used in computer vision. An increasing body of research contends that the Swin-Transformer, which inherits the notion of CNN hierarchical receptive fields, may be the ideal replacement for CNN. Specifically, Swin is separated into four stages, each of which results in a smaller input feature map and a larger receptive field. Each stage consists of a Patch Merging module and a Swin-Transformer Block. The role of Patch Merging is to downsample the image, similar to the pooling layer in CNN. The Swin-Transformer Block consists of Window Multi-Head Self-Attention,Shifted-Window Multi-Head Self-Attention, Layer Norm, MLP and Residual Connection.

Swin-Transformer and MLP are used to transform the image in order to obtain the final image embedding, then image embedding is utilized to calculate product similarity.

3.3   Contrastive Learning Objective

Since identical or different product always occur in pairs in this product mining task, we apply Cosine Sentence (CoSENT) to explicitly distinguish the difference among items. Inspired by Circle Loss, we add weight and margin to CoSENT to increase the weight of difficult pairs and separate them from each other. Inspired by Curricular Loss, we gradually increase the weight of the difficult sample pairs during the training process, so that the model gradually focuses on the difficult sample pairs. The following is an introduction to CoSENT, Circle-CoSENT and Curricular-CoSENT respectively.

CoSENT. The essence of CoSENT is comparative learning based on sample pairs, loss function is as follows:

$$\mathcal{L} = \log\left(1 + \sum_{(i,j)\in\Omega_{pos},(u,v)\in\Omega_{neg}} e^{\lambda\left(cos(e_u,e_v)-cos(e_i,e_j)\right)}\right) \qquad (4)$$

where $\Omega_{pos}, \Omega_{neg}$ are positive sample pairs set and negative sample pairs set, respectively. e_u represents representation of product u. λ is a hyper-parameter set to **20** in our experiment.

The optimization goal of CoSENT is to increase the cosine similarity of positive sample pairs while decreasing the cosine similarity of negative sample pairs. By subtracting the cosine similarity of positive sample pairs from the cosine similarity of negative sample pairs, it increases the distance between positive and negative sample pairs. The benefit of CoSENT is that the threshold for identifying whether a sample pair is a positive or negative pair does not need to be predetermined.

Circle-CoSENT. We add weight and margin to CoSENT, the loss function of Circle-CoSENT is as follows:

$$\mathcal{L} = \log\left(1 + \sum_{(i,j)\in\Omega_{pos},(u,v)\in\Omega_{neg}} e^{\lambda\left(\omega_{neg}\left(cos(e_u,e_v)+m_{neg}\right)-\omega_{pos}\left(cos(e_i,e_j)-m_{pos}\right)\right)}\right)$$
$$(5)$$

$$\omega_{neg} = \frac{cos(e_u,e_v)+1}{2}, \omega_{pos} = 1 - \frac{cos(e_i,e_j)+1}{2} \qquad (6)$$

where $\omega_{pos}, \omega_{neg}, m_{pos}, m_{neg}$ are positive sample pairs weight, negative sample pairs weight, positive sample pairs margin, negative sample pairs margin, respectively. $\omega_{neg}, \omega_{pos}$ imply respectively that negative sample pairs are more difficult the closer they are to 1 and positive sample pairs are more difficult the closer they are to 0. Furthermore, we hope that the positive sample pair will be accurately predicted even if m_{pos} is subtracted and the negative sample pair will be correctly predicted even if m_{neg} is added, further separating the positive and negative sample pairs.

Curricular-CoSENT. We compel CoSENT to master the straightforward sample pairs before moving on to the challenging ones, the loss function of Curricular-CoSENT is as follows:

$$\mathcal{L} = \log\left(1 + \sum_{(i,j)\in\Omega_{pos},(u,v)\in\Omega_{neg}} e^{\lambda\left(f\left(cos(e_u,e_v)\right)-f\left(cos(e_i,e_j)\right)\right)}\right) \qquad (7)$$

$$f\left(cos(\cdot,\cdot)\right) = \begin{cases} cos(\cdot,\cdot), & \text{if } (\cdot,\cdot) \text{ is easy sample pair} \\ cos(\cdot,\cdot)\left(t + cos(\cdot,\cdot)\right), & \text{if } (\cdot,\cdot) \text{ is hard sample pair} \end{cases} \qquad (8)$$

where t grows gradually from 0 to 1. Negative sample pairs greater than a particular threshold and positive sample pairs under a particular threshold are challenging samples.

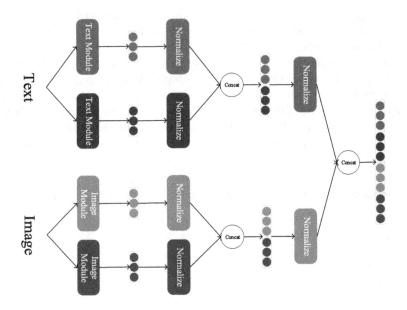

Fig. 3. Model ensemble

3.4   Model Ensemble

We use four models for integration, RoBERTa-Base for text representation $\mathbb{R}^{128}$, RoBERTa-Large for text representation $\mathbb{R}^{128}$, Swin-Transformer for image representation $\mathbb{R}^{256}$, and Swin-Transformer for image representation $\mathbb{R}^{512}$. Separate concatenations of the two text representations and the two image representations are performed, and then the text representation is concatenated with the image representation. Note that normalization is required before each concatenation. The model ensemble is shown in Fig. 3.

4   Experiments

4.1   Dataset

We conduct experiments on CCKS2022 identical product mining competition dataset. The training set contains 71,452 product information and 57,741 pairs of labeled product pairs data, and the validation set contains 16,876 product information and 20,707 pairs of unlabeled product pairs data, and the test set contains 17,132 product information and 15,909 pairs of unlabeled product pairs data. The product information data contains ten features such as id, industry_name, cate_name, cate_id, cate_name_path, cate_id_path, image_name, title, item_pvs, and sku_pvs.

Furthermore, we divide the local-train set, local-valid set, and local-test set on the basis of the training set in the ratio of 8:1:1.

4.2   Data Pre-processing

We primarily preprocess the product information data's item_pvs feature. First, we remove the redundant values and overlength values from them. Then, as new features, we copy the values of brand, item number, and model number from item_pvs. Finally, we remove some symbols to shorten the text.

4.3   Experimental Setup

We choose RoBERTa-Base, RoBERTa-Large, and Swin-Transformer-Large as our pre-trained models. For the text module, we set the learning rate to 2e–5, the batch size to 128, the epoch to 30, the maximum sequence length to 256, and the threshold is set to 0.8. And for the image module, the learning rate is 1e–5, the batch size is 32, the epoch is 50 and the threshold is set to 0.76.

In addition, while training the model, we only unfreeze the last three layers of RoBERTa and the last two layers of Swin-Transformer.

4.4   Post-processing

We add some rules to do further threshold processing when concatenating the final text representation and image representation. For example, if the brand and model number of two products differ but the image similarity is low, we may choose to increase their threshold. In addition, if two products have a high image or text similarity and the same brand, we choose to lower the threshold.

4.5   Experimental Results

The main results on local-valid data are shown in Table 1. As can be seen from the table, the Circle-CoSENT, Curricular-CoSENT and K-Gram Exponential Decay (KGED) we adopted have some improvement on the local-valid data. The image module performs best on local-valid data, with an F1 score of 90.21%.

The experimental results of our methodology using validation data are shown in Table 2. We can find that Circle-CoSENT has some degradation on validation data, and we guess that this may be due to the difference between the two datasets. Therefore, we only utilize the ordinary CoSENT, subsequently. Text model ensemble and image model ensemble represent the ensemble of RoBERTa-Base and RoBERTa-Large, and the ensemble of Swin-Transformer-Large and Swin-Transformer-Large, respectively. The results of Text model

Table 1. The main results on local-valid data.

Model	P	R	F1
RoBERTa	87.36	84.27	85.79
RoBERTa + Circle-CoSENT	86.20	86.70	86.45
RoBERTa + Curricular-CoSENT	86.90	85.90	86.40
RoBERTa (KGED)	87.34	86.73	87.03
Swin-Transformer	**88.41**	**92.20**	**90.27**

ensemble (KGED) are better than those of Text model ensemble, which proves the effectiveness and robustness of KGED. Additionally, the model ensemble effect has improved significantly, indicating a higher level of complementarity between the input from various modalities. This further demonstrates the effectiveness of our concatenate-based multimodal information fusion method in this task. Given the decreasing effectiveness of Model Ensemble (KGED) with post-processing, we infer that the current image model ensemble is implemented more effectively with text model ensemble than it is with text model ensemble (KGED). The model ensemble and post-processing combination, with an F1 score of 90.57%, makes the best results overall.

Table 2. The main results on valid data.

Model	P	R	F1
RoBERTa	82.65	83.51	83.07
RoBERTa + Circle-CoSENT	82.11	83.05	82.58
Text Model Ensemble	84.36	84.78	84.57
Text Model Ensemble (KGED)	85.09	85.57	85.33
Image Model Ensemble	85.49	86.15	85.82
Model Ensemble	88.50	90.69	89.58
Model Ensemble + Post-processing	**90.23**	**90.92**	**90.57**
Model Ensemble (KGED) + Post-processing	89.96	90.52	90.24

5   Conclusion

In this paper, we apply multimodal representation learning to product matching. For the text representation module, we propose K-Gram Exponential Decay scheme with CNN to refine text representation. In order to enhance the distance between matched and unmatched product pairs, we also utilize sample pair-based contrastive learning. Last but not least, we combine the two text representation modules with the two image representation modules to lower the variance of the separate models and enhance the ability of the product to be represented. The experimental results demonstrated that our model performs significantly with an F1 score of 90.57% on the validation set and 90.77% on the test set, and is ranked first in the identical product mining competition for CCKS2022. Our long-term research goal is to improve the K-Gram Exponential Decay in the text representation module such that, when combined with the image representation module, it can better represent product.

Acknowledgement. This work was supported by the grants from National Natural Science Foundation of China (No. 62072423), and the USTC Research Funds of the Double First-Class Initiative (No. YD2150002009).

References

1. Zhang, N., et al.: AliCG: fine-grained and Evolvable Conceptual Graph Construction for Semantic Search at Alibaba. In: Proceedings of the 27th ACM SIGKDD Conference on Knowledge Discovery Data Mining, pp. 3895–3905 (2021). ACM, Virtual Event Singapore. https://doi.org/10.1145/3447548.3467057
2. Fang, Y., Wang, J., Jia, L., Kin, F.W.: Shopee price match guarantee algorithm based on multimodal learning. In: 2021 IEEE International Conference on Computer Science, Artificial Intelligence and Electronic Engineering (CSAIEE), pp. 84–87 IEEE, SC, USA (2021). https://doi.org/10.1109/CSAIEE54046.2021.9543217
3. Sun, Y., et al.: Circle loss: a unified perspective of pair similarity optimization. In: 2020 IEEE/CVF Conference on Computer Vision and Pattern Recognition (CVPR), pp. 6397–6406 IEEE, Seattle, WA, USA (2020). https://doi.org/10.1109/CVPR42600.2020.00643
4. Huang, Y., et al.: CurricularFace: adaptive curriculum learning loss for deep face recognition. In: 2020 IEEE/CVF Conference on Computer Vision and Pattern Recognition (CVPR), pp. 5900–5909. IEEE, Seattle, WA, USA (2020). https://doi.org/10.1109/CVPR42600.2020.00594
5. Tracz, J., Wójcik, P.I., Jasinska-Kobus, K., Belluzzo, R., Mroczkowski, R., Gawlik, I.: BERT-based similarity learning for product matching, pp. 66–75 (2020)
6. Li, J., Dou, Z., Zhu, Y., Zuo, X., Wen, J.-R.: Deep cross-platform product matching in e-commerce. Inf. Retrieval J. **23**(2), 136–158 (2019). https://doi.org/10.1007/s10791-019-09360-1
7. Li, H., et al.: Path-based deep network for candidate item matching in recommenders. In: Proceedings of the 44th International ACM SIGIR Conference on Research and Development in Information Retrieval, pp. 1493–1502 ACM, Virtual Event Canada (2021). https://doi.org/10.1145/3404835.3462878
8. Peeters, R., Bizer, C.: Supervised contrastive learning for product matching (2022). https://doi.org/10.1145/3487553.3524254
9. Wu, C., Wu, F., Huang, Y., Xie, X.: User-as-Graph: user modeling with heterogeneous graph pooling for news recommendation. In: Proceedings of the Thirtieth International Joint Conference on Artificial Intelligence, pp. 1624–1630. International Joint Conferences on Artificial Intelligence Organization, Montreal, Canada (2021). https://doi.org/10.24963/ijcai.2021/224

10. Yu, J., Jiang, J., Yang, L., Xia, R.: Improving multimodal named entity recognition via entity span detection with unified multimodal transformer. In: Proceedings of the 58th Annual Meeting of the Association for Computational Linguistics, pp. 3342–3352. Association for Computational Linguistics (2020). https://doi.org/10.18653/v1/2020.acl-main.306

11. Liu, Y., et al.: RoBERTa: a robustly optimized BERT pretraining approach. http://arxiv.org/abs/1907.11692 (2019)

12. Yao, H., Liu, H., Zhang, P.: A novel sentence similarity model with word embedding based on convolutional neural network: sentence similarity model with word embedding based on convolutional neural network. Concurrency Computat. Pract. Exper. **30**, e4415 (2018). https://doi.org/10.1002/cpe.4415

13. Liu, Z., et al.: Swin transformer: hierarchical vision transformer using shifted windows. In: 2021 IEEE/CVF International Conference on Computer Vision (ICCV), pp. 9992–10002. IEEE, Montreal, QC, Canada (2021). https://doi.org/10.1109/ICCV48922.2021.00986

Relation Extraction as Text Matching: A Scheme for Multi-hop Knowledge Base Question Answering

Ziyan Li[1], Kan Ni[1], Haofen Wang[2]([✉]), and Wenqiang Zhang[1]([✉])

[1] Fudan University, Shanghai, China
{ziyanli20,wqzhang}@fudan.edu.cn, kni21@m.fudan.edu.cn
[2] Tongji University, Shanghai, China
carter.whfcarter@gmail.com

Abstract. Chinese Knowledge Base Question Answering (CKBQA) aims to predict answers for Chinese natural language questions by reasoning over facts in the knowledge base. In recent years, more attention has been paid to complex problems in KBQA, including multi-hop questions, multi-entity constrained questions, and questions with filtering or ordering. To this end, in this paper, we propose a KBQA system to generate logic forms and retrieve answers for different types of complex questions. For the single-hop and multi-hop questions, which account for the largest proportion among all questions, we propose a novel path construction method that converts the path construction task into a hop-by-hop relation extraction task via text matching. Our method combines the advantages of both the relation extraction and path ranking methods, which can focus on the order of entity-relations as well as alleviate the problem of exponential growth of candidate paths with the number of hops. Our proposed method achieves the averaged F1-score of 75.70% on the final leaderboard of CCKS-2022 CKBQA task.

Keywords: Knowledge base question answering · Multi-hop relation extraction · Semantic parsing

1 Introduction

Knowledge base (KB) is a structured representation of facts, composed of triplets in the form of $[subject, relation, object]$. In recent years, Chinese Knowledge Graphs have been expanding in number and scale (some of them can be found in OpenKG[1]), and researches based on Chinese Knowledge Graphs have attracted more and more attention. Chinese Knowledge Base Question Answering (CKBQA) is one of those popular research areas, which aims to predict answers for Chinese natural language questions by reasoning over facts in the knowledge base. For example, given the question "蜀道难的作者祖籍在哪里?

---

[1] http://openkg.cn/.

N. Zhang et al. (Eds.): CCKS 2022, CCIS 1711, pp. 191–201, 2022.
https://doi.org/10.1007/978-981-19-8300-9_21

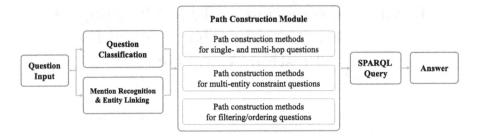

Fig. 1. The overall framework of our KBQA system.

"(Where is the ancestral home of the author of *Shu Dao Nan*?), the answer "陇西县 "(Longxi County) can be accessed by triplets "[蜀道难_（李白作古体诗）, 作者, 李白_（唐朝著名诗人）]" and "[李白_（唐朝著名诗人）, 祖籍, 陇西县]".

Mainstream KBQA methods can be roughly classified into two categories: Semantic Parsing-based (SP) methods and Information Retrieval-based (IR) methods. SP-based approaches convert natural language questions into executable queries (also known as logic forms) [1]. Traditional semantic parsing-based approaches typically build the logical form of a given question step by step, including utilizing question syntax analysis [2,9], entity linking [10], relation extraction [3,11] or KB grounding with reinforcement learning [5]. Information retrieval-based methods first extract a topic-entity-centric subgraph from the knowledge base, and then reason over the subgraph or rank the candidate entities for the final answer [4,6,8].

In the current CKBQA task, the questions have diverse types and complex structures, including single-hop questions, multi-hop questions, multi-entity constraint questions, questions with filtering and ordering, etc. Due to the complexity and diversity of the questions, it is difficult for information retrieval-based methods to cover all question types, and most of the top-ranked methods in the CKBQA competition of previous years were semantic parsing-based methods. [7,12]. Following this, we propose a semantic parsing-based KBQA system that uses different methods to construct SPARQL queries for different question types. Our KBQA system consists of four modules, namely the *question classification module*, the *entity linking module*, the *path construction module*, and the *answer retrieval module*. Specifically, given a natural language question q, we first obtain the question category c and the linked entities $\mathcal{E}$ by the question classification module and the entity linking module. Then, in the path construction module, according to the question category c and the number of linked entities $|\mathcal{E}|$, we use different path construction methods to generate the SPARQL query for q, and finally, we execute the query to get the answers $\mathcal{A}$ by the answer retrieval module. The framework of our system is presented in Fig. 1.

Among all question types, single- and multi-hop ones account for the largest proportion of all questions, which is the main focus of this paper. However, for multi-hop questions, the number of candidate paths grows exponentially with the number of hops, which can seriously degrade the efficiency and performance of the system. To address this, these methods have to keep the path count within a reasonable range by pruning the candidates, which increases the system complexity and may exclude the correct path from the candidates. In our system, to address this problem, we design a path construction method for single- and multi-hop questions that converts the path construction task into a hop-by-hop relation extraction task via text matching. Our method combines the advantages of both the relation extraction and path ranking methods, which can focus on the order of entity-relations as well as alleviate the problem of exponential growth of candidate paths with the number of hops.

2   Methodology

2.1   Question Classification

In our KBQA system, we design different path construction methods for different types of questions, so we begin with the question classification. Based on the structural features of the SPARQL queries, we classify the questions into 6 categories, namely, 1-, 2- and 3-hop questions, multi-entity constraint questions, multi-entity constraint+2hop questions, and filtering/ordering questions. In addition, we ignore some categories with too few occurrences, such as questions of more than 3-hop.

An n-hop question ($n = 1, 2, 3$) is one where the linked entity count $|\mathcal{E}| = 1$ (this unique entity is also termed the topic entity) and the number of triplets from the topic entity to the answer is n. A multi-entity constraint question is one where the linked entity count $|\mathcal{E}| > 1$ and the answer is constrained by all linked entities. A multi-entity constraint+2hop question is one where the number of linked entities $|\mathcal{E}| > 1$ and the answer is one hop away from the intermediate query variable that all linked entities constraint. A filtering/ordering question is one that requires filtering or ordering answers based on the figures that appear in the question. In Table 1, we present the question classifications, their examples, and their percentages in the training set.

To obtain the question category, we first adopt a pretrained BERT-base model to encode the question and take the [CLS] token embedding of the last hidden state in BERT as the question representation. This 768-dimensional question embedding is then fed into a 768×512 fully-connected layer, followed by a 512×6 fully-connected layer to fetch the logits, and finally the logits are passed through a softmax layer to obtain the probabilities of different categories. We select the label with the maximum probability as the question category.

2.2   Entity Linking

Entity linking in KBQA aims to identify the mentions in the question and link them to the corresponding entities in the knowledge graph, which can be separated into two sub-tasks: mention recognition and entity linking.

Table 1. Question Categories and Examples

Category	Proportion	Example of a question
1-hop	62.6%	李白祖籍是哪里? Where is Li Bai's ancestral home?
2-hop	12.0%	《悲惨世界》的作者的血型是? What was the blood type of the author of *Les Misérables*?
3-hop	0.4%	拉格朗日中值定理提出者所在国家的主要民族是什么? What is the main nationality of the country in which the proposer of the Lagrange's median theorem is settled?
multi-entity constraint	19.4%	周杰伦和钟兴民的共同创作的歌曲是? What is the song co-written by Jay Chou and Zhong Xingmin?
multi-entity constraint +2-hop	2.8%	李安导演的获得奥斯卡最佳外语片奖的电影翻译成英文叫什么? What is the name of the film directed by Ang Lee that won the Academy Award for Best Foreign Language Film translated into English?
filtering/ordering	2.7%	浙江国际大酒店附近2公里景点的营业时间是多少? What are the opening hours of the attractions within 2 km of Zhejiang International Hotel?

Mention recognition aims to identify mentions in questions that can be linked to entities, which we achieve with a model-based and rule-based method. In the model-based method, we consider the mention recognition as a sequence labeling task and implement it with a BERT+CRF model, in which we feed the question into a BERT-base model followed by a CRF layer to obtain the "BIO" label for each token. In the rule-based method, we use regular expressions to extract the time, distance and price from the question, such as "2006 年 6 月 "(Jun 2006), "5千米 "(5 km) and "100 块钱 "(100 yuan).

After obtaining the mentions of the questions, we need to link them to entities or literals in the knowledge graph. Due to errors in mention recognition and the fact that the question may not contain the full entity mention, we utilize fuzzy text matching based on BM25 algorithm to align mentions. Specifically, we use Elasticsearch as the query engine and design three indexes: *pkubase_entity*, *pkubase_literal* and *pkubase_mention* (as shown in Table 2). In designing the index structure, we use a 3-gram tokenizer with the purpose of considering word order within a 3-word range to improve the accuracy of the linking.

Given a mention predicted by the mention recognition model, we first use the mention to retrieve the highest scoring entity name from *pkubase_entity* and dictionary key from *pkubase_mention*. Then, we compare the similarity of these two items with the mention, and add the entity to the entity linking result if the entity name is more similar, or add the first 5 entities from the mention-to-entity dictionary to the entity linking result if the key is more similar. After that, we retrieve the highest scoring literal from *pkubase_literal* and add it to the entity linking result.

Table 2. Index information in Elasticsearch

Index	Quantity	Description
pkubase_entity	9,147,117	Entities in the knowledge graph whose in- and out- degree sums are greater than or equal to 2
pkubase_mention	12,989,848	Keys in the mention-to-entity dictionary provided with the knowledge graph
pkubase_literal	13,065,032	Literals in the knowledge graph that are less than 20 in length

2.3   Path Construction

Path construction aims to select the appropriate methods to construct executable SPARQL queries based on the question category and the entity linking result. In our KBQA system, we classify the path construction methods into three categories:

1. For single- and multi-hop problems, we propose a path construction method based on Sentence-BERT, which converts path construction into a text matching task that extracts relations hop-by-hop to construct SPARQL queries.
2. For multi-entity constrained questions, we first generate candidate queries based on linked entities, and then use the queries that can retrieves entities from the knowledge graph as the final SPARQL queries.
3. For filtering/ordering questions, we construct SPARQL queries based on templates.

Single- And Multi-hop Questions. For single- and multi-hop questions, we convert the path construction into a text matching task and extend the path by extracting relations hop-by-hop until it matches the problem category. In this way, our method can focus on the order of entity-relations as well as alleviate the problem of exponential growth of candidate paths with the number of hops.

Given an n-hop question q and its topic entity e, we first retrieve the relation set R_1^{head} with e as the head entity and the relation set R_1^{tail} with e as the tail entity from the knowledge graph. We convert the relation r in R_1^{head} to the text "e 的r "(r of e) and the relation in R_1^{tail} to "r 是e "(r is e). All texts form a candidate text set T_1 and a text t_1^i corresponds to a unique query triplet qt_1^i, which is either "$< e >< r_1^i >?var1$" or "$?var1 < r_1^i >< e >$". Then we feed q and texts in T into a same BERT model (Sentence-BERT) to obtain their embeddings. After that, we select the query triplet qt_1^* corresponding to the text t_1^* that has the smallest L2 distance from the question in the embedding space. If the question is a single-hop one ($n = 1$), we return the SPARQL query "select distinct ?var1 where $\{qt_1^*\}$".

If the question is a multi-hop one ($n > 1$), assuming the current hop count is x ($1 < x \leq n$), we use the previous predicted query triplet qt_{x-1}^* to retrieve the relation set R_x^{head} and R_x^{tail} (by executing "select distinct ?r_x where $\{qt_{x-1}^*$.

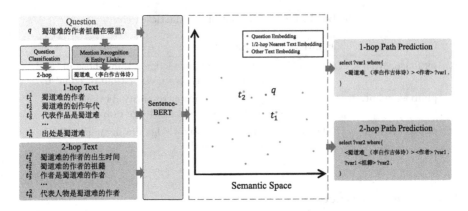

Fig. 2. An example of our path construction method for single- and multi-hop questions.

$?var_{x-1} \ ?r_x \ ?var_x\}$" or "select distinct $?r_x$ where $\{qt^*_{x-1} \ . \ ?var_x \ ?r_x \ ?var_{x-1}\}$'). Then, we convert them to the text "是" or "是". Similar to the previous step, we use Sentence-BERT to predict the query triplet qt^*_x for the x-th hop, which is either "$?var_x < r^*_x > ?var_{x-1}$" or "$?var_{x-1} < r^*_x > ?var_x$". After that we let $x = x + 1$ and repeat the above steps until $x = n$. And after n iterations, we will get the SPARQL query "select distinct $?var_n$ where $\{ \ qt^*_1 \ . \ \cdots . \ qt^*_n \ . \ \}$".

For example, given the question "蜀道难的作者祖籍在哪里？", its category "2-hop" and its topic entity "蜀道难_（李白作古体诗）", we can retrieve R^{head}_1 that includes relations such as "作者" (author), "创作年代" (creation era) and "文学体裁" (literary genre), and R^{tail}_1 that includes relations such as "代表作品" (representative work) and "出处" (provenance). Next we convert these relations to texts "蜀道难的作者" (author of *Shu Dao Nan*), "蜀道难的创作年代" (creation era of *Shu Dao Nan*), "代表作品是蜀道难" (representative work is *Shu Dao Nan*), "出处是蜀道难" (provenance is *Shu Dao Nan*), etc. We then feed the question and all texts into Sentence-BERT, and get the most similar text to the question t^*_1 = "蜀道难的作者" and the query triplet qt^*_1 = "<蜀道难_(李白作古体诗)> <作者> $?var_1$". Since this is a two-hop question, we will perform one more iteration. With qt^*_1, we can obtain the relation set R^{head}_2 and R^{tail}_2 for the 2-th hop, and the corresponding text set T_2, which contains "蜀道难的作者的出生时间" (birth date of *author of Shu Dao Nan*), "蜀道难的作者的祖籍" (ancestral home of *author of Shu Dao Nan*), "作者是蜀道难的作者" (author is *author of Shu Dao Nan*), "代表人物是蜀道难的作者" (representative person is *author of Shu Dao Nan*), etc. Again, we feed these texts into Sentence-BERT and obtain t^*_2 = "蜀道难的作者的祖籍" and the corresponding triplet qt^*_2 = "$?var_1$ <祖籍> $?var_2$". Finally, we combine qt^*_1 and qt^*_2 to get the SPARQL query "select distinct $?var_2$ where $\{$ <蜀道难_(李白作古体诗)> <作者> $?var_1$. $?var_1$ <祖籍> $?var_2$. $\}$".

Compared with previous path ranking methods [7,12], our method focuses only on the relations of the current hop in each iteration, where the number of relations is the number of candidates, avoiding the problems arising from the exponential growth of the quantity of candidate paths. In addition, by converting relations in R^{head} and R^{tail} to texts, our method can focus on the order of entity-relations (i.e., whether the topic entity or intermediate query variables appear at the head or at the tail of the triplet). For example, for a two-hop question, a relation will appear in the first-hop relation set R_1^{head} and the second-hop relation set R_2^{tail}, such as the relation "作者" for the previous example question. In our method, we will have "作者是蜀道难的作者" for a 2-hop path "<蜀道难_(李白作古体诗)> <作者> $?var_1$. $?var_2$ <作者> $?var_1$" and a quite different text "蜀道难的作者的作者" (author of author of *Shu Dao Nan*) for the path "<蜀道难_(李白作古体诗)> <作者> $?var_1$. $?var_1$ <作者> $?var_2$". Although such a path in this case does not really exist, for relations with a transfer nature such as "父亲" (father) and "老师" (teacher), different positions where entities or intermediate query variables are located can express completely different meanings. However, this entity-relation order is often neglected in previous relation extraction methods [3,11]. In contrast, in our method, we achieve the focus on this order with a simple path-to-text transformation.

Multi-entity Constrained Questions. Multi-entity constraints represent a class of questions where multiple mentions are detected in the question and the answer or intermediate query variables are constrained by multiple entities linked by the mentions. If the constraint is on the answer (that is, the answer variable, $?ans$), we call it a "multi-entity constrain" question, and if the constraint is on an intermediate query variable (i.e., $?var_1$), then there will be one more hop from this variable to the answer, and we call it a "multi-entity constraint + 2-hop" question. For example, "李安导演的获得奥斯卡最佳外语片奖的电影获得了多少票房？" is a multi-entity constraint + 2-hop question, and from its corresponding SPARQL "select $?ans$ where { $?var_1$ <导演> <李安_(华人导演) > . $?var_1$ <主要奖项> "奥斯卡最佳外语片". $?var_1$ <票房> $?ans$. }" we can see that there is an entity "李安_(华人导演)" and a literal "奥斯卡最佳外语片奖" that simultaneously constrains the intermediate query variable $?var_1$ (which represents that movie), and the answer $?ans$ is one hop away from $?var_1$.

Given the mention set M detected in the question, and the corresponding linked entity set E, where e_j^i denotes the j-th entity for mention m^i, we first generate two query triplets for each entity "$?var_1$ $?r_i$ e_j^i" and "e_j^i $?r_i$ $?var_1$". Then, for each m_i we choose a query triplet to form a $|M|$-entity constraint query, and if any entities can be queried from the knowledge graph, we replace r_i with the exact relations and add this query to the candidate SPARQL set. If the question is classified as "multi-entity constraint", we return the SPARQL set directly, and if it is "multi-entity constraint + 2hop", we perform one more relation extraction from $?var1$ to get the last hop relation. In addition, if $|M| = 1$, we treat the "multi-entity constraint" as a single-hop question and the "multi-entity constraint +2hop" as a 2-hop question.

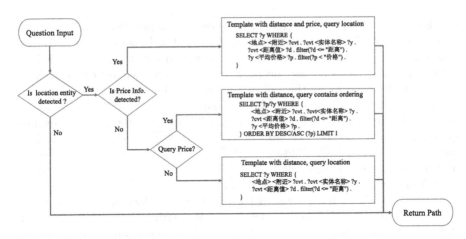

Fig. 3. Template for filtering/ordering questions.

Filtering/Ordering Questions. Among all the questions, there is a category that takes location as the topic entity, filtering or sorting nearby attractions or hotels by price or distance, which we label as "filtering/sorting questions". Since these questions have a strong regularity, we use a template-based approach to construct queries based on their characteristics in syntactic structure. We illustrate the process of constructing query from the template in Fig. 3, where the conditional judgments are based on the results of mention recognition or keyword matching.

2.4 Answer Retrieval

After path construction, if there is only one SPARQL, we execute the query in the knowledge base to get the answer, and if there is more than one, we take the union of all answers. Finally, a pair of brackets or quotation marks is added to each answer depending on its type.

3 Experiment

3.1 Dataset

Our method is evaluated on the CCKS 2022 CKBQA dataset. The training set contains 7625 questions with SPARQL and answer annotations. And the performance is evaluated on a test set containing 869 questions. The evaluation metric is the average F1 score. The given knowledge graph is pkubase, containing 66 million triplets and more than 20 million entities, which we deployed in gStore.

3.2 Experiment Details

Question Classification. To obtain the training data for question classification, we first convert the SPARQL to the abstract path by replacing entities and relations with placeholders. For example, we convert SPARQL "select distinct $?var_2$ where $< 蜀道难\_(李白作古体诗)> < 作者> ?var_1 . ?var_1 < 祖籍> ?var_1$. " to "$e_1 - r_1 - ?var_1\ ?var_1 - r_2 - var_2$". Then, we manually label the abstract paths with categories, which greatly reduces the annotation work.

In the training stage, we used 85% of the data for training and 15% of the data for validation. We use cross-entropy loss function and train 10 epochs with the Adam optimizer. The learning rate is set to 2e-5 for BERT layers and 5e-5 for other layers. We report the validation result in Table 3.

Table 3. Question Classification results on validation set, where MHC stands for Multi-Entity Constraint and F/O stands for Filtering/Ordering.

Category	1hop	2hop	3hop	MHC	MHC+2hop	F/O	Total
Accuracy	98.2%	86.9%	16.7%	93.7%	65.6%	100%	94.6%
	697/710	119/137	1/6	207/221	21/32	31/31	1076/1137

Entity Linking. To obtain training data for mention recognition model, we compare the question sequences with the entities or literals in SPARQL, tag the matching entity names or literals as mentions, and manually annotate the mismatched questions. In the training stage, we used 85% of the data for training and 15% of the data for validation. We train 10 epochs with the Adam optimizer and the learning rate is set to 5e-5. We evaluate the model on validation set and obtain an average F1 score of 93.54%.

Path Construction. Of the three methods of path construction, only the single/multi-hop questions require a trainable model. To obtain training data, we first retrieve the relation set R^{head} and R^{tail} from the knowledge graph by the topic entity (1-hop) or the query triplets of the previous hops. Then we convert the gold query triplet to text as the positive sample t^+ and convert up to 10 random relations from R^{head} or R^{tail} to text as the negative sample t^-. Take the question "蜀道难的作者祖籍在哪里? " as an example, "蜀道难的作者 " and "蜀道难的作者的祖籍 " are positive samples for 1 and 2 hop, while the other texts are negative samples.

Since our goal is to make the distance of positive samples from the question smaller than that of negative samples, we use TripletLoss as the training objective, as shown in Eq. 1:

$$Loss(\boldsymbol{q}, \boldsymbol{t}^+, \boldsymbol{t}^-) = \max(dis(\boldsymbol{q}, \boldsymbol{t}^+) - dis(\boldsymbol{q}, \boldsymbol{t}^+) + m, 0) \tag{1}$$

where $\boldsymbol{q}$, $\boldsymbol{t}^+$ and $\boldsymbol{t}^-$ represent the BERT embeddings for the question, positive and negative samples, $dis(\cdot, \cdot)$ calculates the L2 distance between embeddings and m denotes the margin between $dis(\boldsymbol{q}, \boldsymbol{t}^+)$ and $dis(\boldsymbol{q}, \boldsymbol{t}^+)$.

In the training stage, we used 85% of the data for training and 15% of the data for validation. We train 10 epochs with the Adam optimizer and the learning rate is set to 2e-5. Then we evaluate on the validation set and achieve an accuracy of 93.3%.

Answer Retrieve. Since each module uses a separate training set, we cannot split a separate validation set for answer retrieval from the original training set and therefore we only validate the overall performance of our KBQA system on the test set. Finally, we achieve an average F1 score of 75.70% on the test set as the final result.

4   Conclusion

In this paper, we propose a KBQA system to generate logic forms and retrieve answers for Chinese natural language questions. To parse and answer complex questions of diverse types, we designed and integrated four modules in our system, namely, path classification, entity linking, path construction, and answer retrieval. For single- and multi-questions, we propose a novel path construction method that can focus on the order of entity-relations as well as alleviate the problem of exponential growth of candidate paths with the number of hops. Finally, our proposed method achieves an averaged F1-score of 75.70% on the final leaderboard of CCKS-2022 CKBQA task.

Acknowledgments. This work is supported by the National Natural Science Foundation of China (No. 62176185) and the Fundamental Research Funds for the Central Universities (No. 22120220069).

References

1. Berant, J., Liang, P.: Semantic parsing via paraphrasing. In: Proceedings of the 52nd Annual Meeting of the Association for Computational Linguistics, pp. 1415–1425. The Association for Computer Linguistics (2014). https://doi.org/10.3115/v1/p14-1133
2. Chen, Y., Li, H., Hua, Y., Qi, G.: Formal query building with query structure prediction for complex question answering over knowledge base. In: Bessiere, C. (ed.) Proceedings of the Twenty-Ninth International Joint Conference on Artificial Intelligence, pp. 3751–3758. International Joint Conferences on Artificial Intelligence Organization (2020). https://doi.org/10.24963/ijcai.2020/519
3. Chen, Z., Chang, C., Chen, Y., Nayak, J., Ku, L.: UHop: an unrestricted-hop relation extraction framework for knowledge-based question answering. In: Burstein, J., Doran, C., Solorio, T. (eds.) Proceedings of the 2019 Conference of the North American Chapter of the Association for Computational Linguistics: Human Language Technologies, pp. 345–356. Association for Computational Linguistics (2019). https://doi.org/10.18653/v1/n19-1031

4. He, G., Lan, Y., Jiang, J., Zhao, W.X., Wen, J.: Improving multi-hop knowledge base question answering by learning intermediate supervision signals. In: Lewin-Eytan, L., Carmel, D., Yom-Tov, E., Agichtein, E., Gabrilovich, E. (eds.) Proceedings of the Fourteenth ACM International Conference on Web Search and Data Mining, pp. 553–561. ACM (2021). https://doi.org/10.1145/3437963.3441753

5. Lan, Y., Jiang, J.: Query graph generation for answering multi-hop complex questions from knowledge bases. In: Jurafsky, D., Chai, J., Schluter, N., Tetreault, J.R. (eds.) Proceedings of the 58th Annual Meeting of the Association for Computational Linguistics, pp. 969–974. Association for Computational Linguistics (2020). https://doi.org/10.18653/v1/2020.acl-main.91

6. Li, Z., Wang, H., Zhang, W.: Translational relation embeddings for multi-hop knowledge base question answering. J. Web Semant. **74**, 100723 (2022)

7. Lin, F., et al.: Knowledge-enhanced retrieval: a scheme for question answering. In: Qin, B., Wang, H., Liu, M., Zhang, J. (eds.) CCKS 2021 - Evaluation Track. CCKS 2021. CCIS, vol. 1553, pp. 102–113. Springer (2021). https://doi.org/10.1007/978-981-19-0713-5_12

8. Saxena, A., Tripathi, A., Talukdar, P.P.: Improving multi-hop question answering over knowledge graphs using knowledge base embeddings. In: Jurafsky, D., Chai, J., Schluter, N., Tetreault, J.R. (eds.) Proceedings of the 58th Annual Meeting of the Association for Computational Linguistics, pp. 4498–4507. Association for Computational Linguistics (2020). https://doi.org/10.18653/v1/2020.acl-main.412

9. Sun, Y., Zhang, L., Cheng, G., Qu, Y.: SPARQA: skeleton-based semantic parsing for complex questions over knowledge bases. In: Proceedings of the Thirty-Fourth AAAI Conference on Artificial Intelligence, pp. 8952–8959. AAAI Press (2020)

10. Yang, Y., Chang, M.: S-MART: novel tree-based structured learning algorithms applied to tweet entity linking (2016)

11. Yu, M., Yin, W., Hasan, K.S., dos Santos, C.N., Xiang, B., Zhou, B.: Improved neural relation detection for knowledge base question answering. In: Barzilay, R., Kan, M. (eds.) Proceedings of the 55th Annual Meeting of the Association for Computational Linguistics, pp. 571–581. Association for Computational Linguistics (2017). https://doi.org/10.18653/v1/P17-1053

12. Zhen, S., Yi, X., Lin, Z., Xiao, W., Su, H., Liu, Y.: An integrated method of semantic parsing and information retrieval for knowledge base question answering. In: Qin, B., Wang, H., Liu, M., Zhang, J. (eds.) CCKS 2021 - Evaluation Track. CCKS 2021. CCIS, vol. 1553, pp. 44–51. Springer (2021). https://doi.org/10.1007/978-981-19-0713-5_6

Research on Salient Reasoning
for Commonsense Knowledge

Mingxu Ma[1](✉), Guangshuo Wu[2], and Jingli Yang[3]

[1] XiaohongshuTechnology Co., Ltd., Shanghai 200001, China
mamingxu@xiaohongshu.com
[2] School of Bussiness, University of Shanghai for Science and Technology,
Shanghai 200093, China
[3] Shanghai Amarsoft Enterprise Credit Reference Co., Ltd., Shanghai 200092, China

Abstract. Salient reasoning of commonsense knowledge can help search engines better understand users' search intentions and improve users' search experience with intelligent product recommendation. Existing reasoning methods only use triple classification to determine the rationality of different entities in the knowledge graph, ignoring the significant changes between entities due to different search scenarios, and thus cannot infer the user's true search intent. In order to solve the above problems, this paper tries various methods to improve the performance of the salient commonsense reasoning model, and proposes a multi-task learning model based on entity type discrimination and entity commonsense saliency reasoning, and at the same time proposes a Prompt-based commonsense saliency inference model. The model proposed won the first place in both the preliminary and semi-finals in the commodity commonsense knowledge saliency reasoning track of the 2022 China Conference on Knowledge Graph and Semantic Computing.

Keywords: Salient reasoning · Multi-task · Prompt

Commonsense saliency reasoning of commodity entities is a technical hotspot in the scenario of intelligent commodity recommendation in e-commerce platforms. By associating and displaying products with strong saliency to users, products that are more suitable for users can be returned, and the user's search experience can be improved at the same time.

Today, major e-commerce platforms capture the relationship between user search demands and products by building a knowledge graph of products [1]. E-commerce knowledge graphs usually contain a large number of structured data triples related to entities and commonsense. However, most of the existing triplet reasoning methods often only focus on the rationality of commonsense, ignoring the saliency among commodity entities.

In the knowledge graph evaluation task for digital commerce held by CCKS in 2022, the commonsense knowledge saliency reasoning task is one of the subtasks, the purpose is to study the significant relationship between user groups, purchase scenarios and commodities, so as to enhance the user's search experience and improve the efficiency of the e-commerce platform. From the perspective of e-commerce platforms, commonsense saliency reasoning between commodities can identify products that better meet user needs, mine users' search demands on e-commerce platforms, increase the retrieval efficiency of target commodities, and improve user stickiness and search experience. to bring greater economic benefits. From the user's point of view, being able to search for products that are more in line with their own intentions can save search time and improve user satisfaction.

Salient reasoning of commonsense has made some progress in e-commerce platforms, but there are still some problems: (1) Most commodity knowledge graphs are constructed manually or semi-automatically. Due to the influence of subjective and other factors, the types of some commodity entities exist mislabeling problem. (2) The commonsense saliency reasoning task is difficult, and the saliency between entities often changes due to the switching of the environment. Therefore, with the influence of the subjective factors of different annotators and other factors, the annotation quality of the dataset has certain defects.

In view of the above problems, in order to enable the model to identify the commonsense entity triple data with strong saliency, the reason that the saliency label is low is due to the error of entity type labeling, this paper proposes an Ernie-based entity type discrimination and commonsense saliency MultiTask-Ernie, a joint learning model for gender inference, learns entity errors in triplet structured data through an entity type discrimination task to improve the model's inference performance for commonsense saliency. At the same time, this paper proposes a saliency inference model CSI-Prompt based on prompt learning, considering the gap between pre-training and fine-tuning. CSI-Prompt transforms the saliency inference problem into an MLM task, alleviating the problem of task inconsistency when the model is pre-trained and fine-tuned. At the same time, this paper revises the data through data statistical rules to help improve the model's inference performance for commonsense saliency. The method proposed in this paper won the first place in both the preliminary and semi-finals in the CCKS commodity commonsense knowledge saliency inference track in 2022, and at the same time verified the performance and competitiveness of the model proposed in this paper.

1 Related Work

Pretrained models have very impressive performance on text classification tasks. The introduction of Transformer [2] and BERT [3] models has greatly promoted the development of pre-training models in the field of NLP. In the field of Chinese NLP, Xiao proposed the ERNIE-Gram model [4], in the pre-training stage, the model jointly models entity information and N-gram, and integrates fine-grained word information and coarse-grained n-gram information to improve the model's ability to understand Chinese semantics. Cui proposed MacBERT to implement an n-gram masking mechanism using similar words to close the gap between the pre-training and fine-tuning stages [5].

Recently, prompt learning [6] has gained attention in small-scale data tasks. This type of method moves the downstream task closer to the pre-training task through templates and prompt words to reduce the gap between the downstream and pre-training stages. Schick transformed this classification task into a reading comprehension task and demonstrated the effectiveness of cue learning in classification tasks [7].

In the classification direction of triple structured data, Yao proposed the KG-BERT model [8], the algorithm constructs the model input by splicing entities and relations through [SEP] connectors, and learns the category of triple relations through BERT. Xie proposed a GenKGC model that takes both NLU and NLG into consideration [9], the model learns triple entity information to generate the relationship between conforming entities. On the basis of prompt learning, Lv proposed PKGC [10], the model combines soft templates to construct the input of triple structured data, and introduces entity descriptions to enhance the model's understanding of entities, thereby enhancing the model's inference performance. Qu proposed PMI-tuning [11], where the model infers the sufficiency and necessity between entities and relations through the latent knowledge distribution learned in the pre-training stage, and infers the direct commonsense saliency scores of triple entities.

2   Data

2.1   Data Sources

The data used in this article comes from the AliOpenKG knowledge graph, which consists of Taobao product attributes and product descriptions, including more than 1.8 billion triples, as many as 670,000 core concepts, 2,681 types of relationships, and 16 million entities.

2.2   Significant Definitions

Salience: When asked about a concept, the commonsense that contains the concept most likely to come to mind.

Sufficiency: The object holds in most cases of subject and predicate verb.

Necessity: The subject is almost the only reason why the predicate and object hold.

In this evaluation task, the data will be distinguished strictly according to whether it is significant or not. For data that meet the sufficiency or necessity, if it does not meet the significance conditions, it will be marked as insignificant. This triplet will be marked as significant if and only if both necessity and sufficiency are strong [12, 13].

2.3   Data Annotation Analysis

The task of this competition is divided into two stages: preliminary and semi-finals. The preliminary data set is only marked once. Due to the influence of some factors, the commonsense saliency annotation of the data and the annotation of entity types are not completely accurate.

The rematch test set is scored by annotators using a Likert scale: usually true, occasionally true, rarely true. The scores corresponding to the three options are 1 point, 0.5 points and 0 points respectively, and the final result is the average of the three labeled values. If and only if the average score is greater than 0.5 points, the commonsense saliency of the corresponding triples will be marked as significant.

3   Method

Considering the difference between the pre-training and fine-tuning paradigm in the two stages of pre-training and fine-tuning, and in order to improve the generalization performance of the model in the saliency inference task, this paper proposes a Prompt-based commonsense saliency inference model (Prompt-based commonsense saliency inference model, CSI-Prompt). At the same time, in order to allow the model to capture that the saliency label between two entities with strong saliency is non-salient due to the wrong entity type annotation, this paper proposes a multi-task joint learning based on Ernie's entity type discrimination and saliency reasoning. In order to enhance the algorithm's discrimination of entity types, this paper proposes a separate model ED-Ernie for entity type discrimination to improve the algorithm's saliency reasoning performance for commonsense. In addition, this paper combines data statistical laws and auxiliary algorithms to improve the effect of commonsense saliency inference.

Due to the difference between the initial and semi-final evaluation data sets, this paper adopts different saliency inference strategies in the two stages. Different from the preliminary round, the semi-finals did not use too many model structures and methods to improve and optimize the reasoning ability of the algorithm for commonsense saliency, but it did not affect the performance of the proposed algorithm itself.

3.1   CSI-Prompt

As shown in Fig. 1, the proposed Prompt-based CSI-Prompt model is divided into three parts: data construction layer, inference layer and output layer. The data construction layer uses [SEP] to splice and fill the data into the template, and map the labels at the same time. The inference layer uses ernie-gram-zh model inference to identify the label probabilities mapped at template [x]. The input layer computes the final saliency, computes the loss, and optimizes the model.

3.2   MultiTask-Ernie

Figure 2 shows the multi-task joint learning model proposed in this competition. In the data construction layer, the algorithm constructs commonsense saliency inference data; retains the entity category in the strongly saliency triplet data, marks the entity category of the insignificant triplet data as unknown, and marks

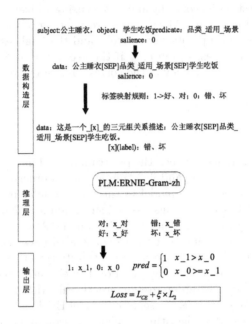

Fig. 1. CSI-Prompt Model

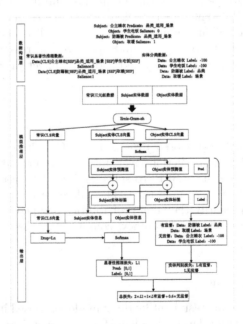

Fig. 2. Multi-task joint learning Model

the entity category in the insignificant triplet data as unknown. Entities undergo semi-supervised learning. The reasoning layer obtains commonsense saliency and entity category, and introduces entity information into commonsense reasoning, so that the model captures the reason why the label of strongly saliency triples due to entity type error is not saliency. The output layer outputs the triple saliency and entity category, and at the same time assigns weights to different losses, calculates the losses, and optimizes the model.

4 Experiments

4.1 Data Distribution

This section visualizes the number of samples, labels, relationships, word frequencies, and some special data in the data to elicit subsequent links.

Quantity and Relationship Distribution. As shown in Tables 1 and 2, it is divided into the distribution of the number of samples in the training set, the initial and semi-final test sets, and the distribution of the saliency label relationship.

Table 1. The distribution of the number of datasets

Dataset	Quantity
Training set	20435
Preliminary test set	10000
Rematch test set	50000

Table 2. commonsense saliency label distribution for the training set

Relation	Not salience	Salience
Category_applicable_scenario	10989	4614
Category_applicable_character	1727	1029
Category_matching_category	1002	432
Character_implication_scene	424	218
Total_num	14142	6293

Word Frequency Distribution. As shown in the Fig. 3a and b, the word frequency distribution of the first 20 words in the three datasets after entity segmentation on the Subject and Object sides, respectively, in order to make the results obvious, the intersection words between the initial and semi-final datasets and the training set are marked with different colors. It can be seen

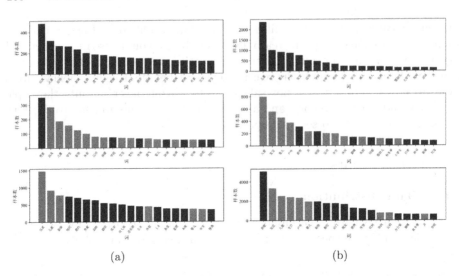

(a)   (b)

Fig. 3. Dataset object word distribution

that the word frequency distributions of the three datasets are roughly the same, and the proportion of training data is different from that of the preliminary and semi-finals. Therefore, the preliminary and semi-final data sets can test the generalization performance of the model.

In the head data in Fig. 3a and b, the proportion of children's data in the preliminary competition data is roughly the same as the distribution of the training set, which prompted the statistics and discussion of the laws of children's data in the preliminary competition process, and based on this greatly improved the performance of the model in this competition.

Data Correction. As shown in Fig. 4, in the training data, there are some data with a very unbalanced proportion of categories. For example, in the figure "*尿*_predicate_", * represents other words. This part of the data indicates that in the train data, * has no effect on the significant change of this sample. Therefore, based on the characteristics of this part of the data, some data that do not conform to this statistical law are corrected, such as the data in Fig. 4: *玩具*_predicate_儿童家家 .

Experimental Setup. In this competition experiment, the batch_size is set to 64, the learning rate is set to 1e–5, the pre-training model is ERNIE, and the preliminary data set is randomly divided 9:1 into the local training set and test set according to the distribution of labels and relationships. The Weight Decay is set to 0.01, the warmup is set to 0.1, the optimizer is AdamW[14], the learning rate Schedule is set to Liner, and the SEED is 2022. This evaluation task uses Precision, Recall and F1-score to evaluate the inference effect of the model on

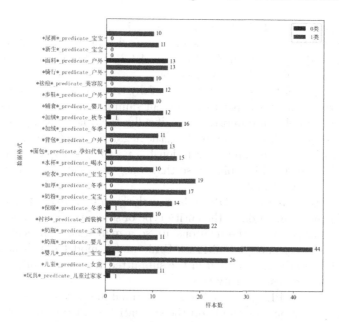

Fig. 4. Statistical Partially Unbalanced Data

the commonsense triple saliency task. The F1-score is calculated as:

$$F1 = \frac{2 \times P \times R}{P + R} \tag{1}$$

4.2 Main Model

This article tried a variety of methods during the competition. In order to more clearly highlight the role of the proposed model and related methods, only the following models were selected for comparison and description:

(1) KG-series models: KG-BERT, KG-Macbert, KG-ERNIE based on BERT, Macbert, Ernie.
(2) PKGC model: a soft template-based prompt model and the introduction of entity description class information to improve the model's ability to understand entities.
(3) MultiTask Ernie model. A multi-task joint learning model that combines entity type discrimination and commonsense saliency reasoning. This model is only used in the preliminary evaluation process.

4.3 Main Method

In addition to the model attempts, this paper has made attempts in data augmentation, data sampling, learning rate optimization, adversarial training, multitasking, etc. The specific methods used are:

(1) Data Correction (DC): In the data analysis and statistics, it was observed that the label distribution of some data existing in the data is extremely unbalanced. As shown in Fig. 4 in Sect. 4.1.3, this point can be highlighted, so the data were analyzed. Correction.

(2) Data Augmentation (DA): In order to fully train the model and fully understand the data, this paper uses different sampling methods for positive and negative samples in proportion, specifically: the original samples of positive samples are 1.5 times over Sampling, the negative samples are extended from the positive samples, and the relationship part in the triple rule data in the KG-BERT method is replaced, so that 3 negative samples can be extended from 1 positive sample.

(3) Entity Discrimination (ED): In data analysis and statistics, this paper finds that in the training data, the entity type of some data does not correspond to the entity type in the relationship, so a multi-task joint learning model MultiTask is proposed MultiTask-Ernie and a model ED-Ernie dedicated to entity discrimination, and in the submitted results, the inference results were corrected using entity types.

(4) Pseudo Label (PL) [15]: Use the local optimal model to predict the saliency of the evaluation data, and add the evaluation data with higher confidence to the training set to improve the model performance.

(5) Statistical Rules (SR)

In addition to the above methods, the following methods are not adopted in this paper:

(1) Cross-validation.

(2) FGM [16], PGD [17], EMA method. In the rematch, this article also tried FGM confrontation training, but the effect was that the line was reduced by 3 thousand points, and the performance of confrontation training during the game was unstable. The EMA method has a small improvement and is not used.

(3) Convert classification to regression. In the process of the competition, this paper tried multiple models and multiple cross-validation to construct floating-point value labels of the training data set for subsequent regression tasks, but the method eventually showed local overfitting and insufficient online performance.

For the model using the above method, a prefix will be added in front of the model, for example DA-KG-Bert means KG-Bert trained after data correction.

4.4   Experimental Results

Preliminary Evaluation Results. As shown in Table 3, the algorithm proposed in this paper achieved the best commonsense triple inference performance in the preliminary competition. Under the original data, the Ernie model shows high competitiveness in the KG series, so the pre-training model selected in this paper is mainly Ernie. Compared with KG-Bert, KG-Ernie improves the F1

Table 3. Experimental results of the preliminary round

Model	Precision	Recall	F1-Score
KG-Bert	0.6420	0.5340	0.5810
KG-Macbert	–	–	0.6069
KG-Ernie			0.6233
CSI-Prompt-Bert	–	–	0.5980
DA-KG-Ernie	–	–	0.6567
DC-DA-KG-Ernie	0.6551	0.7950	0.7183
DC-DA-CSI-Prompt	0.6431	0.7850	0.7070
DC-DA-MultiTask-Ernie	0.7072	0.7729	0.7386
PL-DC-DA-Ernie	0.6773	0.8171	0.7407
PL-DC-DA-MultiTask-Ernie	0.6732	0.7886	0.7467
SR-ED-PL-DC-DA-KG-Ernie	0.7300	0.8343	0.7787
SR-ED-PL-DC-DA-MultiTask-Ernie	0.7297	0.8350	0.7788

score by 4.23% , thanks to the entity information and n-gram features learned by Ernie during the pre-training process. The Prompt-based Bert method CSI-Prompt-Bert has a significantly higher F1 score than KG-Bert, showing the competitiveness of Prompt in downstream tasks.

In order to improve the model's understanding of the data, the data-enhanced DA-KG-Ernie model improved the F1 score by 3.34% . During the preliminary round, for some special data, statistical rules were used to adjust the significance of this part of the data, such as the special data in Fig. 4. Training on the revised data, DC-DA-KG-Ernie's F1 score on the preliminary test set is 71.83% and DC-DA-CSI-Prompt is 70.70% , proving the effectiveness of the training set revision. The F1 score of the multi-task learning model DC-DA-MultiTask-Ernie proposed in this paper reaches 73.86% , which reflects the improvement of the generalization performance of the model by the entity discrimination task, and also verifies the correctness of multi-task decision-making. On this basis, this paper uses pseudo-labels to predict the evaluation data, and adds samples with high confidence to the training set. The PL-DC-DA-Ernie reaches 74.07% , and the multi-task model reaches 74.67% . When manually inspecting the test set data, it is found that the multi-task model cannot completely solve the problem of incorrect correspondence between entities and triples. Therefore, this paper adds an entity discriminant model on top of multi-task, that is, ED-Ernie is used to evaluate the data set. The entity is discriminated, the inference result is repaired, and some rule discrimination is added. Under the above rules, the F1 score of the SR-ED-PL-DC-DA-KG-Ernie model is 77.87% , and the F1 of the proposed multitask model SR-ED-PL-DC-DA-MultiTask-Ernie reaches 77.88%.

In summary, the experimental results on the preliminary data set verify the performance of the multi-task model proposed in this paper, verify the

Table 4. Results of the rematch experiment

Model	Precision	Recall	F1-Score
DC-DA-KG-Ernie_1	0.5664	0.7981	0.6626
DC-DA-CSI-Prompt	0.5532	0.8093	0.6571

correctness of decision-making using entity discrimination tasks, and also verify the stability and effectiveness of some methods.

Results of Rematch Evaluation. Table 4 shows the evaluation results of the semi-final model of this competition. During the online submission process, it was found that the entity discrimination and rules of the preliminary round would lead to a decrease in the F1 score. Affected by time constraints and other factors, this paper did not conduct tuning and evaluation of the multi-task learning model and some methods, and only used the preliminary round to perform relatively stable. model, so only the single-model effect of the final submission is shown.

As shown in Table 4, DC-DA-KG-Ernie using data expansion and data correction achieves a single-model F1 score of 66.27%, and DC-DA-CSI-Prompt achieves an F1 score of 65.71%. The evaluation scores prove the correctness of the data processing decision in this competition, verify the correctness of the data set repair decision, and prove the correctness of the model CSI-Prompt proposed in this paper.

5   Conclusion

The algorithm in this paper has achieved the first place in both the preliminary and semi-finals in the commodity commonsense knowledge saliency reasoning track of the 2022 China Conference on Knowledge Graph and Semantic Computing. In terms of model, the problem of entity mislabeling is solved by adding entity discrimination, and a multi-task joint learning model combining entity type discrimination and commonsense saliency reasoning is proposed, so that the model captures the label of entity triple data with strong saliency as insignificant s reason. At the same time, this paper converts the classification problem into a mask prediction problem to address the difference between the two stages of model pre-training and fine-tuning. The model proposed in this paper greatly improves the performance of a single model on the saliency inference task. In terms of data, the data is repaired through data distribution and statistical laws, which improves the generalization ability of the model in the initial and semi-finals. At the same time, the research idea of saliency reasoning proposed in this paper can recommend products with stronger correlation in the product knowledge graph to users, which has certain practical significance for the study of product intelligent recommendation.

References

1. Liu, Q., et al.: Knowledge graph construction techniques. J. Comput. Res. Dev. **53**(3), 582–600 (2016)
2. Vaswani, A., et al.: Attention is all you need. arXiv:1706.03762 (2017)
3. Devlin, J., et al.: BERT: pre-training of deep bidirectional transformers for language understanding. arXiv: 1810.04805 (2019)
4. Xiao, D., et al.: ERNIE-Gram: pre-training with explicitly N-Gram masked language modeling for natural language understanding. arXiv: 2010.12148 (2020)
5. Cui, Y., et al.: Revisiting pre-trained models for Chinese natural language processing. arXiv: 2004.13922 (2020)
6. Liu, P., et al.: Pre-train, prompt, and predict: a systematic survey of prompting methods in natural language processing. arXiv:2107.13586 (2021)
7. Schick, T., Schutze, H.: Exploiting: cloze questions for few shot text classification and natural language inference. arXiv: 2001.07676 (2020)
8. Yao, L., Mao, C., Luo, Y.: KG-BERT: BERT for knowledge graph completion. arXiv: 1909.03193 (2019)
9. Xie, X., et al.: From discrimination to generation: knowledge graph completion with generative transformer. arXiv:2202.02113 (2022)
10. LV, X., et al.: Do pre-trained models benefit knowledge graph completion? a reliable evaluation and a reasonable approach. In: Proceedings of the 60th Conference on Association for Computational Linguistics, pp. 3570–3581 (2022)
11. Qu, Y.C., et al.: Commonsense knowledge salience evaluation with a benchmark dataset in E-commerce. arXiv:2205.10843 (2022)
12. Chalier, Y., Razniewski, S., Weikum, G.: Joint reasoning for multi-faceted commonsense knowledge. arXiv:2001.04170 (2020)
13. Romero, J., et al.: Commonsense properties from query logs and question answering forums. arXiv:1905.10989 (2019)
14. Loshchilov, I., Hutter, F.: Decoupled weight decay regularization. arXiv:1711.05101 (2017)
15. Lee, D.H.: Pseudo-label: the simple and efficient semi-supervised learning method for deep neural networks workshop on challenges in representation learning. ICML **3**(2), 896 (2013)
16. Miyato, T., Dai, A.M., Goodfellow, I.: Adversarial training methods for semi-supervised text classification. arXiv:1605.07725 (2016)
17. Madry, A., et al.: Towards deep learning models resistant to adversarial attacks. arXiv:1706.06083 (2017)

Retrieval-Then-Parsing: A Two-Stage Model for SQL Generation in Financial Domain

Nengzheng Jin[1,2], Dongfang Li[1,2], Junying Chen[1,2], Yubin Qiu[2], and Qingcai Chen[1,2(✉)]

[1] Harbin Institute of Technology (Shenzhen), Shenzhen, China
[2] Harbin Institute of Technology (Shenzhen) and Tuling Joint Laboratory, Shenzhen, China
qingcai.chen@hit.edu.cn

Abstract. Querying financial databases with natural language has been a strong requirement for financial company staff in recent years. The common method for this task is to transform the natural language into structured query language (SQL), which is referred to as semantic parsing. In this paper, we propose a two-stage model for semantic parsing in large financial databases. The two-stage model consists of an integrated table retriever that is used to retrieve related tables from a large database and a knowledge-enhanced semantic parser that utilizes a knowledge base for SQL generation. Experimental results show that our model achieves decent performance, which ranks the first place on both development and test datasets of CCKS 2022 evaluation task 11.

Keywords: Table retrieval · Semantic parsing · Table question answering

1 Introduction

Semantic parsing, which refers to transforming natural language utterances into logical forms (e.g., SQL) that can be executed by the machine, has been applied in various domains [3,6,7]. Along with the rapid development of digital intelligence in the financial domain, the internal data of financial companies is increasing rapidly. Hence, a human-friendly natural language interface to query financial database becomes more and more important for the staff of financial enterprises.

Recently, HundSun, a financial technology company, has released a semantic parsing dataset as an evaluation task of CCKS 2022, which aims to promote related techniques in the financial domain. Given a user's question, it is required to transform the question into a SQL query. Different from previous public datasets [6,7], the HundSun dataset does not indicate which tables are related to the given question. Hence, a table retrieval model becomes necessary to retrieve related tables from a large database.

N. Zhang et al. (Eds.): CCKS 2022, CCIS 1711, pp. 214–220, 2022.
https://doi.org/10.1007/978-981-19-8300-9_23

To tackle the problem of SQL generation in large databases, we propose a two-stage model that consists of an integrated table retriever and a knowledge-enhanced semantic parser. The integrated table retriever is integrated with a classification-based retrieval module and a heuristic-based retrieval module. The knowledge-enhances semantic parser utilizes the financial knowledge base provided by the HundSun dataset to accomplish SQL generation. The detail of the two-stage model is introduced in Sect. 2, and the experiment part is shown in Sect. 3.

2   Methodology

2.1   Overview

Given a user's question and databases, we first retrieve the database tables that are related to the question through a table retriever, which is integrated with a classification-based retrieval module and a heuristic-based retrieval module. Two modules are simply integrated by hand-crafted rules. Then, based on the retrieved tables, the user's question is transformed into a SQL query by a knowledge-enhanced semantic parser (as shown in Fig. 1).

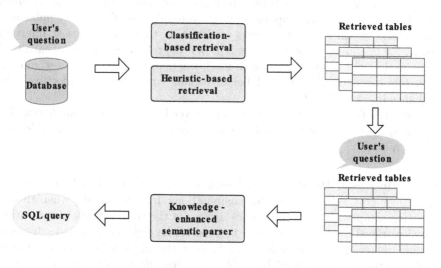

Fig. 1. An overview of our two-stage model. The first stage is the retrieval stage, the second stage is the semantic parsing stage.

2.2   Table Retriever

Classification-Based Retrieval. We observe that the questions that are related to the same tables usually have the same pattern or keyword. Hence, we formulate the retrieval task as a question classification task. Each kind of table combination that consists of one or more tables is treated as a class. Given a question, a BERT-based model [2] is used to predict its related tables through performing classification on the question (as depicted in Fig. 2).

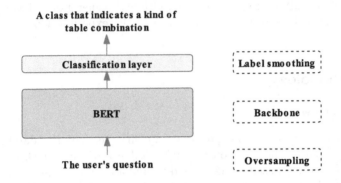

Fig. 2. The architecture of classification-based retrieval module

Considering that the distribution among the table combinations is imbalanced, we adopt an oversampling strategy to reduce the effect of the imbalance. Specifically, we first find the table combination that has the most questions (mark the maximum of questions as N), then the related questions of each table combination will be over-sampled to reach the number of N. Moreover, in order to reduce overfitting, we adopt label smoothing which refers to injecting a disturbance into the class label.

The classification layer is a small multi-layer Perceptron that predicts a class for the question. Through classification, we can retrieve the related tables of a question finally.

Heuristic-Based Retrieval. Although efficient, classification-based retrieval fails to generalize to unseen table combinations. In other words, when there is a testing sample whose tables do not appear in the train set, the classification-based retrieval module is not able to predict the right class for the discussed sample. Hence, we propose a heuristic-based retrieval module to retrieve unseen table combinations. Inspired by [1,5], we define three main heuristic rules to score a table combination for the given question, which are *question-table exact match score, question-column exact match score, question-column value match score.*

- **Question-table exact match score:** if a phrase in the question exactly matches the name of a table in the candidate table combination, then the question-table exact match score is added with 100, and 0 otherwise.

- **Question-column exact match score:** if a phrase in the question exactly matches the name of a column from the candidate tables, then the question-column exact match score is added with 5, and 0 otherwise.
- **Question-column value match score:** if a phrase in the question exactly matches the value of a column from the candidate tables, then the question-column value match score is added with 3, and 0 otherwise.

Finally, three kinds of scores will be summed up to be the final matching score between a question and a candidate table combination. The candidate table combination with the highest score will be treated as the related tables of the question.

2.3 Knowledge-Enhanced Semantic Parser

Semantic parsers usually follow the encoder-decoder framework, where the encoder is used to encode the question and its related tables, and the decoder is used to generate structure query language autoregressively. Recently, researchers [1,5] have proposed schema linking to capture the matching relationship between the question and its related tables, which is proved to be an effective technique. Specifically, the schema linking is to link the mentions in the question to schema content (e.g., table names, column names). As we discussed in Sect. 2.2, the links include question-table exact match, question-column exact match and question-column value match, etc. The links are usually modeled by a relation-aware Transformer encoder or graph neural network (GNN) encoder. LGESQL [1] is a representative method in this technique route, which outperforms previous methods by a large margin.

However, there are two issues that LGESQL does not solve. First, LGESQL does not support value generation. Second, it fails to extract the schema links when the mention in the question is slightly different from the schema content. For example, when the user uses the alias of a column in the question, the model might fail to generate the right column in the SQL query.

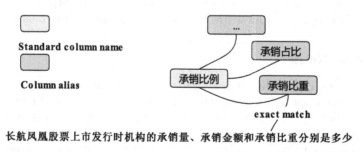

Fig. 3. The utilization of financial knowledge base for fuzzy schema linking

For the first issue, we implement a pointer network [4] on the LGESQL model for value generation, which enables the model to copy the tokens in the question as the value of "where condition" in the SQL query.

Then, for the second issue, we utilize the financial knowledge base that is provided in the HundSun dataset to enable more flexible schema linking. As depicted in Fig. 3, the financial knowledge base provides aliases for standard column names. Hence, we use these column aliases for fuzzy schema linking, which helps the semantic parser generate correct columns.

3   Experiment

3.1   Dataset

We conduct the experiments on the HundSun dataset that is released as a CCKS evaluation task. It is a Chinese text-to-SQL benchmark where each question is related to one or two tables. As shown in Table 1, there are 3966 samples in the train set, 1000 samples in the development set, and 2000 samples in the test set. To a certain extent, the test set is out of distribution because a lot of questions and tables in the test set are different from those in the train/dev set.

Table 1. The statistic of the dataset

	Train Set	Dev Set	Test Set
# of samples	3966	1000	2000
# of samples with 1 table	3068	766	–
# of samples with 2 tables	898	234	–

In detail, each sample in the dataset consists of a question and a corresponding SQL query. For example, given the question "Which company is Wang Zheng the secretary of the board of directors", the corresponding SQL query is "select chinameabbr from lc_stockarchives where secretarybd='Wang Zheng';".

3.2   Table Retrieval

In Table 2, we report the retrieval performance of our models on the development set. We adopt accuracy as the metric, which is equivalent to recall@1 that is commonly used in information retrieval domain. Both of them measure the correct ratio of first-ranking predictions.

As shown in Table 2, the classification-based retrieval module achieves much higher accuracy than the heuristic-based retriever. However, it fails to generalize to unseen tables on the test set. Hence, we use the heuristic-based retrieval module to tackle the robustness attack on the test set.

Table 2. The retrieval performance of table retrieval modules

Module	Dev Acc.
Classification-Based Retrieval	0.957
+Ensemble learning	**0.971**
Heuristic-Based Retrieval	0.619

3.3 Semantic Parsing

On the development set, we simply use the classification-based retrieval module to retrieve the related tables for semantic parsing. However, on the test set, we integrate the classification-based retrieval module and heuristic-based retrieval module by hand-crafted rules to achieve better generalization ability.

Based on the retrieved tables, we ensemble 12 knowledge-enhanced semantic parsers to produce SQL queries. The exact match accuracy of the SQL queries generated by our model is shown in Table 3.

Table 3. The exact match accuracy of the models on the leaderboard. We name the models after their teams and order them by the performance on the final test set.

Model	Dev	Test
Ours	**0.846**	**0.4460**
SystemAndMe	0.805	0.2870
HUST_ZL	0.832	0.2870
Langboat	0.844	0.2845

The exact match accuracy represents the ratio of the predicted SQL queries that are consistent with the gold SQL queries on every SQL clause. As shown in Table 3, our model achieves the best exact match accuracy on both development set and test set.

4 Conclusion

In this work, We propose a two-stage model that consists of an integrated retriever and a knowledge-enhanced semantic parser. It achieves exact match accuracy of 0.846 on the development set whose distribution is consistent with that of the train set. However, the accuracy of the test set is much lower. This is because the distribution of the test set is largely different from that of the train set. Hence, how to enhance the generalization ability of the table retriever and the semantic parser might be an important topic in future research.

References

1. Cao, R., Chen, L., Chen, Z., Zhao, Y., Zhu, S., Yu, K.: LGESQL: line graph enhanced text-to-SQL model with mixed local and non-local relations. In: ACL (2021)
2. Devlin, J., Chang, M.W., Lee, K., Toutanova, K.: BERT: pre-training of deep bidirectional transformers for language understanding. In: NAACL (2019)
3. Katsis, Y., et al.: AIT-QA: question answering dataset over complex tables in the airline industry. ArXiv abs/2106.12944 (2021)
4. Vinyals, O., Fortunato, M., Jaitly, N.: Pointer networks. In: NIPS (2015)
5. Wang, B., Shin, R., Liu, X., Polozov, O., Richardson, M.: RAT-SQL: relation-aware schema encoding and linking for text-to-SQL parsers. In: ACL (2020)
6. Yu, T., et al.: Spider: a large-scale human-labeled dataset for complex and cross-domain semantic parsing and text-to-SQL task. In: EMNLP (2018)
7. Zhong, V., Xiong, C., Socher, R.: Seq2SQL: Generating structured queries from natural language using reinforcement learning. ArXiv abs/1709.00103 (2017)

Structured Design Solves Multiple Tables of NL2SQL

Xianwei Yi[(⊠)], Ruijie Wang, Hanyi Zhang, and Shiqi Zhen

iFLYTEK Co., Ltd., Hubei 430000, China
necther@qq.com

Abstract. NL2SQL (NLP Language To SQL) is a cutting-edge research direction of natural language processing, which converts natural query statements input by users into executable SQL statements. CCKS2022 proposes a multi-database multi-table NL2SQL task for the financial domain. For this task, this paper proposes a SQL generation method based on semantic parsing. The method adopts the multi-stage iterative generation mode of "question-database name-table name-column name-SQL statement", uses semantic parsing and semantic similarity learning methods in acquiring table names, and generates and selects SQL statements based on the same query Multi-input statement for integrated filtering. At the end of the competition, the label replacement method was adopted, that is, the tables and columns in the SQL statement were replaced with tags to reduce the difficulty of generation.

Keywords: NL2SQL · Text generation · Semantic similarity

1 First Section

1.1 Background

There are various databases at present, but SQL statements have strong generality. SQL statements provide convenience for developers to access the database, but also limit the query of the database by non-professional users. In recent years, with the rapid development of artificial intelligence and natural language processing, the emergence of NL2SQL has provided a new idea for non-professional users to query databases. This technology has attracted more and more attention from researchers, and the demand for implementation has also increased rapidly.

NL2SQL, the full name is Natural Language to SQL, also known as Text2SQL. Simply put, it converts the user's natural language query into an executable SQL statement given a database (Context). In order to promote the research and development of NL2SQL, The 2022 China Conference on Knowledge Graph and Semantic Computing (CCKS 2022) will hold a financial NL2SQL evaluation task. This evaluation has the following difficulties:

(1) **multi-table connection:**
The sql statement is more complex and requires fields such as order by, groupy by, limit, and agg.

(2) **The distribution of the test set and the training set is different:**
(3) According to the analysis, most of the question query tables and columns in the test set have not appeared in the training set, and the problem of weak generalization ability of the generative model is particularly prominent.
(4) **The question and sql language are inconsistent:**

The question is in Chinese, and the sql is marked in English.

To address the above difficulties, we propose a system for structured ENCODER input [1], structured LABEL [2], and correction of irregularly generated results. Firstly, the pre-training model is pre-trained again, so as to enhance the semantic understanding of the SQL statement structure. Then, the corresponding database name is generated through the model, and the table name under the database is provided as a priori knowledge to the model to generate the corresponding table name., the column name corresponding to the table name and the sample problem construct a structured input, and the sql is used as a label after a special MASK, which reduces the generation pressure and enhances the generalization ability. Finally, the sql is corrected based on semantic similarity. The method proposed in this paper has the following three innovations:

(1) **Iteratively generate database name, table name, sql:**
Due to the large number of table names and column names in the data set, the sql is more complex, and it is difficult to generate sql directly by using the question. Therefore, the column names and table names are constrained in the model input, and the column names and table names in the generated SQL must exist in the input, which solves the difficulty of generating lists out of thin air and improves the accuracy of generating SQL.
(2) **Generate the sql of the mask structure:**
If the table names and column names are directly spliced as input [3], the model will lack the generalization ability, and if there are new table names and column names, it cannot be generated correctly. Therefore, the table and column names in the input are bound to symbols, respectively. For example, the input is: question + T: Table 1 + C1: Column 1 + C2: Column 2, and the output is: Select C2 from T, where the position of the column name can be randomly replaced multiple times to improve the generalization ability of the model.
(3) **Post-processing sql using text similarity:**
If there is a situation where the generated column corresponds to the wrong table, you can use this column to perform text similarity matching with a column in another table, and replace the column with the highest similarity.

1.2 Data Description

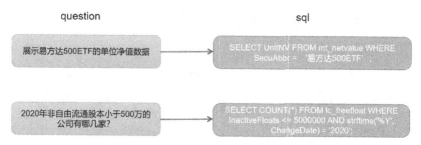

Fig. 1. NL2SQL question answering data example

The question and answer data is shown in Fig. 1. The labeled data provided in this competition comes from 3 scenarios in the financial field (stock, fund, macro), including 3966 training sets, 1000 validation sets and 2000 test sets. The sql statement of the data has multi-table connection, agg, order by, group by, and functions, etc. The average length of the sql statement is 1, and the longest is 2. The data distribution is shown in Figs. 2 and 3.

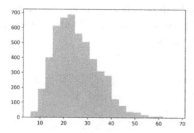

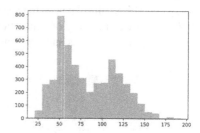

Fig. 2. Question length distribution   **Fig. 3.** Sql length distribution

2 Model and Method Introduction

2.1 System Structure

The overall iterative architecture of our method is shown in Fig. 4, and we adopt a three-stage training approach using the SeqSeq architecture [4]. Since the dataset is a multi-database and multi-table query, the first stage generates the dbname through the question, the second stage uses the question and all the tables in the dbname obtained in the first stage as input to generate the table corresponding to the current qeustion, and the third stage uses the question, table, and cols are used as input to generate the SQL query statement corresponding to the question.

Phase one:

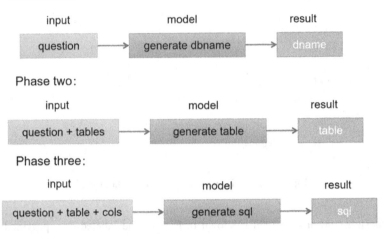

Fig. 4. Iterative model hierarchy example

2.2 Specific Design of Input and Output

The sql generation we designed is shown in Fig. 5. In the input, T1 and T2 are the two tables corresponding to the question, and X and Z are the columns in Table 1 and Table 2, respectively. The results that need to be generated will be generated using T, X Replacing with Z reduces the difficulty of generation while avoiding the model's over-reliance on the character order of tables and columns in the input.

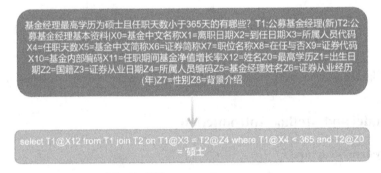

Fig. 5. SQL generate input example

3 SQL Correction Method

3.1 Text Similarity

As shown in Fig. 6, first construct candidate columns through all column names in the table, use the generated column names and candidate column combinations as model input to obtain vector representations [5], and then calculate the cosine similarity, and select the candidate column with the highest similarity.

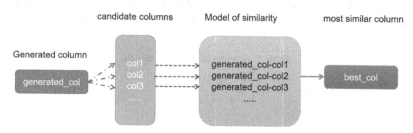

Fig. 6. Correction of column names

3.2 Querying the Database by Value to Correct the Column Name

As shown in Fig. 7, the columns in Generated sql are incorrect. Shanghai corresponds to the province instead of the nationality. Therefore, we construct a candidate query query. If the statement can be correctly queried in the database, its column will be used for the generated column. Replace to get an executable sql statement.

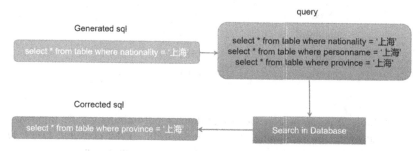

Fig. 7. Query the database to modify the column name

4 Experiments

This section introduces our experiments, including experimental parameter settings and analysis of experimental results.

4.1 Experimental Parameter Settings

For the generative model, we use the mt5-base [6], bart, and unilm [7] models as the initial pre-training model, and the dataset is divided by 5-fold cross-validation. The maximum encoding length is 512, the maximum decoding length is 200, and the batch_size is 8. Use Adam as the optimizer and the learning rate is set to 5e-5.

4.2 Experimental Results and Analysis

We use 4,000 labeled data as the training set, and 1,000 validation sets in the A list as the evaluation data for experimental verification, and use the acc value as the evaluation index. We used unilm, mt5, and bart as generative models for experiments.

Table 1. Results of different models

Model	ACC
unilm	0.769
bart	0.773
mt5	0.787

The prediction results of different models are shown in Table 1. It can be observed that unilm and bart have similar prediction results, and the result of mt5 is the best. We tried to use corpus for pre-training, and randomly masked SQL statements as input [8] to predict the correct SQL statements.

Table 2. Results after pre-training

Model	ACC
unilm	0.785
bart	0.788
mt5	0.801

From Table 2, it can be concluded that domain pre-training greatly improves the results of downstream fine-tuning, which can help the model converge faster, learn relevant domain knowledge, and improve the accuracy of generation.

5 Conclusion

Database question and answer has a wide range of applications in the financial field, which can greatly improve the convenience of non-professional users to query the database and improve the application of the database. Based on the NL2SQL evaluation data set provided by the sponsor of CCKS 2022, this paper proposes an NL2SQL method based on multi-stage structured generation, and achieved the second place in the final.

References

1. Herzig∗, J., Shaw, P., Chang, M.-W., Guu, K., Pasupat, P., Zhang, Y.: Unlocking Compositional Generalization in Pre-trained Models Using Intermediate Representations (2021)

2. Andreas, J.: Good-enough compositional data augmentation (2020)
3. Scholak, T., Schucher, N., Bahdanau, D.: PICARD: Parsing Incrementally for Constrained Auto-Regressive Decoding from Language Models (2021)
4. Mike, L.: BART: denoising sequence-to-sequence pre-training for natural language generation, translation, and comprehension. In: Proceedings of the 58th Annual Meeting of the Association for Computational Linguistics (2021)
5. Gao, T., Yao, X., Chen, D.: SimCSE: Simple Contrastive Learning of Sentence Embeddings (2021)
6. Xue∗, L., et al.: mT5: A massively multilingual pre-trained text-to-text transformer (2020)
7. Li, D., et al.: Unified Language Model Pre-training for Natural Language Understanding and Generation (2019)
8. Choi, D., Shin, M.C., Kim, E., Shin, D.R.: RYANSQL: Recursively Applying Sketch-based Slot Fillings for Complex Text-to-SQL in Cross-Domain Databases (2021)

The Method for Plausibility Evaluation of Knowledge Triple Based on QA

Shutong Jia and Jiuxin Cao[✉]

School of Cyber Science and Engineering, Southeast University, Nanjing 211189, China
{shutong_jia,jx.cao}@seu.edu.cn

Abstract. At present, most of the methods for knowledge graph completion (KGC) task highly rely on external knowledge base or graph representation learning. However, how to complete this task without using any external prior knowledge is still a huge challenge and difficulty. To this end, we propose a novel framework which converts the plausibility evaluation of knowledge triple task to the question and answer (QA) task with the thought of KG-BERT and prompt learning. We also test the effect of different question types on the results. Secondly, by fine-tuning two pre-trained language models BERT-wwm-ext and ERNIE-Gram on these generated sequences, so that they can complete the QA task. We won the 5th place at CCKS 2022 track 1 rematch stage, which proved the effectiveness of our method.

Keywords: Knowledge graph completion · Knowledge triple · Pre-trained language model · Question and answer

1 Introduction

Nowadays, the construction of large-scale knowledge base (or knowledge graph) provides the underlying support for many NLP tasks. However, due to its large scale and incompleteness, how to complete the knowledge base has become a very significant task. The completion of knowledge graph mainly includes two aspects: the salience prediction of knowledge triples' plausibility evaluation and link prediction. In this paper, we mainly focus on the problem of evaluating the plausibility of knowledge triples.

At present, some existing methods highly rely on the external knowledge base to train the language model from scratch [1] or rely on the data set provided by the task to build the knowledge graph [2] to complete the task. However, on the one hand, the construction of external knowledge base needs a lot of manpower and time, and it is difficult to judge its noise level due to the existence of subjective factors. On the other hand, it is difficult to deal with the gap problem between the test set and the train set while building the knowledge graph through the existing train set. In addition, the cost of equipment and time for training model through the external knowledge base are also expensive.

Many pre-trained language models such as BERT [3], RoBERTa [4], ERNIE-Gram [5] have presented great brilliance in natural language processing (NLP) tasks, how to

N. Zhang et al. (Eds.): CCKS 2022, CCIS 1711, pp. 228–235, 2022.
https://doi.org/10.1007/978-981-19-8300-9_25

make full use of the common knowledge contained in the pre-trained language model to make up for the gap between the train set and the test set is an urgent problem to be solved. In this paper, we use the thought of KG-BERT [6] and prompt learning to transform the knowledge triples' plausibility evaluation task into QA task. Through the above way, we could make the input closer to the natural language question, and as a result, we could better capture the implicit knowledge contained in the pre-trained model without the help of external knowledge base and graph representation learning. The main contributions of this paper are as follows:

- With the thought of KG-BERT and prompt learning, we transform the plausibility evaluation of knowledge triple task into the question and answer (QA) task, so that the input is closer to natural language question, which can effectively mine the implicit knowledge contained in the pre-trained language model. In addition, we also test the effect of different question types on the evaluations results.
- Through fine-tuning the pre-trained language model on these generated sequences, two models QA-BERT-wwm-ext and QA-ERNIE-Gram are given to complete the QA task.
- A large number of experiments have proved the effectiveness of our method in completing the plausibility evaluation of knowledge triple task, and we won the 5th place at CCKS 2022 track 1 rematch stage without using any external prior knowledge.

2 Related Work

The plausibility evaluation of knowledge triple task is one of the important parts, but there are not many researches yet. Most of the early related works only rely on the structural similarity of knowledge triples. The representative models include TransE [7], TransH [8] and RotateE [9], which evaluate the plausibility of triples through the distance among the head entity, relationship and tail entity. With the advance of the pre-trained language model and the rise of graph representation learning, more and more researchers also use the above methods to solve the KGC problem. KG-BERT [6] first transformed knowledge triples into text sequences and input them into the pre-trained language model, but it is too easy to fully capture rich linguistic knowledge in pre-trained model. StAR [10] combined the thought of Sentence-BERT [11] with graph embedding. PKCG [12] applied prompt learning to the integrity of knowledge map. However, most of the above work rely on open source knowledge base or graph representation learning, ignoring the problem of model train under limited conditions and the invisibility of test set for model.

In order to address the above problems, this paper transforms the plausibility evaluation of knowledge triple task into the QA task, so that the model input is more similar to the normal question, and could better obtain the rich semantic knowledge contained in the pre-trained language model.

3   Method

3.1   Task Conversion

Problem Description. Given a knowledge triple (head entity, relation, tail entity), the goal of plausibility evaluation of knowledge triple task is to judge whether there is a relation (r) between the head entity (subject) and the tail entity (object), and the order of the head entity and the tail entity cannot be reversed.

Question Generation. In this paper, we transform the plausibility evaluation of knowledge triple task to the QA task. Based on this, the question generation module is designed to convert knowledge triples into corresponding questions according to their relationship category. Specially, for the given dataset[1], we define the corresponding question generation template, which are shown in Fig. 1.

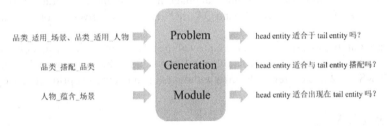

Fig. 1. Problem generation module

After that, we can get the question sentence $s = \{w_1, w_2, ..., w_l\}$ for a knowledge triple, where l means the length of s. After adding two special token [CLS] and [SEP], the sentence would be changed like this $s = \{[CLS], w_1, w_2, ..., w_l, [SEP]\}$. Then we fine-tune our QA-BERT-wwm-ext and QA-ERNIE-Gram model on these generated sequences.

3.2   The Plausibility Evaluation

We can get the output of $h = \{h_0, h_1, ..., h_l, h_{l+1}\}$ by QA-BERT-wwm-ext and QA-ERNIE-Gram model, then through formula (1) and (2), we finally get the output label y.

$$x = \text{FCN}(h) \tag{1}$$

$$y = \text{Sigmoid}(x) \tag{2}$$

where FCN means the fully connected layer. And we use the binary cross-entropy loss to train our model (Fig. 2).

---

[1] https://tianchi.aliyun.com/competition/entrance/531955/information.

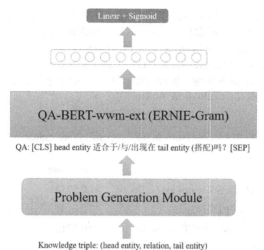

Fig. 2. The overall structure of our model

4 Experiment

4.1 Dataset and Experiment Settings

We conduct our experiment on CCKS 2022 track1 dataset[1]. The specific content of the data set is shown in Table 1, which contains four relation categories: 品类_适用_场景(category_applicable_scene), 品类_适用_人物(category_applicable_ character), 品类_搭配_品类(category_match_category) and 人物_蕴含_场景(character_implication_scene). Each instance in the dataset is labeled as 1 or 0, which means a knowledge triple is salience or not. Because the gold labels for test set are not given, we random choose 10% of original dataset as dev set to select model. And the number of instances in each category in original dataset is also shown in Table 1.

Table 1. Statistics of original dataset

Relation category	1	0
品类_适用_场景(category_applicable_scene)	4614	10989
品类_适用_人物(category_applicable_character)	1029	1727
品类_搭配_品类(category_match_category)	432	1002
人物_蕴含_场景(character_implication_scene)	218	424

In this paper, we choose the BERT-wwm-ext [13], ERNIE-Gram [14] as our model backbone and select KG-BERT-wwm-ext (KG-ERNIE-Gram) and Sentence-BERT-wwm-ext (Sentence-ERNIE-Gram) as baseline models to compare. And we use Adam [15] as optimizer to fine-tune pre-trained model. In addition, the hyper parameters setting in our experiment are as follows: batch_size: 32, max_length: 32, learning rate: 1e-5. We adopt F1 score as the evaluation metric.

Table 2. The main results in out experiment (preliminary contest)

Model	F1 score
KG-BERT-wwm-ext	0.5742
KG-ERINE-Gram	0.6131
Sentence-BERT-wwm-ext	0.5719
Sentence-ERINE-Gram	0.6151
QA-form-BERT-wwm-ext	**0.5890**
QA-form-ERINE-Gram	**0.6694**

4.2 Results and Analysis

The main results in our experiment as shown in Table 2. As can be seen, the performance in KG-BERT-wwm-ext (ERNIE-Gram) and Sentence-BERT-wwm-ext (ERNIE-Gram) is similar. Under the same environment, the performance of ERNIE-Gram is much higher than BERT-wwm-ext. We speculate that the training mode of ERNIE-Gram may be more suitable for this task. It is worth mentioning that the both F1 score of our two models exceed baseline models. Among them, the F1 score of QA-BERT-wwm-ext model is about 1 points higher than baselines models, and the F1 score of QA--ERNIE-Gram model is more than 5 points higher than baseline models, which proves that the effectiveness of our method that transforms the plausibility evaluation of knowledge triple task into a QA task.

In addition, we also test the influence of different question types on results, as shown in Table 3, and we use ERNIE-Gram with better performance as the model backbone default.

It can be seen from Table 3 that different question types have a great impact on the results. Through numerous experiments, we finally chose the type 9 as template to generate question sequences from original knowledge triple, and won the 5th place in the CCKS 2022 track 1 rematch stage, with the F1 score of 0.6124.

Table 3. Experimental results of different question types (preliminary contest)

Type	Form	F1 score
Type 1	Head entity 适合于 tail entity 吗?(common) Is the head entity suitable for tail entity? (common)	0.5705
Type 2	Head entity 与 tail entity 存在显著性关系吗?(common) Is there a salience relationship between head entity and tail entity? (common)	0.5924
Type 3	Head entity 与 tail entity 存在适用、搭配或蕴含的关系?(common) Is there a relationship between head entity and tail entity that is applicable, matched or implied? (common)	0.6208
Type 4	Head entity 适合于 tail entity 吗? (品类_适用_场景/人物) Is head entity suitable for tail entity? (category_applicable_scene/character) Head entity 适合与 tail entity 搭配吗? (品类_搭配_品类) Is head entity suitable for matching with tail entity? (category_match_category) Head entity 适合在 tail entity 吗? (人物_蕴含_场景) Is head entity suitable for tail entity? (character_implication_scene)	0.5881
Type 5	Head entity 适用于 tail entity 吗? (品类_适用_场景/人物) Is head entity applicable to tail entity? (category_applicable_scene/character) Head entity 适合与 tail entity 搭配吗? (品类_搭配_品类) Is head entity suitable for matching with tail entity? (category_match_category) Head entity 适合出现在 tail entity 吗? (人物_蕴含_场景) Is head entity suitable for tail entity? (character_implication_scene)	0.6669
Type 6	Head entity 是否适合于 tail entity (品类_适用_场景/人物) Whether the head entity is suitable for the tail entity (category_applicable_scene/person) Head entity 是否适合与 tail entity 搭配 (品类_搭配_品类) Whether the head entity is suitable for matching with the tail entity (category_matching_category) Head entity 是否适合出现在 tail entity (人物_蕴含_场景) Whether the head entity is suitable for the tail entity (character_implication_scene)	0.6040
	Head entity 适合于 tail entity ? (品类_适用_场景/人物) Head entity is suitable for tail entity? (category_applicable_scene / character)	0.6003

(*continued*)

Table 3. (*continued*)

Type	Form	F1 score
Type 7	Head entity 适合与 tail entity 搭配? (品类_搭配_品类) Is head entity suitable for matching with tail entity? (category_match_category)	
	Head entity 适合出现在 tail entity？(人物_蕴含_场景) Head entity is suitable for tail entity? (character_implication_scene)	
	Head entity 适合于 tail entity (品类_适用_场景/人物) Head entity is suitable for tail entity (category_applicable_scene/character)	0.6194
Type 8	Head entity 适合与 tail entity 搭配 (品类_搭配_品类) Head entity is suitable for matching with tail entity (category_match_category)	
	Head entity 适合出现在 tail entity (人物_蕴含_场景) Head entity is suitable for tail entity (character_implication_scene)	
Type 9 we used	Head entity 适合于 tail entity 吗? (品类_适用_场景/人物) Is head entity suitable for tail entity? (category_applicable_scene/character)	**0.6694**
	Head entity 适合与 tail entity 搭配吗? (品类_搭配_品类) Is head entity suitable for matching with tail entity? (category_match_category)	
	Head entity 适合出现在 tail entity 吗? (人物_蕴含_场景) Is head entity suitable for tail entity? (character_implication_scene)	

5 Conclusion

In this paper, we explored how to complete plausibility evaluation of knowledge triple task without using any external knowledge base and graph representation learning. We propose a simple but effective method to solve this problem. With the help of KG-BERT and prompt learning thought, we transformed this task into the question and answer (QA) task, then through fine-tuning the pre-trained language model, two models QA-BERT-wwm-ext and QA-ERNIE-Gram were given to complete the QA task. We finally achieved the 5th place in CCKS 2022 track 1 rematch stage, which proved the effectiveness of our proposed method. Future work includes exploring how to apply this method to other fields and how to set corresponding questions according to specific tasks.

References

1. Wang, X., et al.: KEPLER: a unified model for knowledge embedding and pre-trained language representation. Trans. Assoc. Comput. Linguist. **9**, 176–194 (2021)
2. Zhang, S., et al.: Quaternion knowledge graph embeddings. Adv. Neural Inform. Process. Syst. **32** (2019)

3. Lee, K., Devlin, J., Chang, M.-W., Toutanova, K.: BERT: pre-training of deep bidirectional transformers for language understanding. In: Proceedings of NAACL-HLT (2019)
4. Liu, Y., et al.: Roberta: a robustly optimized bert pretraining approach. arXiv preprint arXiv: 1907.11692 (2019)
5. Sun, Y., et al.: Ernie: enhanced representation through knowledge integration. arXiv preprint arXiv:1904.09223 (2019)
6. Yao, L., Chengsheng M., Yuan, L.: KG-BERT: BERT for knowledge graph completion. arXiv preprint arXiv:1909.03193 (2019)
7. Antoine, B., et al.: Translating embeddings for modeling multi-relational data. Adv. Neural Inform. Process. Syst. **26** (2013)
8. Wang, Z., et al. "Knowledge graph embedding by translating on hyperplanes. In: Proceedings of the AAAI Conference on Artificial Intelligence, vol. 28, no. 1 (2014)
9. Sun, Z., et al.: RotatE: knowledge graph embedding by relational rotation in complex space. In: International Conference on Learning Representations (2018)
10. Wang, B., et al.: Structure-augmented text representation learning for efficient knowledge graph completion. In: Proceedings of the Web Conference 2021 (2021)
11. Nils, R., Gurevych, I.: Sentence-BERT: sentence embeddings using siamese BERT-networks. In: Proceedings of the 2019 Conference on Empirical Methods in Natural Language Processing and the 9th International Joint Conference on Natural Language Processing (EMNLP-IJCNLP) (2019)
12. Lv, X., et al.: Do Pre-trained Models Benefit Knowledge Graph Completion? A Reliable Evaluation and a Reasonable Approach. Findings of the Association for Computational Linguistics: ACL 2022 (2022)
13. Cui, Y., et al.: Pre-training with whole word masking for chinese BERT. IEEE/ACM Trans. Audio Speech Lang. Process. **29**, 3504–3514 (2021)
14. Xiao, D., et al.: ERNIE-gram: pre-training with explicitly N-gram masked language modeling for natural language understanding. In: Proceedings of the 2021 Conference of the North American Chapter of the Association for Computational Linguistics: Human Language Technologies (2021)
15. Diederik, P.K., Ba, J.: Adam: A Method for Stochastic Optimization. ICLR (Poster) (2015)

Author Index

An, Bo   12

Bao, Hongyi   21

Cao, Jiuxin   228
Chen, Chao   180
Chen, Enhong   180
Chen, Junying   214
Chen, Qingcai   214
Chen, Wei   180
Chen, Yang   78
Chen, Yilin   127
Chen, Yuefeng   78
Cheng, Chuang   1
Cheng, Gong   70
Cui, Pingfei   98

Dai, Haoyu   127

Feng, Changkai   180

Gu, Yuang   127

Han, Chenchen   172
Han, Han   47
Han, Lin   98
He, Shizhu   154
He, Yaohan   39, 87
He, Zhenkun   107
Hua, Rui   1

Ji, Jiangzhou   39
Jia, Heng   172
Jia, Jinkang   120
Jia, Peipei   107
Jia, Shutong   228
Jin, Nengzheng   214

Kang, YangYang   163

Lan, Man   78
Li, Dongfang   214
Li, Jinlong   39, 87
Li, Peng   30
Li, Xiao   70

Li, Ziyan   191
Liang, Zhancheng   107
Liu, Hongyi   87
Liu, Huihai   98
liu, Jie   148
Liu, Kang   154
Liu, Ziqian   120
lv, Xiaodan   12

Ma, Miaomiao   47
Ma, Mingxu   202

Ni, Kan   191
Ning, Xingxing   148

Peng, Song   30, 47
Pu, Keyu   87

Qin, Ying   30, 47
Qiu, Yubin   214

Ren, Yupei   78
Ruan, Guoqing   21

Sun, Jiadong   21

Teng, Ben   12

Wang, Haofen   191
Wang, Jingting   127
Wang, Ruijie   221
Wang, Xinyan   1
Wang, Xuepeng   12
Wang, Yexiang   163
Wang, Yongbo   138
Wei, Jiaqi   120
Weng, Yixuan   154
Wu, Guangshuo   202
Wu, Shuang   120
Wu, Tianxing   127
Wu, Zhanglin   30

Xia, Yunni   138
Xu, Jian   21
Xu, Jingyi   127
Xu, Tong   180
Xu, Xin   21

Yang, Hao   30, 47
Yang, Jingli   202
Yang, Wenming   57
Yang, Yixiao   87
Yi, Xianwei   221
Yin, Le   57

Zhang, Hanyi   221
Zhang, Ke   70
Zhang, Min   30, 47
Zhang, Weidong   30, 47
Zhang, Wenqiang   191
Zhang, Xinxin   12
Zhang, Yadong   78

Zhao, Fubang   163
Zhao, Jun   154
Zhao, Yupeng   148
Zhen, Shiqi   221
Zhou, Xuezhong   1
Zhou, Yanmao   138
Zhu, Junhao   30, 47
Zhu, Ming   30
Zhu, Minjun   154
Zhu, Qiang   1
Zhu, Shutong   127
Zhu, Ting   30
Zhu, Yipeng   127
Zou, Jiali   57

Printed in the United States
by Baker & Taylor Publisher Services